Wisdom in Buddhism

Cultivating The Mind of Peace

Edward Horner

Mind of Peace Publications

© Canadian Outdoor Press
First printing 2020 10 9 8 7 6 5 4 3 2 1

All Rights Reserved. No part of this publication may be reproduced in any form, without written permission by the publisher, except by a reviewer who may quote brief passages.

The Publisher
   Mind of Peace Publications
      - An imprint publication of Canadian Outdoor Press
      Riverdale, Toronto, Canada.
           www.canadianoutdoorpress.ca

Title
   Wisdom in Buddhism

ISBN
   978-1-7771539-1-5

Cover photo by Audrey C. Jolly

Web links change, get updated, corrected and edited. They also, get hijacked, re-directed break or disappear altogether. For those reasons, despite the best efforts of the authors and editors, we cannot be held accountable for the accuracy of any links suggested in this book.

Table of

Forward ix
How to Use This Book xxiii
1. Communication 1
    1.1 Characteristics of Conversation 4
2. Timeline Perspective 19
3. Values, Morality and Ethics 35
    3.1 Universal Responsibility 49
    3.2 Wisdom and The Five Precepts 53
    3.3 Wisdom and The Paramitas 73
4. Humility and Humour 79
    4.1 Humour 87
    4.2 The Five Remembrances 90
    4.3 Wisdom and The Three Mental Defilements 94
    4.4 Ignorance, the First Mental Defilement 95
    4.5 Overcoming Ignorance 102
    4.6 Greed, the Second of the Mental Defilements 105
    4.7 Hatred, the Third Mental Defilement 107
    4.8 The Five Stages of Wisdom 111
5. Ultimate Limit Events 119
    5.1 Fake News and Post-Truth 127
    5.2 Our View of the World 136
    5.3 Wisdom in Ageing 137
6. The Illusion of Permanency 145
7. Compassion and its Role in Wisdom 155
    What is Compassion? 155
    How to Raise Compassion for Others 156
    A Story of Compassion 160

Contents

8. Bias in Wise Decision Making 167
   - 8.1 The Decision, Unpacked 168
   - 8.2 Mental Biases 175
9. Theory of Mind 197
   - 9.1 Motivation, Skills and Resource Analysis in Wise Decision Making 203
10. Emotional Stability And Wisdom 209
    - 10.1 Mental Re-Training 217
    - 10.2 Modify Thinking 219
    - 10.3 Modify Habits 221
11. Meditation, Concentration and Patience 227
    - 11.1 The Four Noble Truths 227
    - 11.2 The First Noble Truth 228
    - 11.3 The Second Noble Truth 235
    - 11.4 The Third Noble Truth 242
    - 11.5 The Fourth Noble Truths 243
    - 11.6 The Eightfold Path 245
    - 11.7 Meditation, Concentration and Patience 262
12. Learning 279
    - 12.1 Seven Steps to Reinforce Wisdom 290

Final Thoughts 295
Wisdom from The Buddha 298
Self-Assessment Tools 313
Bibliography 322
About the Author 327
Other Books From Mind of Peace Publications 331
Index 334

"Man has two windows to his mind; through one he can see his own self as he is; through the other he can see what it ought to be. It is our task to analyze and explore the body, the brain and the mind of man separately, but if we stop here we derive no benefit, despite our scientific knowledge."

~ Mahatma Gandhi

"I travel to many places around the world, and whenever I speak to people, I do so with the feeling that I am a member of their own family. Although we may be meeting for the first time, I accept everyone as a friend. In truth, we already know one another, profoundly, as human beings who share the same basic goals; We all seek happiness and do not want suffering."

~ The 14th Dalai Lama
How To Practice: The Way to a Meaningful Life

Forward

ON THE NIGHT OF ON APRIL 18, 2020, a gunman, 51 year old Gabriel Wortman, went on a shooting rampage across central Nova Scotia, in Eastern Canada, leaving 22 dead in his wake. It began sometime before 10:26 pm at which point the police were called to the town of Portapique, in Colchester County, where they discovered the bodies of 13 victims and ended some 13 hours later at a gas station in Enfield, 150 kilometres distant, where Wortman was shot dead by police. In total, Wortman killed 22 people.

That morning, when I turned on the news and learned of this tragic event, I was shocked, literally flabbergasted. For the next few minutes, my toast cooled on the plate and my coffee sat, untouched, cooling at my elbow, as I took in the reportage and tried to make sense of what had taken place. The details were few, motivation was unknown, the man's name not yet divulged. Why had this happened?

I listened to shocked reporters as they dutifully dissected what few details they had. Victims names had not yet been released, pending notification of their families. Theories were put forward, the 'why's all trying to be answered, but no one had all the details yet. The scope of the event had not yet been fully realized. Most of Canada, a country where these types of events are mercifully rare, although not unknown, was reeling from this bombshell.

At times like this we hope to conjure up that little bit of wisdom that our parents had hoped for us. Surely, my brain should be able to come up with something from 16 years of schooling (not to mention 18 years of almost daily meditation practice) that would help navigate this morass of disbelief; some intelligent path to follow as my world spun before me. But, like the 2017 Las Vegas Shooting, the Walkerton Tragedy, Columbine, 9/11, École Polytechnique, Challenger, Bhopal, Three Mile Island or the assassination of Kennedy, there was, at first, nothing to be had. There seemed no process upon which I could rely that would help me work through what-the-hell unfolded the previous day and how I ought to access an uncertain future.

I imagine a lot of people in Canada went through something similar that morning, each, in their own way, seeking some wisdom, trying to make sense of what happened, trying to figure out what went wrong.

There is never one single reason that explains why anything of major import occurs. When writers, researchers, science reporters, inside investigators and hundreds of others examined, dissected and turned over every scrap of evidence having to do with the Challenger Disaster of 1986, it was clear that no single event or decision fully accounted for the explosion of the space shuttle and the loss of all seven of its crew members. No single event or process, alone, accounted for that failure. Rather, it was a series of things going wrong, sometimes along a single chain of events and other times along multiple chains of events that all led to that singular calamity. So it would be with this mass murder.

Trying to parse Portapique the next day or even the following week, proved futile. Not all the facts would be in, no analysis had yet been done, not all the players were talking and emotions were running high. Examination too closely and too early would yield false starts, dead ends, lame theories and all manner of misinformation. That morning I got lucky, in retrospect. It seems I was wise to sit, calm myself and give this story time to unfold.

———————

One thing about writing a book, almost any book, is that once it nears completion, you almost always have to rewrite the introduction or preface. What you thought the book was going to address has altered, twisted and turned. The book takes on a life of its own and evolves as information and story unfold to become something not quite intended, but in its own way better, larger and more inclusive.

It's also true that most authors learn a few things along the way and, like the book itself, are changed - often having to confront and hopefully come to terms with their own limitations on a topic. Sometimes they develop a different understanding of themselves. So it has been with this book ... so it has been with me.

I've learned that I'm not an expert on wisdom. In fact, very few things I've done in my life, given the benefit of hindsight, seem to have been anything resembling 'wise' at all. This realization and red-faced admission might, in some circles, disqualify me from even writing about wisdom - or at least having anything relevant to say about it. But, as I've learned over my 65 years of living on this planet, my not knowing about something hasn't stopped me from talking about it, as my long-suffering friends can attest.

Another thing about me is that I'm liberal in my political views and I don't mind sharing those views in this book. Yes, I have biases and preferences. So, if you're thinking that there will be a fair and non-partisan examination of wisdom presented in these pages, you'll be disappointed. Still, I am not shy to point out where liberal views may falter. Simply having a viewpoint does not disqualify one from engaging in a discussion, so long as the biases are recognized and understood.

As I started talking with others and reading about wisdom, it soon became clear that no one is imbued with wisdom at birth. It's not something that one is genetically endowed with, like say, a high IQ, musical aptitude or a predilection to easily solving quadratic equations. No one is born the very model of a *Modern Major-General*.

I also learned fairly quickly that wisdom and intellect, while related, are not at all one-and-the-same. Having some store of life experience plays a key role in the development of wisdom, but only if one examines and extracts learning from those experiences. Simply growing old does not, in itself, confer wisdom. We discuss this in Chapter 5.

One of the main challenges faced with this book was trying to define wisdom and, more specifically, wisdom from a Buddhist perspective. That is the crux of the matter; defining wisdom from one perspective really limits the discussion. What seems apparent and obvious from one POV, sounds false, even egregious, from another. Trying to define this mental construct we call wisdom is slippery, but with enough parameters and a well laid out point of view, we can at least get close enough - or close enough for something to work with.

What I have read of the Buddhist scriptures, the sutras (or suttas), has not been overly helpful, for most references to wisdom were not about every day living and practical sense, but more liturgical allusions - important for sure, but not strictly the 'Buddhist wisdom" I went looking for to help commoners like me, make our way through a difficult world. Wisdom, in the liturgical context, was usually linked to higher states of enlightenment and closely associated with the ultimate aim of Buddhist wisdom, NIRVANA, that state of 'disappearing' from the universe. Noble and lofty goals, not easily dismissed, but from the point of view of a simple practitioner like myself, not particularly useful on a day-to-day basis.

We all want to *appear* wise, to look like we have insight into complicated matters that plague our world, our neighbourhood or even ourselves. Sure, we all have *something* to say, but we want what is said to have pertinence, not necessarily all the time, but when it really matters. When your eight-year-old daughter asks, for example, about gay marriage, you want to have something to add to the discussion. You want to be able to add some important insight, some set of values and considered judgment or a process that shows you're not just some dope with an opinion. Simply expressing an opinion doesn't make you wise – at best, it makes you opinionated. You want to speak in a manner that shows you've looked into it, seen various aspects of the topic and synthesized a thoughtful reply.

Wisdom, at least as a process, is important, not because it gives us the 'right' answer or the 'deep' answer, (although it helps) but because the process itself causes us to slow, centre, calm and be heedful of what we know, what we value and what COMMON GOOD we choose to address. In a way, it's the confluence of three streams; what we've learned in our life, what we value and how we address a common good to maximize its benefits. It's not easy, but in this book I offer some ways that wisdom can arise and be utilized, more-often-than-not from a Buddhist perspective.

At the core of all this wisdom talk is, of course, decision making, advice giving and action taking. What information we bring into our decisions, how it's processed, how it's weighted and filtered, all play a role in our decisions. Understanding the problem, hearing *accurately* the situation and making *ourselves* understood is a key component in wisdom development and for that reason, we start with a deep dive into COMMUNICATION in Chapter 1.

We need to come to terms with the fact that everything changes, not always within our own lifetime, but they will change and our wisdom will be supplemented by that understanding. While no one can predict with complete certainty, what will unfold in the future, looking at the past and examining the present can give us valuable insights into future possibilities. This is discussed, primarily, in Chapter 2 - TIMELINE PERSPECTIVE.

Wisdom-making needs a set of values from which it can draw some sense of 'morality' or 'rightness' as it relates to a common good. From a Buddhist perspective, the widely used Five Precepts discussed in Chapter 3 – VALUES, MORALITY AND ETHICS – fit the bill, but they do not exist in-and-of themselves, for, if we are to take anything from our discussion about wisdom, it's the understanding that all things, including values and any sense of morality, arise from the community which they purport to serve and in which they exist.

Along the way we will need to recognize, develop or restore our sense of humour and humility. Humility reminds us that we do not, in fact *cannot*, know everything that needs to be known in every circumstance, if only because chaos exists and random circumstances can arise at any time. Humility is an antidote to the arrogance which may blind us to new facts and circumstances that, in turn, might limit our understanding of the world and so impede wisdom. This is discussed in some depth in Chapter 4 – HUMILITY AND HUMOUR.

Major and often traumatic events in one's life - events in which one is pressed almost to the breaking point - can, if they are met with resolve and survived, bring about major epiphanies and 'Ah Ha!' Moments. These ULTIMATE LIMIT EVENTS are discussed in Chapter 5.

When we realize - *fully* - that everything is subject to change, then we come to understand that dogma, procedure and policy come to mean little. Everything changes and is subject to entropy - maybe not within our own lifetime, but eventually. Change, is the central theme of all our lives. *IMPERMANENCE* is discussed in Chapter 6.

How can we connect with others and know *their* suffering unless we, ourselves, have had direct, personal experience with such suffering? Not knowing suffering, our wisdom is hampered and limited, but, being human, we know the pain of others, for we endure pain ourselves. *RAISING COMPASSION for Others*, and how that applies to the development of wisdom, is discussed in Chapter 7.

Our early childhood development, our peers, school or religious affiliation have all formed us, to one degree or another and caused us to hold certain biases - inclinations or preferences, that effect how we think, speak, view the world and take action. These biases are important, as they affect our decision making processes. These biases, and how to recognize and how we might deal with them, are discussed in Chapter 8 - *THE ROLE OF BIAS IN WISE DECISION MAKING*.

Sometimes we believe we can 'read' people and do manage a pretty good job of determining if someone means us harm or ill-will, by recognizing social cues – much of the time, but not always. We too often, incorrectly, think that since we are part of the same society, culture, club or organization, we can determine a person's intentions because they think like us. This *THEORY OF MIND* or T.O.M. is discussed in Chapter 9.

When we address major issues, we need a clear mind, as unaffected by emotions and bias as is reasonable, given the circumstances. Our emotions might have set us on a course, but it's the clear mind that is able to assess and make reasonable predictions about that course which is most wise. *EMOTIONAL STABILITY*, what it might look like and how it might be obtained is discussed in Chapter 10.

We will need the ability to focus or concentrate on difficult questions and, from a Buddhist perspective, nothing improves one's ability to concentrate like meditation, so we spend a bit of time looking at that practice as well. Buddhism doesn't treat meditation as some tangental aspect or minor diversionary incident of a larger whole, but as one of the main tenets of the practice. While exhaustive explanations on how to meditate are beyond the scope of this book, we do take a look at MEDITATION, CONCENTRATION AND PATIENCE, in Chapter 11.

Lastly, we take a deep dive into learning; specific, general and ongoing. Understanding and knowing how events are linked and how human nature works, is another important component of wisdom. The ability to understand a topic, know it both intellectually and emotionally is critical if we are to have any chance at addressing it. Ignorance of the issue being addressed blocks wisdom from arising. LEARNING and its relationship to wisdom is discussed in Chapter 12.

It quickly becomes apparent that wisdom - whatever that may turn out to be - is not something you can address with a silver arrow. It turns out to be an elusive idea, that is shaped and massaged by numerous and ever-changing forces, some of which are within our control (largely operating within the confines of our mind) and others which are not.

For all the research, talking, reading and listening I've done about wisdom, it's damned hard to nail down. I'm not even sure most people would recognize wisdom if it hit them in the head with a *baguette*. I make a brazen attempt at setting parameters for this book, for without them, I found myself wandering down some mighty long dead ends that would not have resulted in a book at all.

At times, my trying to corral wisdom seemed to require more of it than I am ever likely to possess. But even that glib observation, suggests a *soupçon* of wisdom. Knowing that in some circumstances there will be things that are unknown or maybe even unknowable is recognition of the need to place qualifications around conclusions. Humbling, to be sure, for who doesn't like certainty?

In one of my earlier chapbooks, *Certainty in Buddhism*, I examined why we get so hung up on being right and how we can learn to live with uncertainty, once we recognize that change is the central theme of all our lives. Wisdom for one day, under specific circumstances, may seem like folly the next. Ironically, getting too attached to wisdom itself may not be particularly wise, for as I tried to come up with the ultimate and enduring definition, it kept slithering away, morphing into something else. More than once I scattered papers across the kitchen floor in frustration.

Another thing about trying to define wisdom is that we can take various approaches on the matter. One good book I read on the topic was Robert J. Stern's, *Wisdom: Its Nature, Origins and Development*. In this book Stern assembles about a dozen contributors who each take a run at defining wisdom, each from their own specific discipline. Each one seemed like a great definition, at least until I got to the next one. By the end I realized how difficult the task of defining wisdom was going to be. Thankfully, I tripped over Paul Baltes and the *Berlin Wisdom Project*.

Baltes, and his team, worked out theories about lifespan and wisdom, practical knowledge about living, and about successful aging and developing. I found his methods to be quite helpful, not because they resulted in some specific, unimpeachable definition of wisdom, but because he took a multi-faceted approach to the topic that would provided a balance of; life experience, intellect, social/cultural context, procedural knowledge, factual knowledge, relativism and uncertainty. His team also interviewed people (mostly college students) and asked them questions that might reveal their views on wisdom.

For example;
"A 14 year old girl wants to move out of her parents house right away. What should be considered in this situation?"

A low-scoring response might be, "She's only 14! She shouldn't be out on her own under any circumstances. Think of the trouble she might run into."

A high-scoring response might be, "She may be living in an abusive home and she recognizes a need to escape to safer surroundings, or her parents might be substance abusers and unable to look after her. While only 14, she may be about to enter an 'arranged marriage' situation that has no future. Maybe she's already of 'of age' for her culture and moving out is no big deal."

In the first, low scoring, response, the answer indicates a limited path of thinking that suggests many biases.

In the second, high-scoring, response, the answer suggests a wide-range of thinking, taking into account the fact that not everything is known about the situation.

In the end, Baltes' definition of wisdom is;

> "Expert knowledge concerning the fundamental pragmatics of life"

Baltes went on to declare that wisdom is, *'good judgment and advice about important but uncertain matters of life.'* Framing wisdom in 'expertise' has a certain value, but, in my opinion still falls short for it fails to recognize the 'emotional' and 'empathetic' aspect of wisdom. Too much 'from the head' and not enough 'from the heart' thinking, speaking and acting denies our humanity, our suffering and our pain and tends to detach us from the problem trying to be solved.

What has also become clear is that in our modern era, technology, science and knowledge have become something of a panacea for a lot of people. Our lives are essentially ruled by technology; we arise with the alarm clock, turn on the electric light, check our email using our smartphone at our bedside, brush our teeth with an electric toothbrush, listen to the FM radio or news podcast to hear what the day might be like. We might have an espresso at home using the Nespresso coffee machine, check what time the bus is due on our NextBus app and then make our way to work, where we spend the day staring at a screen analyzing data and making things happen remotely.

Technology touches so much of our lives that we begin to think that it, alone, is worth pursuit. We forget all the thinking and experimentation that went into its creation is knowledge and *not* necessarily wisdom. We seem confused between simply *knowing* something and being *wise* about something. For all our technological breakthroughs, we seem to have a spotty record when it comes to relieving human suffering, and the relief of suffering, for oneself and for others, is a very large part of Buddhism.

> *"Who is wise? The one who learns from every person."*
> ~ Pirkei Avot 4:1

We have flu vaccines and almost everyone has a smartphone, but we haven't managed to provide clean drinking water for some 1.1 billion people or reliable sanitation facilities for 2.2 billion people or reliable electricity to 1.3 billion. So, it seems fairly clear that our technology doesn't serve everyone.*

We've become so obsessed with telling our own version of a story that we can barely even *tolerate* hearing that of another. This behaviour is encouraged, when, for example, we are on Facebook or Twitter and click on a story, we get not only that one upon which we clicked, but also a few other stories that are related in temper and topic. The search algorithms recognize we might want to read or research material that is critical of a celebrity. It then finds more stories that criticize the particular individual and suggests those articles. What the algorithms *don't* do is run out and look for stories that are in support of the celebrity.

Facebook and Google, to name only two, shape and reinforce our existing ideas by offering more of what we believe and rarely, if ever, offer contra opinion stories.

---

* International Energy Agency - Key world Energy Statistics, 2017

Of course, this is their business model. Twitter and Facebook want to keep you scrolling, scrolling, forever scrolling to the next story that will reinforce your opinions, views and beliefs. The more time you spend surfing their sites, the more they learn about you and that translates into valuable data that they can then use to sell very targeted advertising directed right back at you, in the hopes you'll click on an ad and they get paid.

They also work the other end as well. When you post something on a Facebook page, often you'll get a messages that reads something like, "Get this post noticed. For $25 you can get this post in front of 25,000 users who are interested in this topic." For a fee, they serve up your post to thousands of others who seem to have an interest in the topic you posted about in they hopes they'll get *those* people to click and then the process repeats itself.

We can't really blame them. They're offering us only what we are asking for and need a way to make some money at it, otherwise why bother doing it at all? Still, it does lead us to become further entrenched in our views, thinking or position.

Netflix is another example of our interests being used to feed us more of our specific entertainment diet. After we watch an episode of *Wallander* on Netflix, "Episode 2 begins in 13 seconds" pops up on the screen, even before the credits for episode 1 have finished rolling. This gets you interested in the next episode … and the next … and the one after that. Next thing you know you've binged-watched the entire 13 episodes of season one.

Apple's iTunes takes this 'predictive usage' to a new height when they not only select other music that we might be interested in, based on what we've paid to download from their site, but also from what we've ripped from our personal CDs and loaded into the iTunes app on our personal computers, to offer us entire playlists that are actually pretty good. Who would have thought Nocturne, by Scott Hamilton would be a good follow up to Bob Dylan's Master of War? We don't even have to build our own lists anymore. They then go on to offer us their Apple Radio channels based on the music we have and/or listen to on our computer - for a charge, of course - all the while watching, noting and logging all the music and news we listen to in order to offer us more of their goods.

But this *'selectivism'* isn't limited to our Facebook, Twitter, Netflix and iTunes usage. It's much more widely ingrained in our information and entertainment seeking activities.

Our news media has become politically fragmented, biased and self-serving ... although to be fair, they've always been politically fragmented, biased and self-serving.

Entire news networks and their related news gathering apparatus is geared towards collecting, digesting and relating the news with a not-at-all disguised partisan view point. CNN, The New Yorker, the Washing Post deliver us the news from a Democratic point of view, while Breitbart, Fox and NewsMax deliver the news from a conservative, establishment POV in the US. In Canada the National Post gives us the conservative, vested interest news and we rely on the Toronto Star to deliver and opine on all things liberal.

Party politics has been disseminated since Dutch *Courante uyt Italian, Duytslandt, &c.*(Roughly, 'Events from Italy and Germany') published their first broadsheets in1618. The publisher, Caspar van Hilten, was essentially, a press agent for the army of Maurits van Oranje.

In 1826 William Lyon Mackenzie's, *Colonial Advocate* press was wrecked by Tory yobs in retribution for articles critical of the *Family Compact.* Press affiliation with political parties has been around a very long time, but what *is* new is the fine fragmentation, volume and velocity of the news being delivered. Everything a president or despot says in some far away corner of the world is amplified, retold, twisted and massaged instantly, to suit the agenda of any given news outlet, be it Liberal, Conservative, Alt Right, *Extrême-Gauche* or something else.

The point of all this, of course, is that unless we agree with something, we're not going to take it in. If one newspaper doesn't agree with our conservative view on immigration, then we stop reading it and take up a newspaper or website that *does* agree with us.

We've become very self-selecting in what we read, much to our detriment. We paint our world in the only colours we are interest in. In a way, we become colour blind - eschewing everything unless it's of direct and immediate interest to us. We won't read anything unless it's Red or Blue. We become less exposed to other opinions, interests, topics and people who may think differently from us. We become insular, isolated, intolerant, mono-toned and less willing or able to assimilate new information. Our world becomes ever smaller, less diverse and less accepting. This breeds contempt for other ideas, other music, other news and other lifestyles. Those who do not share our view, or share it with the same enthusiasm and vitality as us, are seen as 'outsiders' and treated with suspicion, at best. It breeds fear.

We have become contemptuous of each other and our differences. Our media consumption habits have made us so. We've become locked into points of view that may be based solely on our TV viewing habits.

> Being able to hear and understand the experiences of others, even when they disagree with us, is a critical skill if we wish to ultimately give rise to wisdom.

Incivility
We have entered an age of incivility and an era of erosion of common courtesy, kind words and sympathy. It has become commonplace, for even leaders of countries, to hurl deeply personal insults at one another, via the internet and broadcast over the airwaves for the entire world to hear. They tweet out scorn and vitriol on a vast scale, childishly comparing, for example, the size of the buttons on their desk to start a nuclear war, as if bigger were somehow better. Inconsiderate tweets and ill-conceived Facebook posts are *d'rigour.*

Some state leaders act as if their words are perfunctory. It's a sad state of affairs that we've come to expect and even accept Discourtesy, Denial, Deflection and Deceit from our leaders. I've come to refer to these personality types as suffering from D4 disorder.

> Sadly, cogent thought, rational words, reasoned discussion and actions rarely seem to take place anymore, at least in the public/political space. We have become so unwise in our dealing with each other, indeed even in dealing with ourselves, that we no longer, recognize wisdom when we see it – unless it happens to exactly agree with out own thinking.

We can't paint everyone with the same brush. To be sure, there are exceptions - notable exceptions, at that. The president of France, Emmanuel Macron has learned, to a large extent, that dividing, maligning and insulting people is not going to help his country. To a great extent, his message of unity, not speaking in extremes and at least *acting* reasonable, during the last French election, is what brought him to the *Palais de l'Élysée*. Then there's John Hume/David Trimble, Barrack Obama, Gloria Steinem, Alice Walker, Thomas Merton and of course, Mahatma Gandhi and Aristotle to name but a few wise and considered individuals who, in the public sphere, have made a positive difference within their lifetimes.

These are people who have demonstrated deep thought before uttering their words and actions - at least when it matters - for we are all allowed our foibles, indiscretions and missteps. We are all allowed our humour and idiosyncrasies. However, where the rubber hits the road, it's the ability to think deeply, over a wide ranging landscape, using the 12 pillars of Buddhist wisdom to synthesize meaningful, lasting solutions to problems, that really counts. It's this thinking, this *wisdom*, that we are sorely lacking in contemporary, public discourse and indeed, in our private lives.

That super-suite of attributes that constitute the *compound mind* of; concentration, foresight, life experience, humility, compassion, emotional stability, learnedness, historian, disseminator of information and reasoned opinion, debater, orator and humanitarian has, historically, been rare in any society, but it seems all the more so today. Bringing together those qualities, in good quantity seems a Herculean task and it's often left to random chance – but not always.

> When 'belief' enters our mind, especially a belief that diminishes others, demeans them, separates 'them' from 'us' and creates a negative environment, it should be accompanied with compassion, evidence, and skillful thinking.

How to Use This Book

WE CAN, WITH DILIGENCE AND INTENT, BECOME MORE WISE. We can, with cultivation and thought, raise and sustain those circumstances that encourage and promote deep thinking. What those circumstances might be and how they might be sustained is what this book is all about. In what ways can Buddhism and the dharma - teachngs of The Buddha - help foster wisdom and how could that wisdom be applied in our everyday lives?

In our opening chapters, we will work towards an understanding of wisdom, beginning with the mundane, everyday understanding of wisdom and what the OED has to offer. We will then go on to examine what can be brought to bear upon that definition from a Buddhist perspective. What, for example, are the positive ethics and values that can be referenced and where do Buddhist values intersect? What is the common good to which this wisdom is being applied?

We will look at trying to 'balance' the needs of the many with the rights of the few. We will examine intrapersonal needs, interpersonal needs and even extra-personal needs as they fluctuate over the immediate and long term.

The Glossary
Holding specific jargon in mind while reading a book of this type is difficult. For this reason a glossary is included, near the back of the book, that defines and/or explains key terms. The first time a word or phrase is used, it will be in SMALL CAPS and *italicized* to indicate that there is further material available.

Citations
It's hard to drag people along from one book to someone else's document or research paper and for that reason I've tried very hard to accurately reflect conclusions of documents cited.

Footnotes
Every effort has been made to ensure the accuracy and relevancy of the footnote references, however links change, get updated, the material to which they refer may be altered or deleted, the links go dead or occasionally get re-directed to other websites. For these reasons, the author and editors cannot be held accountable for the footnote links or the accuracy of the material they reference. At the time of publication, these footnotes were accurate.

Key Point Summary
At the end of each chapter or section, there will appear a Key Point Summary chart of the main ideas covered.

Index
Beginning on page 332 is a comprehensive index that will allow the reader to cross-reference important terms, names and ideas.

Key Point Summary

There Are No Silver Arrows	<ul><li>Defining wisdom in a few simple words is a mug's game. There is no single thing that defines wisdom</li><li>Wisdom, a we will learn, is a bricolage of traits, skills and attitudes that must be developed over time and consciously applied</li></ul>
Selectivism	<ul><li>To our detriment, we have become very self-selecting in our reading and media consumption</li><li>We no longer seem able to tolerate the views and opinions of others</li><li>Our selectivism breeds contempt/fear, for others</li></ul>
Media Fragmentation	<ul><li>Our new media has become ultra-fragmented and partisan in the extreme, rarely reporting on events without a political angle that may or may not be disclosed.</li></ul>
Our Words Matter	<ul><li>What we say, and how we say it, makes a difference to how people perceive us</li><li>We too easily use words to harm others</li><li>We often use words to create division and mistrust</li></ul>
Technology	<ul><li>Our unrelenting push for greater technological development has not always provided benefits to everyone</li></ul>
Civility	<ul><li>Too often our leaders demonstrate poor judgment in how they communicate with others and their habits are often echoed by their entourage and followers</li><li>Frequently our leaders exhibit untrained emotional responses that do not recognize long-established courtesies</li></ul>
No One is Wise Every Day	<ul><li>No one can be 'wise' all day long, seven days a week. We are allowed our idiosyncratic behaviours, foibles and quirks. We are allowed to make snap decisions about what we want for breakfast without giving it the same consideration about who we might vote for</li><li>We *all* suffer from slack thinking on occasion</li></ul>
No One is Born Wise	<ul><li>Wisdom and intellect, are not the same thing</li><li>Wisdom is a balancing of attitudes and skills that we are rarely, if ever, born with. They are taught and learned throughout our lifetime and only through constant practice and applied effort do they strengthen</li></ul>

1. *Communication*

Bringing Light to Discourse - the Ability to Communicate

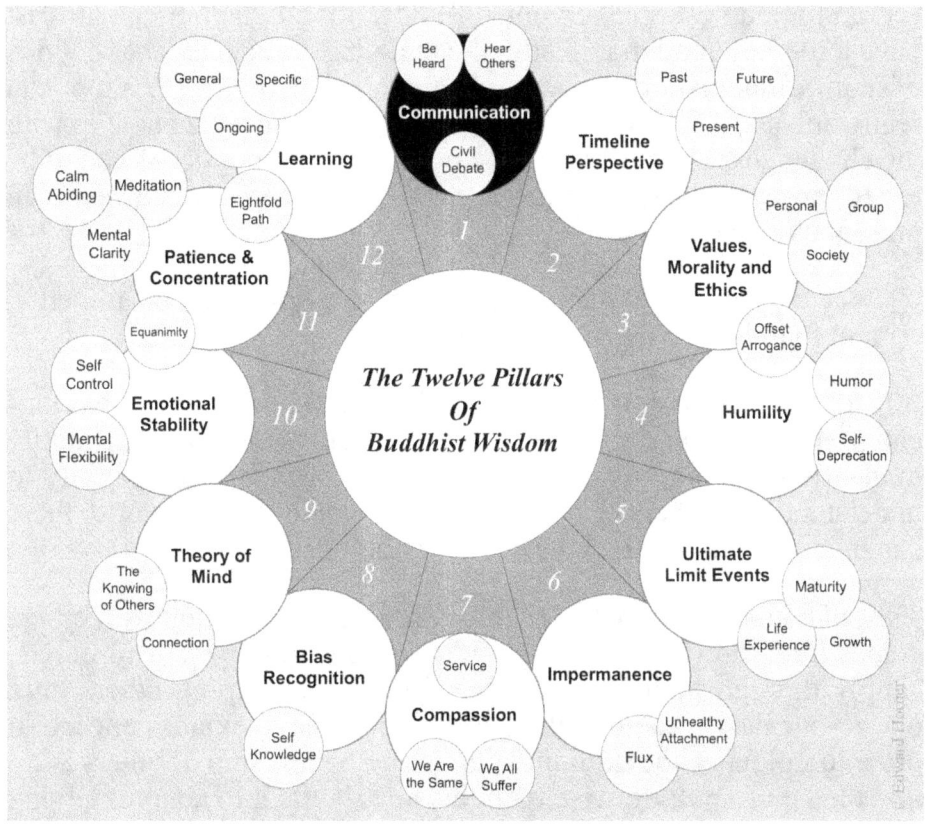

THE FIRST CRITICAL ASPECT OF WISDOM, Buddhist or otherwise, is being able to express oneself and take in *and hear* the opinions and ideas of others because we don't operate in a vacuum. Rather, we are born into, and deeply influenced by, our culture, society, cohort, parents, church, siblings, education system, politicians, and even TED speakers.

- Not being able to express ones ideas in a coherent and clear manner is not conducive to raising wisdom.

- Not being able to *hear* and *understand* what others have to say is not encouraging of wisdom.

When you can have an exchange of ideas, an understanding of others, and are able to make yourself understood, wisdom can at least have a foothold and manifest in the real world. Indeed, what good is wisdom, Buddhist or otherwise, hoarded in the mind? Wisdom can really only exist where it can be applied in the real world to help with the challenges that face us everyday. Thoughts and ideas need to be tested, proven and applied in the real world where their benefit can present and *prove* wise.

> Wisdom must be *proven*, put to the test, dismantled, examined and found fit-for-purpose claimed.

It is for this reason that we begin our look at wisdom with communication in general and conversation in particular. Without the ability to clearly transmit our understanding of the world and an ability to understand that others also have an understanding of the world, there can be no direct exchange or transmission of wisdom.

This, of course is where being able to hold a conversation with others comes in. Rarely can any individual bring great benefit to others, simply through their own efforts. Obviously, helping others on a one-to-one basis is a good thing, but being able to express oneself in order to influence the thinking, words and behaviours of others is really the key to putting wise thoughts and words into action. Giving change to a homeless person in your neighbourhood clearly benefits that individual and, from a Buddhist perspective, is an act of merit that affects karma, but being able to speak convincingly and clearly at a fundraising event that might raise hundreds, thousands or even hundreds of thousands of dollars for the homeless is better still.

As noted in the introduction we have entered into an age of incivility. We are in a time of social and civil degradation. I'm not writing about apocalyptic events, but we are witnessing a coarsening of words and confused thinking. We are on the verge of a Civility Conflict. Of course humans always seem to be in a time of conflict, but the various forms we can summon forth now are greater than ever before, with wide ranging ramifications; psychological discord, disinformation, internet trolling, media partisanship, political conflict, simmering hostility among the races, even dissension between the sexes. But the conflict that should concern us most is the assault on reasoned thought and civil discourse, for a de-valuing of these civil attributes, comes a lesser ability to solve the other issues.

When we are confused and uncertain, we can too easily be influenced by charismatic leaders who may not have our best interests at heart. When we are at sea, we may grasp at the straw that seems most palpable, most likely to bear our weight, even if it's not in our best, long-term interests to do so. When we are fed a diet of *DELUSIONS*, we may be too easily led by our greed and hatred. Even smart, skeptical people can be conned if the ruse is tailored to their prejudices and biases.

When we take less time to think before speaking, we can, today, spread our poor choice of words around the globe, perhaps not fully realizing the almost immediate impact. For example, posting a photo of a friend acting foolish at a party, with a few choice words of derision, will live on the internet for a lifetime, influencing people's opinions of you and your friend for years to come, affecting your social lives, career opportunities and maybe even your families.

Mentioning, on Facebook, that you hate your job, even if your privacy setting is "friends only," you still run the risk of someone telling someone else that you hate your job and it can so easily get back to your boss and that may well be career-limiting or even career ending.

Wisdom is Encouraged When We Avoid ...	
Words which DECEIVE	• Words that avoid the truth and seek to deceive others
Words which are DIVISIVE	• Words spoken to create rifts between people or groups
Words which are HARSH	• Words spoken to shock or harm others
Words wIthout HUMILITY	• Words spoken to aggrandize oneself beyond proportion or to take credit from others

These four simple guidelines require that we stop and think, before we speak. This is seemingly simple, but, in fact, generally proves quite difficult. It requires a practiced skill and awareness of our thought process and, as we discuss later in the book, an element of patience.

When speaking with others, we rarely enjoy any pauses in conversation. We always seem to want the silences filled with something, *anything*, so long as it's filled. We seem to feel that, "dead air," is to be avoided at all costs. These simple guidelines around speech are expanded upon in Chapter 11.6 – The Eightfold Path - Right Speech.

Now, more than ever before, we need to choose our words wisely, offer counsel which is well considered, take actions that create harmony and build mutual trust. Every society knows (or once knew) that living together required decency, kindness and civility towards one another, but in societies like that which we've built in the West, we've become so focused on the gain of material goods, money or status in order to satisfy the insatiable desires of the individual that this civility is too often seen as uncomfortable, limiting, week, unworthy or in some way unseemly. Today, little value is placed on skillful speech and this has lead to a degradation of common human decency, kindness and care for one another. How you think and what you say *does* make a difference.

Yet, human decency and kindness, in this day where everything can be amplified and accelerated through our technology, is more important than ever before.

> Knowing how to have a conversation with someone that doesn't send one party or the other spinning off into an abyss, feeling dismissed, mis-understood, demeaned or devalued is a crucial component of Buddhist wisdom.

1.1 *Characteristics of Conversation*

When people converse, one or the other party may sometimes wonder, "When is he/she going to get to the point?" Well, fact of the matter is, sometimes there is no 'point' to get to. Sometimes, a conversation doesn't have a point, moral, reason or any justification. Sometimes, not-withstanding the previous point, we just talk for the sake of talking; perhaps to reveal something of ourselves, our passions or dislikes or to feel a sense of connection or to tell how we feel without any judgement or reply even being necessary. Sometimes no decisions need be offered or made, no 'solving' needs to be done. Although it doesn't sound very 'Buddhist' it's simply an exchange for sheer social joy and for that reason alone, it has value and, in my opinion, would not be considered 'idle chatter' in the Buddhist context.

When we speak with others, beyond a simple, "Hi. How's it going?" the conversation typically has an ebb and flow. Sometimes the conversation will be short while other times it may be long and wandering covering a wide range of topics. Sometimes, as noted earlier, there may be no particular point to a conversation at all, beyond connecting with one another, while other times the nature and outcome of a conversation will be apparent from the outset - having a certain goal to achieve.

Scope

The scope of a conversation might be wide or narrow. For example, two engineers may have a very specific conversation about whether a grade 5 or grade 8 bolt will be best suited for fastening hand rails onto a pedestrian bridge. Other times a conversation may cast a wide net. Two businesswomen may discuss how best to market a product, including; ethical sourcing, pricing variables, distribution channels, after-market sales and service and market positioning.

Quality

Sometimes we feel, 'obliged,' to have a conversation and when we do, the discussion may be shallow and not overly enthusiastic. We may only be interested in saying what is expected of us, or quickly hearing what the other person has to say, and then be on our way. The topic or topics are touched upon lightly and without vigour. Other times, when a topic or person deeply interests us the conversation may be fully engaged in and plumb the depths of a topic or topics with enthusiasm and zeal with each participant bringing their knowledge and experience to bear.

Character

When we speak upon topics that we are well acquainted with, the character of the conversation may be smooth and seamless, quick paced and focused. On the other hand, when we speak on topics we are less familiar with and using the time to 'explore' the topic, our conversations may be less smooth, a bit choppy or fragmented as we search for the words to use and a way in which to express ourselves. We may occasionally backtrack over points to clarify and refine. We may have blind paths which we run down that yield no way forward and we need to backtrack and start down another avenue. These conversations are often infused with terms like, "Now, I'm just thinking out loud here ..." or "Clearly, I'm not an expert on this, but ..." in order to get the point across that the topic being spoken of is being explored.

A smooth interaction with someone flows easily from one topic to another, each feeling comfortable expressing their ideas, opinions, observations or comments and receiving the same from their conversation partner.

At times, a conversation may feel adversarial, where one person may feel hurt, dismissed, or undervalued. The conversation may feel out of balance with one side being more dominant while the other feeling they may not have fully participated.

In ancient Japan, Samurai warriors, were skilled in the use of weapons of war such as swords, knives, bow and arrow and, of course, hand-to-hand combat. These warriors, who were feared and respected for their fighting skills had special social standing, but they were also expected to train and become efficient in the arts, such as flower arranging, tea ceremonies and conversation.* Demonstrating their power in battle, then being able to contain and channel that power in delicate matters such as a tea ceremony and eloquent conversation demonstrated discipline of the mind and development of the spirit.

---

* Japanese Samurai culture and code of conduct (Bushido) evolved to include the idea of artist-warrior. It was during the Muromachi era (1338-1573) that Samurai training began to include the formal and highly ritualized tea ceremony and flower arranging to add refinement and balance to the warrior persona.

Intent

Everyone knows that our words can be hurtful, dismissive, callous, cold and uncaring, but they can, with good intentions and considered choices, also be used to garner warmth, love, compassion, understanding, support and kindness for your conversation partner. It's all about intent.

In order to help in selecting wise words, look for areas of common interest and common philosophy. We can't always agree on everything, but some common ground can almost always be found. Where it can't, there is no wisdom in inflaming the emotions of others with ridicule, harsh words or name calling. Rather, seek to mend fences, build trust and harmony with your conversation. If you've offended someone in the conversation, own up to it, apologize and move on.

In short, the nature of a conversation is formed by the interplay of scope, quality, character and intent. The wisdom is determining how to manage these components to get the best from a conversation at any given time in any given place. To seek a smooth, engaged, energized, meaningful and balanced exchange of ideas within a conversation, should be our goal.

In This Moment

When we enter into a meaningful conversation with someone, it should be a priority. We might turn off our television, radio or cell phone. We might ask that we not be interrupted except for urgent matters. We might set aside a specific time and place where the conversation can take place. Above all, we need to be present, in the moment and focused.

No one wants to be in the middle of making an important point in their conversation and have the recipient look down at his or her cell phone to read an incoming text. It's disrespectful of the point being made and of the person making it. Still, we see this all the time.

We often see people seemingly deep in conversation at our local Starbucks yet with rare exception are the cell phones *not* on the table in front of them, ready to relay some piece of information from the outside world to distract them from their talk. Some people seem literally addicted to their cell phone and its use, actually suffering withdrawal symptoms if separated from their internet provider for even a few short moments.*

> *"Understanding is the heartwood of well-spoken words."*
> ~*The Buddha*
> Kimsila Sutta

What all this seems to indicate is that we are having difficulty engaging with others in meaningful conversation, in part, because we have this pressing, almost burning, belief that we are 'needed' somewhere else or that something elsewhere requires our urgent attention. Yet this belief is rarely based on any reality. To be sure, a call from the day care centre telling us little Johnny fell off the slide is an urgent matter, deserving our immediate attention, but do we really need to respond to Mary's 'check in' at the new location of Lady Marmalade, on Broadview, for breakfast with her husband, to look at a picture of their poached eggs and toast? What is important and urgent is too often confused with background noise.

Our untrained and unfocused minds are simply unable to 'settle' and be in the present moment as our ego is trying to manufacture some reason for us to be elsewhere doing 'important' things, or seeking some novel experience. We are undisciplined and unaccustomed to the idea of being in one place and engaging in something for more than just a few minutes.

Decorum
It seems quaint to speak of aplomb, decorum, composure or poise in todays slap-dash, superficial, distracted world, but decorum is how we behave towards others in civilized society. Politeness and civil behaviour towards others is a sign of respect and worthiness towards

---

* Withdrawal symptoms include; anger, tension, depression, irritability and restless ness. Signs and Symptoms of Cell Phone Addictions - www.PsychGuides.com

them. It also shows a respect towards yourself and *your* fundamental good nature.

You occasionally hear the term, "Polite for politeness sake." This suggests disingenuous politeness that comes from a fundamental lack of respect for others and even in yourself. When you do not believe that others have inherent good qualities or attributes, you may pay lip service to polite behaviour and words, but this is more a reflection on how you feel about yourself. You may feel too important or grand to speak with another who does not share your social status, income range, job title or ideas. You are polite only so far as is required by social dictum and not because you value others.

When you come to be comfortable with your own ideas and your own place in the community, then you can become more comfortable with others, show them respect, politeness and compassion.

> Showing other people respect, through your body language, dress and sense of decorum never insults them, but rather, it enhances their own sense of value and the feeling that they are being respected.

Really Listen
Listening is much harder, than speaking. Yet, it's imperative that we fully hear and understand people if we are to offer wise advice, suggest a wise course of action, make a rebuttal to their suggestions or offer a constructive, respectful counter argument.

> When we undertake conversation, we need to have an open mind, allow words or ideas we might not agree with, to hang in the air. We have to be 'big' and allow room for those ideas, even when we don't agree with them. But, if we are truly interested in learning about other people, new ideas, ways of doing things and new ways of thinking, then this is a skill we need to develop.

Once people both feel and believe that they've been 'heard,' and understood, then they will stop fighting to be heard. There will be a letting down of defences and a warming up of trust, and until trust can arise there is no real exchange of ideas, no meaningful conversation. Without this trust, there isn't likely to be an environment where wisdom, if it has arisen, would even be heard, let alone acted upon.

Sometimes, when we are not fully present in a conversation, we may find ourselves listening with the intent of formulating what to say next. But this is not really listening. This is being self-centred and dismissive of your conversation partner.

When listening, you can let the other person know that you hear and understand their points by occasionally nodding, saying "I understand," and repeating back - paraphrasing - what you've come to understand. When a person tells you she's upset that she was passed over for promotion, you might make eye contact, nod and paraphrase, "Yes, yes, I hear that. You're upset about that decision." It sounds a bit trite, but it does let the person know they've been heard and you at least understand her point.

Another way to be an active listener is to probe deeper with relevant questions where your understanding is not clear. Examples might include, "Can you tell me a little more about that?" or "How was that resolved the last time it came up?" You're not asking the person to defend herself, but to provide further information and clarification so you can better understand her point, position or feelings.

Watch body language. True, it's not 'listening' per se, but how an individual sits, stands, moves and reacts may give some insight to their thinking or emotional state - at least for an astute observer. If you think you saw a sudden pull back of the individuals head or arms, after you repeated back a point or paraphrased her previous comment, you might follow up with, "It looks like you had a bit of a reaction to my comment. Did I misunderstand the point you were making?"

Pay attention to *your* body language as well. Sitting with legs and arms crossed might send a signal that you are not receptive to ideas. Rolling your eyes, sighing, fidgeting might all suggest to your conversation partner that you're not fully listening. Be present and respectful.

Listening is Not Agreeing

Just because you hear, clearly, and understand a person's point doesn't mean that you will agree with them. People don't always need you to agree with them, they only need to know that their ideas have been heard, understood and considered. Active listening, repeating back their story and asking questions is usually proof enough that they've been heard.

Sometimes a conversation may, indeed, change your mind. It may give you pause to reflect or alter your thinking in some way. This is good. It shows you've been listening and you're open to new ideas. The revelation may not come during, or immediately after, the conversation, but it might come days or even weeks later after it's "sunk in." You may need time to view the world through the filter they've provided before you come to agree with their point of view. An old work colleague of mine, P. Tucker would occasionally suggest we take a bit of 'soak time,' before coming to any conclusions.

> The wisdom in listening is that we learn about others, what motivates them, what drives them, what ideas they may have to improve a situation. Without fully understanding what they are offering, we can't be in a position to offer any real help.

Listening, from a Buddhist perspective, allows greater understanding of the problems of others. When we understand the conditions of others, we can better speak or act to help reduce their suffering or at least make their circumstances better in some way, if it's within our power.

Consider Your Partner

Having a conversation with friends can some times be easy, freewheeling and comfortable. You have shared a lot of common experiences and know one another well. There may be some areas that you've learned are easy to converse about and some areas which are difficult or irritating. The talk will ebb and flow accordingly.

Often, there will be specific topics that are comfortable; sports, cars, the weather, vacation spots, etc. These may come up time and time again and when they do, you might feel like you've been over this ground before and it's a bit humdrum. Maybe there is an opportunity to explore new common ground and find new common experiences that you can talk about.

You may share a bit of a competitive streak among your friends or business associates. When one or another starts a new business or sets out on a new adventure, perhaps it's related in a friendly, but competitive manner. There's nothing wrong with this, so long as you maintain good intent and do not use the new venture to create ill-will amongst yourselves. Those who have done well use their words cautiously and avoid making others feel inadequate. With some sensitivity and skill you can have conversations that might spur each other towards higher goals, give each other new ideas and new ways of doing things.

> When you meet someone new, conversations can be a little awkward at first. You don't know the common ground. Telling a person you've just met that you, "Had the best burger of my life at lunch and you simply must try Burger's Priest," is a bit awkward when you discover they're vegetarian.

Ask Questions

Take time to ask engaging questions about the topic you're discussing. Sometimes questions can be used to explore another avenue of conversation. Sometimes they are for clarification or more information. Whatever the reason, asking questions allows the other person to speak and express their opinion or point of view. It may allow them to display expertise or provide a unique insight.

Take care not to sound like your cross-examining your conversation partner. No one wants to feel they are being 'put on the spot' by having to answer difficult questions without having given enough thought to their response.

When listening to the answer, don't speak. It's shocking how often people start talking over an answer to a question they just asked. It's quite remarkable, really, yet it happens all the time. We might start to answer their question and in with a few seconds, they're talking again - right over us. Instead, keep eye contact, nod, say, "uh huh," or some other expression to indicate you get the point or points being made. *You* asked the question, so fully listen to the answer, even when you don't like what you hear.

Conversation is Not Therapy

As we've noted, we talk with a lot of people, for a lot of reasons. Sometimes, when we have something important or painful to say, we turn our conversation into a therapy session. We may want to talk with a friend about a problem, circumstance or difficult condition. When we do this, it puts the other person in a difficult spot, with them, perhaps, believing that they need to come up with an answer, offer advice or help in some way. It's very limiting when one party thinks they need to ride to the rescue of the other with sound advice.

Another difficulty with some conversations, is that we may begin to intrude upon the privacy of another. We may, quite innocently, ask questions like, "Why did you and Mary split up?" or "How is it you got fired from your job?" These types of questions, uninvited, tend to be invasive. They may put the person 'on the spot' feeling they must provide some sort of answer. They may feel set upon, ambushed or set up. At best they may just be uncomfortable. Unless invited to have this type of conversation, it's best not to ask these questions as it may only aggravate your partner or cause them to suffer more.

Even if you really, *really* want to know the answer, it's better not to ask. Best to stick with other more neutral topics; a recent book you read, a new movie release, a class you're taking or want to take. There are many things to speak about, without invading someones privacy.

Still, if your conversation partner *wants* to talk about his or her difficulties, the good conversationalist can adapt, listen, give rise to compassion, express sympathy and, if asked, provide whatever advice they believe is helpful. We discuss this further on in chapter 9.1 Motivation, Skill and Resource Analysis in Wise Decision Making.

When Conversation Is Therapy

There are times when we might feel there is no one we can talk to about problems in our life. We might believe that there is something wrong with how we interact with the world or that we are misunderstood or we are not valued. We may feel 'stuck' or 'blocked' in our relationships. We may have come to a creative impasse where we can't move forward with a book, painting, sculpture or project at work. Often, speaking with friends may only exacerbate the problems. That's where talk therapy, in the form of psychotherapy, may prove invaluable.

In therapy, clients learn a new language in which they can better express themselves in a more profound manner, as they and their therapist explore the difficulties. This can be a liberating experience, extending and enhancing interactions with friends, employers, family and others. Beyond this, talk therapy will allow them to see their inner goodness, perhaps for the first time, and know they are valued and have much to offer the world. This is transformational, life enhancing and, in some cases, may be life saving.

> When we feel there is no one else to talk too, or we feel that we need another way forward, there is significant wisdom in asking for help and turning to a professional psychotherapist.

Conversation isn't Bargaining

We often hear the term 'transactional' in relation to a conversation in business. It means that we are entering into a conversation in order to extract a transaction, some sort of deal, from each of the participants. There is nothing wrong with this idea, so long as both partners understand what they're getting into. The difficulties arise when one of the parties isn't aware of the situation and feels, 'set up.'

For example, Bob and Mary might be having a lunch-time conversation at work about how staff resources are being stretched tight and they both recognize how tough it is to meet deadlines. Then Bob asks Mary asks for help. At best, Mary may feel set up and obligated to help, but she can't help, due to her own deadlines. She has to decline and simply say, "Sorry, but as we both know, our resources are stretched. I can't help." Bob has to respect this and not press the point. Mary wasn't aware of the nature of the conversation until Bob made it clear it was transactional in nature.

> Don't set people up. Let them know the nature of the conversation, if it's going to be transactional.

To conclude this section, we need to recognize that speaking with others is done for a lot of reasons, but first and foremost, from a Buddhist perspective, we want to listen to others so that we may have better understanding of them, find some way to help them (if we can) and further understand the human condition. What we don't need to do is talk over people, use unwise words, make people feel small or dismissed. We don't want to be harsh or untruthful for none of that builds trust and without trust, little can be done.

Key Point Summary - Communication

Communication Mastery	• The greater our mastery of conversation, hearing and being heard, without debilitating emotional reactions, the greater the likelihood that we will be able to make wise choices about the circumstances at issue
Wisdom and the Common Good	• Wisdom doesn't exist in and of itself. It exists as part of a greater whole and is derived from and serves the common good • Conversations help to shape wisdom and bend it to the benefit of the community
Scope	• The conversation can cast a wide net, be very focused, or somewhere in between
Quality	• Depending upon our interest in the topic, the conversation may be undertaken with enthusiasm and energy or apathy and disinterest
Character	• Conversations may proceed smooth and quick or, depending upon familiarity with the topic, haltingly with dead ends and false starts
Intent	• Engage in conversation with the intent of enriching both parties
Decorum	• Display courtesy and politeness in conversation • Let your partner know you value and respect them and their view
Listening	• Active listening allows the speaker to know they are valued and are being heard
Consider Your Partner	• Engage in conversation to build trust and to learn • Allow for ideas that do not agree with yours
Conversation Isn't Therapy	• Avoid putting people into the difficult position o listening to your problems and feeling they have to help solve them • If you need therapy, turn to professional providers
Ask Questions	• Where possible, try to speak less and listen more • Ask probing questions to gain greater insight and allow your partner room to fully respond
Point of Conversation	• Conversation builds trust, understanding and allows space for wisdom to arise

2. Timeline Perspective

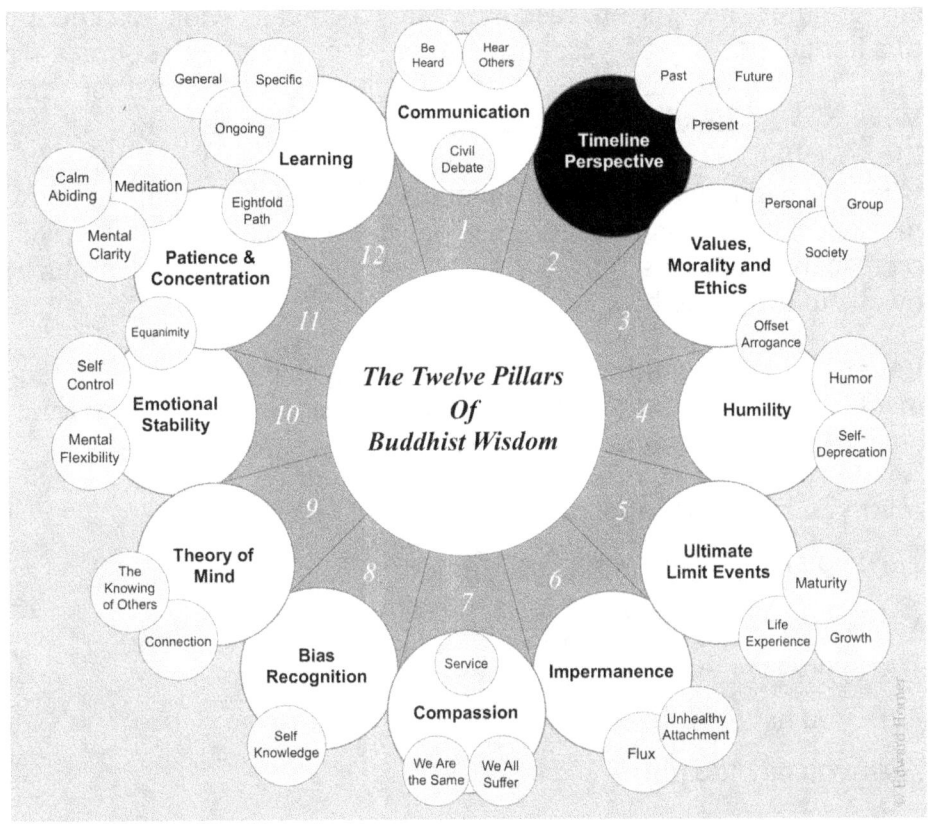

TIME, AS EXPERIENCED BY HUMANS, is generally divided into past, present and future, and experienced in a linear fashion from 'past,' through 'present' to 'future,' unidirectionally.

This is a useful, working division. Few among us would try to deny that using the term 'tomorrow' has value. Similarly, we would universally acknowledge the usefulness of saying, 'yesterday,' as in "Yesterday, we enjoyed a Greek salad on Danforth Avenue." There is no important ambiguous aspect when saying, 'yesterday,' or 'tomorrow.' Philosophers, theoretical physicists and cosmologists may want to split hairs and argue among themselves, but for everyday, earthly living, past and future – yesterday and tomorrow, are well understood.

Further we distinguish the 'present,' or 'now,' in very much the same way we distinguish yesterday and tomorrow. It represents a segment along a timeline - in this case a moving segment. Along a timeline of a human life, say 85 years, the 'present' segment begins soon after birth, but we only become aware of it sometime in the first year. When we are first born, we really only experience the 'now' of our life. We don't seem to have much cognition of a post or future. It's when we begin to develop our mental abilities that we come to know past and future. At any rate, the 'present' is relatively short-lived, representing perhaps only a few seconds or a few minutes and it dwells in the space between past and present.

Eating a meal, might be something we experience as a 'present moment' event, even though it may occupy some past element of time, essentially being a moment of 'thens.'

First you have your appetizer,

Then you have your soup,

Then you have the main,

Then you have desert,

Then you have coffee,

Then you pay the bill.

Essentially a series of moments, strung together, creating a 'present' event, in this case *the meal*, lasting maybe an hour. Were a person to call us up on our cell phone and ask what we were up to, at the moment, we would typically say, "We're having dinner," and it would be understood that the dinner event is in the present, in the 'now,' despite the fact that some of the meal moments were clearly in the past while others would be in the future.

'Now,' as noted above, might be experienced as a few seconds or a few minutes, but everyone generally understands that what lies between the 'past' and the 'future' is a short, moving line segment of time, known as 'the present.'

We don't usually experience any 'leaks' of past into present or present into past or vice-versa. Time, as experienced by human beings, flows in one direction with no cross over of past, present or future. However, *subjectively*, we sometimes feel or believe that there is some cross-boundary seepage of time.

In the example of the meal, the moment of desert and the moment of coffee may cross over and seem as a single unit of time, even though they are, outwardly, discrete in their nature. Our brains and our sense organs, as imperfect as they are, provide some ambiguity in how we experience *the now*.

Most people will have had the experience of a few seconds lasting for minutes or an afternoon having flown by as if it were only a few minutes. These are human experiences that are very much affected by our brains and sense organs, but this is not really a 'leakage' of time.

As we live our lives, (that 85 years mentioned earlier) piling event upon event, present moment upon present moment, the timeline behind us (the 'past') gets longer and longer while that timeline in front of us (the 'future') gets shorter and shorter, but the 'present' always remains more or less the same. It's like driving a car from one point to another. The car represents our 'present' while the road behind us is the 'past' and the road ahead represents the 'future.' The present moment of our life timeline is what we are experiencing right now, in the car.

Take, as another example, reading this book right now, in the moment, starting with the first word of the sentence, then going to the next, then the next, then the next, etc. Just like having a meal, it's a set of 'thens' that build the event of 'reading' in the present - each word communicating some shared experience. As the pages turn, the

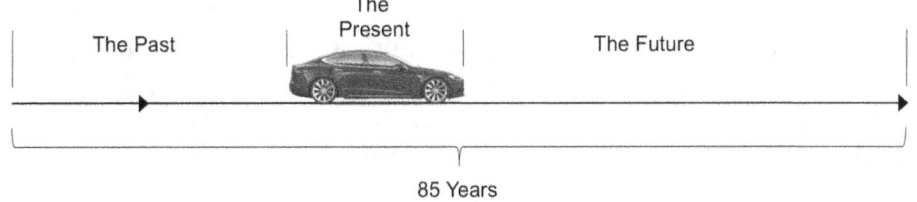

85 Years

present becomes the past while the unturned pages are the future. The pages we've already read pile up, getting thicker and thicker, while the unread pages become fewer and fewer. Essentially our 'present' is the word, sentence, paragraph or page we are reading.

Of course, when we get right down to it and begin to do a deep analysis of 'now,' it becomes very clear that, 'now,' only lasts a split-second. It appears, rushes by and into the past in the blink of an eye, lost to us forever. Still, from a practical point of view, 'now' is what you're experiencing at the moment. The experience of a cup of coffee, the experience of getting on the subway or the experience of signing the divorce papers. Short intervals, but long enough to register with our brains and be experienced.

"The Moving Finger writes; and, having writ,
Moves on: nor all thy Piety nor Wit
Shall lure it back to cancel half a Line,
Nor all thy Tears wash out a Word of it."

~ Omar Khayyám, The Rubaiyat

The Past

In 1928, the US State of Florida was hit with a massive hurricane that, for two hours, shredded houses, upturned boats, stripped the leaves off most of the vegetation, took out power and phone lines and caused property damage on a catastrophic scale. Thankfully, in the early stages, most people heeded the warnings and took cover away from the coast, thus preventing massive loss of life from that quarter.

The hurricane caused massive winds and rain all across Florida, and Lake Okeechobee (70km west of West Palm Beach) was no exception. The region had received an exceptional amount of rain in the weeks prior to this particular storm, so the lake levels were already higher than normal, almost breaching the earthen dam system at it's southern end.

During the initial stages of the hurricane, Okeechobee received even more rain. Then, as the storm centre shifted, the winds turned and began to come from the north. Those high winds, travelling across 50km of open water, pushed waves southward, relentlessly, against the dam which protected the agricultural land and people south of the lake. Places like *Lake Harbour*, *South Bay* and *Belle Glen* were thriving, well populated areas at that time, but they were located directly south of the lake and that location was to prove disastrous.

When the waters began to overtop the earthen dam, erosion began in ernest and soon, the waters of Lake Okeechobee were coursing though the breaches and into the farmland and towns all across the low laying land. As more water poured through, the gaps widened. The result was horrifying. The flood waters, coming at night, took everyone unaware. There was little or no time to evacuate, even if such plans had existed. That evening, at least 2,000 lives were lost in the flood. It remains the most deadly, natural/man-made event in the history of the state.

The point of this story is that when the original earthen dam was built, it was done so with good intentions and with whatever knowledge of geology, weather patterns, dam engineering and risk factors were available. It was decided, wisely, that the farmland and people living on that farmland, should be protected from the frequent flooding the area was prone to and so the dyke was built for the common good of the people and to encourage the local economy.

The building of the dam was, for reasons that made perfect sense at the time, a wise decision that addressed the needs of many stakeholders, over a long timeline, to achieve a common good. The affected communities benefitted and contributed, through their taxes, to achieve flood protection. Wisdom, for the time and place, given the circumstances, prevailed, but in the end it proved to be the wrong choice and loss of human life was the result.

> When we speak of wisdom, we can only speak in terms that make sense for any particular point in time and place, given the circumstances and what is then known or knowable.

There will always be second guessing and that's important to remember, for it's all too easy to look back, point fingers and say, "Ah ha! *That's* where they went wrong," knowing what we know today and enjoying the benefit of hindsight, easier access to information, advances in engineering methods and computing power.

This is not to suggest that we do not look back, make assessments and learn, for wisdom is enhanced when we can incorporate historical perspective, but we need to remember not to be too judgmental around past circumstances and the actions taken at that point in time. Of course, there will always be historic events that are worth deep and comparative study, both for the benefits they may bring us today and in the future, or for the lessons they teach about what we must avoid.

In the case of Lake Okeechobee, looking back with what we know today, we might suggest it would have been wiser to allow the lake to flood naturally and not build towns so close to the flood area and, perhaps, not farm or populate the at-risk land. It's all too easy to second guess the thoughts, words and actions of people who came before us, knowing what we know now. As the old saying goes, hindsight is 20/20.

The Present

When we leave the past behind, and rise through the present and into the future, we leave a lot of stuff behind; friends, jobs, favorite cars, honeymoon trips, homes and countless other items, relationships and circumstances. Some of these we are happy to leave behind and others we are sad to leave behind. Still others bring fear.

- "Should I quit my job and move on to another?"
- "Should I leave my partner and strike out on my own?"
- "Should I sell my car and buy a motorcycle?"
- "Should I retire and move to Arizona?"

- "What will I do when I get out of prison?"
- "Should my family immigrate to Canada?"

Clearly, we are not leaving everything behind all the time, but as the present slips into the past, a lot of things change and a lot of things get dropped. All this 'leaving behind' can be a source of suffering for people. Some people don't like change and the idea of 'loss' brings anxiety. It makes them uncomfortable, cause mental stress, anxiety and, in the extreme, the inability to lead a 'normal' life.

Courage
To some degree, it takes an element of courage to let things drop or fall away when they are no longer needed, desired or available.

Some things we will drop voluntarily. For example we might decide after considerable thought, that although we like our current job and the people with whom we work, we need more challenge or greater opportunity for advancement. We might seek a new job of our own volition.

On the other hand, we might be out of a job because of nothing we did our could have done. As this book goes to press, millions of people around the world have lost their jobs due to COVID-19 and the mental and financial stress is both real and devastating.

In both cases, even though a position is being left behind, they each will have a very different feel and present very different challenges. The first, being voluntary and the second being involuntary means that we will think, speak and act differently about our employment situation.

In the voluntary situation, we may think of ourselves as 'ambitious,' 'upwardly mobile,' a 'go-getter,' or 'motivated.' In the second case, we may think of ourselves as 'victim,' 'innocent bystander,' 'abused,' 'ill-used' or 'disadvantaged' or just plain 'unlucky.' Both of these situations will, each in their own way, require courage and fortitude to proceed from the past and into a future. How we think, speak and act in the present will have an impact on what that future may look like.

Get Your Feet Under You

When things fall away into the past, either from voluntary or involuntary action, we need to explore what the present has to offer. Seek new opportunities, new ways of looking at things and new paths. It's a time to get our feet back under us. We may need help from our partner or relatives, the mental healthcare profession, an employment councillor, a financial advisor or spiritual leader. We often can't let major circumstances drop without getting some form of help.

To be sure, it's a time to reflect on what went wrong. We might want to lay some blame somewhere if that helps us feel better, but we need to take a bit of time to explore those past circumstances, how we ended up there and what we can do today to give ourselves something to look forward to.

We Have What You Have For a Reason

Our past has formed us, moulded us and set us up for what we are today. One doesn't become a concert pianist without practice and instruction. One does not become an F1 driver without first going through Karting, Formula BMW, GP3/GP2 and Formula Test driving.

What we have in the present, is largely a direct/indirect result of what we have done in the past. This goes for our circumstances, mental states, ability to handle stress and loss, financial situation, etc. We have what we have because of what we have done and sometimes what others have done to us. This is known as DEPENDENT ARISING or DEPENDENT ORIGINATION and it simply means that nothing comes of nothing - everything arises because of a combination of things that have occurred in the past.

Get Comfortable Not Knowing Everything

We cannot know everything about every situation. Sometimes we know 'enough,' while other times we don't and sometimes it might even be suggested we know 'too much.' Whatever we think we know is really only that - we *think* we know - because we don't know, what we don't know.

We must always proceed with the deeply understood fact that we *cannot* know everything about what we are doing. NASA did not, and still does not, know everything about putting people into space, but that didn't stop the them from doing it with brave men and women who undertook the challenge. If NASA waited for 'complete knowledge' about near-space travel, Americans would not have visited the moon. Similarly, human trials for new and life-saving medicines would not proceed if the pharmaceutical industry was to wait for 'complete information.'

This complete knowledge can never exist. At the very best, we always proceed with what we think we know, what we estimate the risks to be, what result we reasonably expect, etc. We always weigh the risk against the expected benefit and, when it looks like we have the balance right, proceed. The wisdom comes from recognizing these facts and proceeding with what we think we know today.

Let It Go
We hold onto lot of stuff, material goods not least among them. Cars, stereos, computers, TVs, favourite coffee mugs, ski equipment, paddles, kayaks, books, etc. The list is almost without end. Then there are the mental constructs and situations involving relationships. Our roles as daughter/son, mother/father, aunt/uncle, employee/employer, husband/wife, all change over time. Many of these roles and relationships have fallen away over the years, as they should have, but each of them also represents someone or something that we once were. They are part of our psychic makeup and have defined who we are today. Seeing all those things fall away can be difficult, for they sometimes represented the best of what we thought we might have been.

All these things must be let go, for we change, physically, mentally and spiritually. There has been an evolution of ourselves and we have to become comfortable with what we have become - as difficult as that may sometimes be. To hang on to what we were, is a mug's game, destined to fail and disappoint. The sooner we all recognize our ever-changing relationship with the world and ourselves, the better.

Different roles and relationships arise, often for the better. We evolve. As we age, we develop better emotional regulation, better at sitting down and thinking through a problem, examining relationships between diverse components, and coming to better decisions. What we are today, is often better than what we were twenty years ago, but is largely *dependent* upon what we were twenty years , and fifteen, ten and five.

> Everything that came before today has had some impact on what we have become - some of it good and some less so. The wisdom is in understanding this and coming to know it through direct, personal experience.

The Future

No one can predict the future with any real degree of certainty. We might accurately predict the rising of the sun or the wax and waning of the moon, the ebb and flow of the tides or annual flooding of the Nile, but on a human scale, the everyday comings and going of man, little is assured. When a non-Buddhist speaks of wisdom it's done so almost exclusively in relation to the future and concerns itself with the unknowable future and "best guesses." We might be trying to answer such questions as;

- Should I go to university?
- Should I break up with my partner?
- How can I tell my mother I don't want to see her anymore?
- When will I have grieved enough?

These are mostly the; who, what where when and why's of the future.

When Buddhists speak of wisdom it usually predicated on the best way forward for a) the relief of suffering for ourselves and others and b) how's this going to help with awakening and Nirvana?

Future Anxiety Disorder

This isn't something you're going to find in the DSM-5, but it seems to be a real problem for a lot of people. Future-oriented cognition or

Anticipatory Anxiety–thinking about and especially *worrying* about the future can bring a lot of fear.

- "What if we don't save enough for our retirement?"
- "When will this coronavirus pandemic be over?"
- "Am I marrying the right partner?"
- "What if I don't pass my real estate exam?"
- "Should I take the subway after that incident in the London underground?"

In some ways, the future is a bit like the past - largely unaccessible. Sure, we make plans, work towards a goal, but nothing is assured. A lot of time we get what we want, but other times we don't. Things happen along the track and, in one way or another, we get derailed. It's worse when we have maladapted beliefs like, "Worrying about the future helps me plan and prepare better for it." Perhaps *planning* for the future helps you plan for the future. Worrying about it is a lot like worrying about the past - not particularly helpful and may even be harmful if you can't get out of that deliberation groove.

There is an episode of *Seinfeld*,* in which George is made fun of at work. Lacking a snappy comeback, he ruminates on what he 'should' have said as he drives home from work. With a flash of *"L'esprit de l'escalier,"* he hits upon the perfect retort. Next morning, back at work, he goads the transgressor, from the previous day, into insulting him again, believing he has the best comeback ever and it goes something like this; "Oh yeah, well, that's funny because I just had sex with your wife." The room falls silent. Someone leans over to whisper into George's ear that the man's wife is in a coma.

In this case, George has worried about a future possibility and made plans for a snappy comeback that fell flat. This doesn't even take into account that he lacked a sense of humility or self deprecation that would have allowed him to take the barb in the first place. He also spoke unskillfully, lying and insulting someone in the hope of

---

* *Seinfeld,* TV show. NBC Sitcom. S8E13 "The Comeback." January 30, 1997.

aggrandizing himself. It all fell flat. His worry about the future didn't go so well.

Consider the Future

Future cognition seems to be one of the things that make us rare, if not completely unique, in the animal kingdom, this ability to think ahead, predict, prognosticate and forecast the future. Perhaps it is our lot in the world to worry about the future - perhaps not - either way, we can't really ignore it if only because we've got a brain that is able to differentiate 'today' from 'tomorrow.' There seems to be no way to avoid giving it *some* thought.

We don't want to get paralyzed by what we think we *ought* to do or fall into a debilitating depression, given the almost limitless possibilities, but some form of future is coming our way and we might as well have some influence in order to get what we desire out of it.

From a Buddhist perspective, we need to remember that a lot of our future will be affected by what we've done in the past. What we become is a result of what we've done and what we have been. A good education gives us a better chance to be a management consultant. Practicing guitar, hour after hour, until our fingers bleed, gives us a better chance at being a rock star. Treating people with dignity and kindness today will have an impact on how people treat us in the future. Learning about other cultures, customs and social organizations today will offer better understanding of varying cultures in the future.

All that is good, but we must remember that we can't get too caught up with expectations and desires. What we plan for, may not come to pass. We don't want to become so attached to a specific future outcome that we go to pieces when we don't get what we want or get something we didn't intend. This unreasonable attachment, can be debilitating if not recognized for what it is - an unhealthy greed for getting what we want.

So, let us not leave the future completely to chance. Let's work for what we desire, but not get too bent out of shape if it doesn't go our way. Let's not blame others, point fingers and not take responsibility for our own disappointment. Let it go and try again - maybe have a plan B in your back pocket.

All this talk about past, present and future really comes down to recognizing that our time on this planet is limited - really, really limited. Maybe 85 years, maybe 100 if we are super lucky, but that's about it. As an individual we've not existed for billions of years and then we pop up on Earth because our parents had sex. We exist for maybe 85 years and then we disappear again for who knows how long. Whatever time we have on this planet should be spent well, helping ourselves and others out of suffering, being kind, understanding and steadfast. We all share a common heritage. We are all human beings with eyes, ears, noses, two legs and what-not. What we share in common is vast in comparison to our differences. In the words of Jack Nicholson (Mars Attacks) "Why can't we all just … get along?"

The Forecast
When we look ahead and try to make our best recommendation about a course of action, we might want to think in terms of three scenarios that would follow from taking a specific action;

1. Possible, but *unlikely*, outcome. Low odds, such as 1 in a 100,000 chance of something happening (We could suppose that it's *possible* that the sun won't rise tomorrow, but most unlikely. I'd bet the farm it *will* rise in the morning. Of course, something could happen to change that.)

2. Probable outcome - what seems most likely. More than a 50/50 chance something will happen. (It's *probable* that humanity will continue to burn fossil fuels for the next ten years, more-or-less, as we have been for the past decade. Of course, something could happen to change that.)

3. Desired outcome - that scenario which is desired. What things or circumstances will we have to change if we are to get the outcome we want?

Obviously, there will be no way of knowing *everything* prior to making a decision. We may want to do a bit of research to help us decide about a course of action, look to our past for guidance, but in the end, we make our best choices and then deal with the fallout afterwards.

As we read further in this book, we learn other skills, mental processes and ways of thinking about and seeing the world that will help us make better, *wiser*, choices.

Key Point Summary - Timeline Perspective

Timeline Mastery	• For any given circumstance, the greater our comprehension of its history, present present circumstances and the likely future outcome, the greater the likelihood that we will make a wise choice
The Past	• We should never ignore the past. The past is what has formed us, our past actions, our past words and thoughts have built the foundation upon which our current psyche is built • We need not live in the past, but we do need to heed it if only use it as a reference • The human ability to learn from the past is what offers us a chance to encourage wisdom
The Present	• What we have, right now, this instant, is quite liberally all that we have. Our past is gone and lives on only in our body-memory and thoughts, while the future has yet to manifest • We need a bit of courage to let go of the past • Get your feet under you • Get comfortable not knowing everything • The present is the only place we exist and, as such is the only place where we can work towards enlightenment, attain wisdom, help others and gain relieve from suffering • It is here, in the now, that suffering is experienced
The Future	• The future is unknown and largely unknowable. Sure, there will be things that we can plan for and execute. The sun will rise and set while the planets continue their orbits, set upon their course. Death and taxes will continue to plague us • Still, little can truly be predicted and that's why we worry so much about the 'what ifs' • We need to plan and work towards the future we desire, but don't get too bent out of shape when things don't work out exactly as we had planned • The future, from a Buddhist perspective, is the place where our karmic consequences will manifest. It's a place where our past and present efforts will have some fruition.

*I am what time, circumstance, history,
have made of me, certainly, but I am also,
much more than that. So are we all.*

~James Baldwin
Notes of a Native Son

3. Values, Morality and Ethics

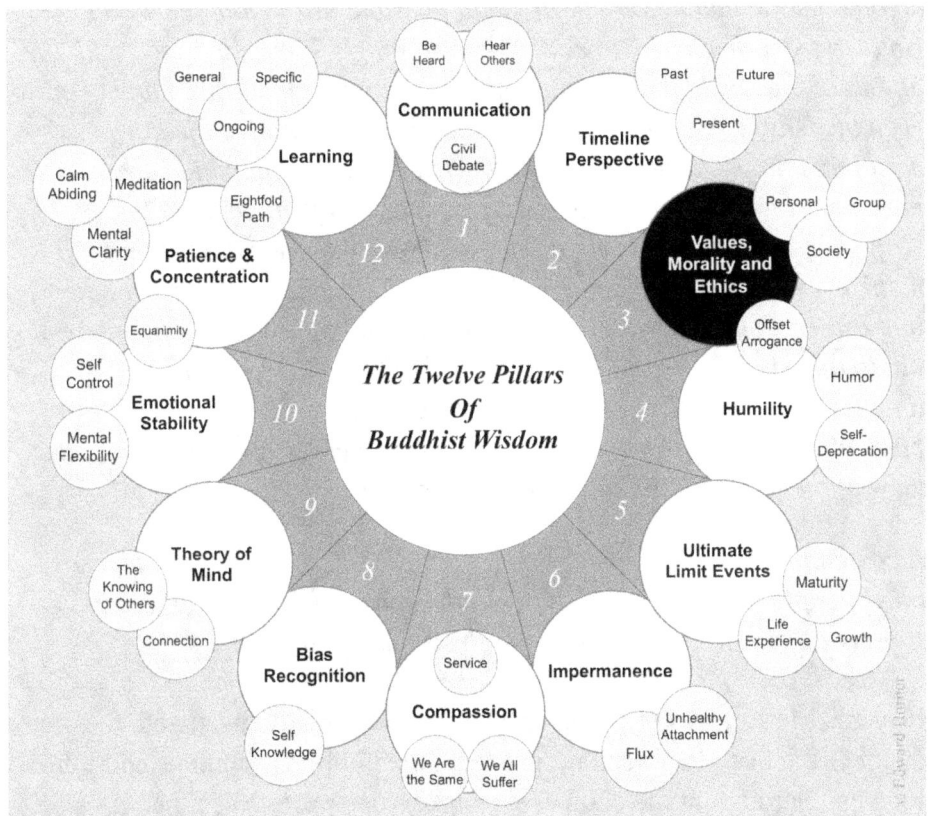

From a Buddhist perspective, we need to recognize that helping others - especially those who are suffering – is fundamental to the Buddhist practice. Buddhism is not alone in its concern over human suffering. Thomas Merton (1915 – 1968) a Trappist monk, theologian, social activist, scholar and writer was keen to use his special position as an 'outsider' to provide meaningful and contemplative discourse on human suffering, albeit from a religious viewpoint.

In Merton's essay, *Events and Pseudo-Events, Letter to a Southern Churchman*, he wrote:
 "Second, there is the nature of my own vocation to the monastic solitary, contemplative life – the vocation of Job! Of course this monastic life

does not necessarily imply a total refusal to have anything to do with the world. Such a refusal would, in any case, be illusory. It would deceive no one but the monk himself. It is not possible for anyone, however isolated from the world, to say, "I will no longer concern myself with the affairs of the world." We cannot help being implicated. We can be guilty even by default. But the monastic and the contemplative life does certainly imply a very special perspective, a viewpoint which others do not share, the viewpoint of one who is not directly engaged in the struggles and controversies of the world. Now it seems to me that if a monk is permitted to be detached from these struggles over particular interest, it is only in order that he may give more thought to the interest of all, to the whole question of the reconciliation of all men with one another in Christ. One is permitted, it seems to me, to stand back from parochial and partisan concerns, if one can thereby hope to get a better view of the whole problem and mystery of man.

A contemplative will, then, concern himself with the same problems as other people, but he will try to get to the spiritual and metaphysical roosts of these problems, not by analysis but by simplicity ..."

It seems Merton was bringing up what we've already discussed, to some degree - the need to sit down, ignore all the hubbub around us and think long and hard about the choices we make - *and that takes time.* As a monastic, Merton was somewhat insulated from the goings-on in the world and so was afforded the luxury of time to sit and contemplate the challenges that plague humanity.

Without veering too far into the convoluted realm of philosophy, we embark, with some anxiety, into values, morality and ethics. By skirting the deep and profound philosophical discussion which is rightly due morality, we run the risk of oversimplifying this topic. But skipping over the topic completely would do a disservice to wisdom. So, on shaky pins, we get going on values, morality, ethics and their role in wisdom.

Values

Values are largely personal judgements or evaluations and represent a set of cognitive and emotional outcomes that are 'ranked' somewhere along a scale of negative to positive.

For example, whatever values we associate with *freedom of the press*, first requires the ability to recognize and understand the mental concepts of what 'freedom' means and the role of journalism in our particular society - that's the cognitive part. Then we need some emotional activity that places that recognition somewhere on a scale from negative to positive. If someone had been treated poorly by the press in the past, they might think of the press in negative terms. If they had been well treated then they might think of the press in positive terms.

In short, we understand what 'freedom' and 'the press' represent and then we emotionally evaluate or judge the concept as 'good,' 'bad' or 'indifferent.' In other words, based upon our personal experiences, *freedom of the press* has value or does not have value or is somewhere in between, according to the individual.

It's important to note that just because emotions are involved, doesn't mean these are messy, emotionally-governed statements of preference (although they may be). It's also important to note that our values will be highly influenced by early childhood development. Our parents, schools, peers, local shopkeepers, librarians, police and church will provide a set of guiding principles and values upon which we might live our lives, but as we mature and begin thinking for ourselves, we begin to see other sets of values from our friends, associates, high school mates, co-workers, different cultures as we travel or read, etc. Our early values are not 'locked in' (although they may be) and will almost certainly evolve over time and with experience.

> Values, then are what we view as good (something we desire or a state which is desirable) or bad (something we avoid). Values are a mental filter that we build over time, through which we interpret everything we see, hear and experience to provide a judgment of good, bad or indifferent for us, as individuals.

When we apply our values-filter to our aspirations, the values help inform and motivate how we might move toward our goals. They are motivational in nature. If we have chosen to believe that a path towards wisdom is a good thing, then our values would direct us towards that goal, motivate and inform how we got there. Our values help us decided that wisdom is 'good' (or desirable) and then helps us determine what thoughts, words and actions will help us obtain 'wisdom.'

While values are, indeed, largely a personal matter, that isn't to say they might not be shared with a community or group. If you value mystery novels, you might join a book club that only reads and discusses mystery novels. In this case the group and the individual share, at least some, common values. Clearly not every group is going to share all it's values with all it's members, that's why we suggest that values are *primarily* an individual matter.

> Values, then, are sets of personal judgments as to what is good, bad or indifferent - and to what degree - that have evolved over time and place. These values are then used to colour how we see the world and determines how we interact with it.

When our values are in harmony with general society, much goes smoothly. When our values are at *odds* with our tribe, we tend to feel out of place, dismissed, oppressed, persecuted, down-trodden, an 'outsider,' etc. The larger society will not typically change to accommodate the individual or minority. Of course, changes within the larger society *do* take place, but generally in a manner both slow and ponderous - rarely quick enough to satisfy individuals or minorities at all times.

When we lack that essential harmony, we may seek out others who share our values, band together and create our own sub-culture within the larger society. For example, Holocaust deniers do not generally fit well into Western society, but you will find no shortage of Holocaust denier groups. For the most part, the deniers, having learned that their values do *not* fit well with society, at large, band together, to support one another, share their views, express their opinions, feed and reinforce their values away from and hidden (or insulated to one degree or another) from the larger society in which they still choose to live.

Morality

Morals have a greater societal component than values. We decide what is 'right' and what is 'wrong' based upon out own set of values, but we may be limited or restrained by what our community deems 'moral.' Morals are a set of prevailing, *community standards* that allow people to live together cooperatively.

For example, a corporation might have a CEO who's personal values are such that pouring raw, untreated effluent into a stream is 'good' because the company can save money by not treating their sewage before its release and therefore improve the returns paid to its investors. The investors might like the idea of greater returns on their investment and turn a blind eye to any negative environmental or human consequences and put their heads in the sand over not paying any 'external' costs associated with the activity of the company in which they've invested. But operating *contrary* to the CEOs values are laws, based upon community standards (morals) that prohibit such actions. Laws, created to protect the common good of the community, are in place to protect the community against dumping untreated waste. These same limits or restrains are also present for the individual.

Where our values and communal morality are in harmony, there is little conflict. Of course where our values and community standards are at odds, conflict will arise. It's worth pointing out that laws, in-and-of themselves, don't make something 'moral.' Usually, the community, at large, decides what is best for the community. Essentially, it decides what is moral and what is not and then enacts laws that constrain individuals in a manner that encourages moral behaviour. Someone acting in accord with the morals of the group would be considered 'moral' while those who were indifferent to the group standards would be considered 'amoral.' Finally those individuals (or entities, such as the corporation noted above) who acted *contrary* to the group standards would be considered 'immoral.'

The standards of the community–the group morality–may call upon the individual to temporarily give up their own short-term interest to the benefit of the group. In the midst of a pandemic, entire populations may be encouraged or, in the extreme, *ordered* to stay at home, not socialize or come into contact with others in order to protect the population at large from a deadly virus. This social isolation buys time for the medical community to find treatments and a vaccine to thwart the effects of the virus.

Laws Change

One hundred years ago, there were many laws in Canada, the US and Britain, that forbade and punished homosexuality. These 'morality laws' have largely been rescinded owing to the enlightened societal norms, evolving over time, to recognize that, in the words of Pierre Elliot Trudeau, *"There's no place for the state in the bedrooms of the nation."* *

Essentially, what we deem 'right' is moral and what we identify as 'wrong' is immoral. We might not go through the day thinking simply in those terms, but that's what running way down in the CMOS.

So, the term, 'morality' might easily be defined as that which concerns right vs wrong defined and influenced by our personal values, but limited or constrained by the community in which we operate. For any given society, community, tribe or family, this may seem relatively straightforward, but there are some complications.

The Oxford Living English Dictionary defines morality as *principles concerning the distinction between right and wrong or good and bad behaviour.* The OLED goes on to suggest, *The extent to which an action is right or wrong.*

It becomes quite clear, early in this discussion that, 'right' for one person may not be 'right' for another. Clearly, right or wrong is a

---

* In 1967, while acting as Justice Minister, Pierre Elliot Trudeau, introduced his controversial Omnibus bill in the House of Commons. Included in the bill were calls for massive changes to the Criminal Code of Canada. Trudeau made an appeal for the decriminalization of 'homosexual acts,' performed in private, telling reporters in a CBC television clip, "There's no place for the state in the bedrooms of the nation," Trudeau went on to say, "What's done in private between *[consenting]* adults doesn't concern the Criminal Code." CBC Digital Archives.

matter not easily settled among all people or communities, yet this idea of morality persists as if it had some special place in the human experience. When it comes to a matter of personal rights and wrongs, we say these are "value judgements" for they involve the choices of the individual. When we talk about the rights and wrongs of society, we say these are 'morality' issues.

Ethics

This is the study or branch of knowledge that deals with moral principles. For the purpose of this book, we turn to the *Cambridge Dictionary of Philosophy*, where we learn that ethics, in part, is is defined as the "moral principles of a particular tradition, group or individual."

Ethics, then, are sets of rules, imposed upon the individual, usually by a sub-group to which the individual belongs, that govern the individuals behaviour or at the very least, suggest how the individual behaves when interacting with the group - and sometimes beyond. For example, rules about how to behave in public office might include;

- not buying land in an area which is confidentially being considered for re-development
- being as truthful as circumstances allow (*arcana imperii* notwithstanding)
- not hiring or appointing relatives where merit tests are not met
- taking money or gifts from lobbyists.

From a 'legal' point of view, most of these activities are not expressly forbidden in every government job. Still, if one was privy to a re-development deal and bought land in the area before it was announced to the public, we would be acting on insider information and be, at the very least, the subject of public scrutiny because it would be *seen* as having a conflict of interest or the *appearance* of a conflict of interest. This is why almost every branch of government has some form of 'Ethics Office,' to offer some level of guidance around what actions may or may not be 'ethical.'

The Ethics Office might be consulted *prior* to taking a questionable action, in order to avoid or minimize any potential conflict of interest. Their advice is rarely binding, but where a questionable action has already occurred the Ethics Office will step in - usually at the request of an injured party - to censure the individual or group who undertook the questionable behaviour.

Ethics are, essentially, rules that tend to be specific to the organization or group and are often codified in a manual, video or some indoctrination procedure. This might best be described as a 'code of ethics' or 'code of conduct.' Some ethics, which may have started out as specific to an organization or group, have over time, come to reflect societal norms with laws to encourage or discourage a particular behaviour.

For example; sexual harassment in the workplace was codified in many organizations well before the lawmakers made sexual harassment in the workplace, illegal.

> *I worked for an advertising firm back in 1978-9 (Directory Advertising Consultants, Toronto) and they had a written policy against sexual harassment in the office, and any reported breach was taken seriously and dealt with quickly, but it wasn't until 1981 that the Ontario Human Rights Code was amended to include workplace protection against such offences.*

A code of ethics might be used in a professional organization which covers, for example, social workers. The worker may be bound by a code of ethics that assures the privacy of a client. But the worker might believe that there is risk to a client or others and disclose their private file to law enforcement in order to intervene to protect the client or others from harm. In this case, the code of ethics may be viewed as 'breached' for the higher purpose of protecting the client based upon the value judgement of the worker. In this instance the worker would have behaved 'unethically' in order to uphold a personal value to protect others from harm. We might call them 'unpro-

	Values *(What is Good)*	**Morality** *(What is Right)*
What Are They?	• A set of beliefs, views and preferences that an individual has evolved over time to help them determine what is good (desirable) or bad (to be avoided) and to what degree	• A societal system of right and wrong and a sense of to what degree
Origin	• Internally derived, usually from direct, personal experience combined with early learning and upheld by the individual	• An overview of the world, as viewed through a societal lens
How is it Used?	• A set of criteria that helps determine goals and how to achieve them	• A societal interpretation of what is right or wrong and to what degree
Degree of Flexibility?	• Usually a set of values will evolve over time in response to new information or circumstances	• Tends to be consistent, but evolution of moral conviction may occur over time
Crossover	• Where individual values are in accord with society's morality, there is little friction	• Where such is not the case, disharmony may exist for both the individual and society
Compliance	• Tending towards high, in that the individual has set their own internal sense of what is good and desirable • Values tend to transcend both time and cultural norms	• Tending towards high, in that they are usually backed up by the rule of law for any given group

fessional' for having violated the code of ethics for his or her profession. Further, depending upon the laws of the community, they may be held accountable for these violations through the courts of law - essentially breaching the standards of the community. On the other hand, some jurisdictions may *compel* the profession to report such suspicions to authorities under community safety guidelines.

Often the terms 'morality' and 'values' are used interchangeably. Sometimes that's accurate enough, but other times it's important to remember that the two are very different things, although the difference can get blurred.

> *Occasionally ethics and values will overlap or conflict. For example, the ethics of a religion might say homosexuality is forbidden, but individuals within the religion may have a different conclusion based on their values, informed by their interactions with society at large. Further, laws (community standards) may make discrimination based upon sexual orientation strictly illegal. Individuals might hide their convictions so they can be part of the greater (religious) group, or they might decide that accepting the ethics of the religion is incompatible with their values and either leave the group or stay and try to change things. In the case of the American military, these conflicts were often swept under the carpet with the DADT policy, "Don't Ask. Don't tell."*

From a wisdom point of view, it's important to understand the differences, for wisdom cannot easily progress without this understanding, since so much of wisdom is trying to address the stated common good, which is usually (not always) defined by the group. Where the common good is obtained and maintained by the efforts of a community, one cannot simply ignore those ethics. From a morality point of view, wisdom cannot easily proceed when the values of the individual are not understood or taken into account by society at large.

Historically, exhibiting 'right' behaviour and accepting the group morality, was a sure way to gain acceptance, while not doing so was a sure way to get ostracized, exiled and almost certainly left for dead. It may be no surprise that behaving in a certain, 'moral' way, as defined by the community or society in which you lived, was, quite literally, a matter of survival. Being tossed out of the hunting group or family unit was essentially a death sentence for our earliest ancestors since living alone, hunting, foraging for food, defending oneself against animals, accident, disease and other tribes would have required a super human effort and would all too often end in early death. For that reason alone there was plenty of motivation to think, speak and act in a way that was acceptable or considered both 'moral' and 'ethical' for your tribe.

Our earliest communities existed in, and of, themselves. They would rarely, come into contact with other groups, tribes or families. Selection of moral principles and codification of ethical behaviour, then, was a matter for the community, tribe or family. So long as everyone more or less agreed, there was no problem.

Today, we live in a vastly more complicated world. Every action my tribe undertakes can have far-reaching effects for other tribes around the world. The CO_2 my tribe releases into the atmosphere travels around the world to affect every other tribe. When there is a stock market crash on one side of the Atlantic, it's felt within hours on the other side. When my water becomes undrinkable, so it is with others who share the well. Sometimes the actions we take to *benefit* our tribe will also benefit others.

Today, we are more intertwined than we have ever been in our past and that *some* sense of universal responsibility or common code of behaviour is good for everyone, indeed maybe even necessary if we are to survive. This *universal responsibility* isn't just for humans, but for all living organisms; fish, plants, protozoa, plankton and what not. Without the survival of those other living things, our human lives will be ultimately unsustainable. One of the great ironies of the vast majority of life is that without eating other living things, there is no life. Even plants depend on consuming the organic matter left behind by decaying creatures and other plants.

> When we re-orient ourselves and recognize that everything is interconnected, we might start making better choices about how we speak and how we behave and we may have a more positive impact on the world where such opportunities arise.

When we recognize and admit to ourselves that our words and actions (or the words and actions of our tribe) may well cause suffering among others, then we begin to cultivate a sensitivity to others who are not necessarily close to us. We have learned from direct, personal experience that words and actions by others can hurt *us*, so there is wisdom in not using words or taking actions that would hurt others.

We may want to avoid language that is divisive, mean spirited or hateful. We may want to behave in a manner that inspires and develops trust.

Were we to ignore the plight of others and act as if our words and actions don't matter, then we begin to see ourselves as separate from others and can no longer recognize their situation. The world becomes harsh. We begin to distinguish small differences in others and make those differences seem important. Have we forgotten we're all going to suffer from sickness, accidents, ageing and death? You'd think knowing this, we'd be more tolerant of others and not make such a big deal of our differences, but rather, work to ease their suffering in the same way we'd hope they'd ease ours.

When we walk on the street or ride the subway, everyone we look at is, superficially, different from us. They may a different skin colour, dress differently, speak a different language and eat different foods, but we are all human beings. We all have two eyes, two ears, one nose, etc. We all suffer from hunger, disease, accidents, pain, ageing and death. We all sense this (even if we don't fully recognize or understand it), but we too often seek to identify superficial differences that separate us, rather than the commonalities that unite us.

> When we dwell on the differences, we tend to inflate them and make them seem more important than they really are. We put up walls and seek to shut others out. But, when we look at our

commonalities, we naturally begin to drop the defences and our compassion arises, almost on its' own, to better know the plight of others.

In the words of the Dalai Lama, in his book Ethics For The New Millennium;

"... Yet it seems to me that while most people are willing to accept the need for unity within their own group and, within this, the need to consider others' welfare, the tendency is to neglect the rest of humanity. In doing so, we ignore not only the interdependent nature of reality but the reality of our situation. If it were possible for one group, or one race, or one nation to gain complete satisfaction and fulfillment by remaining totally independent and self-sufficient with the confines of their own society, then perhaps it could be argued that discrimination against outsiders is justifiable. But this is not the case. In fact, the modern world is such that the interest of a particular community can no longer be considered to lie within the confines of its own boundaries."

So, it becomes clear that what we say and what we do not only affects us, but affects others within our own community and beyond. For this reason, we need to think about what a set of universal ethics might look like, for we are no longer confined to our little corner of the world. How we behave towards one another and what we say to others matters, and it matters a lot.

The vast majority of us live a life that is balanced and bound by tribal morals and personal values. For a paycheque we might weaken our moral stance on selling fur coats at our little retail job or we might eat a turkey sandwich at the company Christmas party even though we might be a vegetarian. On the other hand, we might jump to the defence of a fellow employee where an injustice is done based on our own values that may or may not align with company ethics. We may "stick our neck out" fully understanding that doing so might result in censure, punishment or outright dismissal. We might 'blow the whistle' when we learn that our company has been polluting a local body of water or colluding to fix prices within an industry, etc. The newspapers are awash with stories of employees who have been fired for ratting-out their employers, church leaders and local government officials. While it might be tough on the individual to be the pariah, it rarely goes well for the individual or entity being outed.

The question of which beliefs and behaviours that any given society *should* put forward as moral is the big question. What the community values or accepts as a norm varies widely from place to place and over time. What we might have valued and accepted as the norm 100 years ago, may not be that which we value today. But, are there *some* values that transcend place and time? Are there *some* behaviours and beliefs that, year after year, across cultures and community, are immutable? Are there *some* universal principles of morality or state of existence, to which all can agree? If so, what might they be? In the next section, we spend a bit of time trying to answer that very question.

3.1 Universal Responsibility

This section is, by no means, meant to be definitive or exhaustive. It certainly isn't meant to be scientific. Readers will want to add or take away from what is suggested below, but we need a starting point if a discussion is to be had.

Peace and Peaceful Co-existence
If we were to ask a thousand people if they preferred living a life of peace or a life of war, constant threat of death or maiming, destruction and uncertainty, we could be fairly certain that the vast majority of them would select peace.

Still, can one live with peace under any circumstances? Can a prisoner enjoy his freedom from war and pestilence confined behind bars? Will Republicans and Democrats ever work together again? Can Israel make an enduring peace with Palestine? There will always be costs for a lasting peace, the question becomes what are we willing to give up to enjoy that peace.

Honesty
Again, if asked, "Would you prefer people told you the truth?" it would be fairly certain that most would respond in the affirmative. No one wants to be lied to. When difficult truths need to be told, we'd rather have it given easy, of course, but we'd still prefer to be told the truth, based on verifiable facts. The vast majority of religions, cultures, business and educational centres promote truth, over mis-information, honesty over dishonesty. Our "Post-Truth" world, (discussed in Chapter 5.1) notwithstanding, most of us would prefer to hear the truth. Our legal system and courts are geared to find out the truth. That being said, we are almost all guilty of telling "little white lies" over the course of any given day. How do you not compliment your wife or husband on their new outfit? Where the truth may hurt, divide or demean we often opt for the, "little white lie."

Honour Obligations
When people say they're going to do something for us, we'd all prefer that those things get done within the time frame and in the manner promised. Of course things change and sometimes situations get

beyond our control, but we must act in good faith and with good intention to fulfil our obligations.

Act With Good Intention
No one wants to be treated to someone else's hidden agenda. We'd all prefer to know, up front, what people are up to.

Equal Rights For All
This is a tough one, for while all are people are created equal, they rarely develop as such within their tribe. We all *want* to know that our work is equally valued and equally rewarded. While it seems unlikely, we all *want* to be treated fairly, respectfully and equitably by the police. We all *want* to know that when a crime is committed the courts will act the same way for everyone. Of course, this is rarely the case, but in an ideal world, (and we are a very long way from that) this would be our preference ... unless of course, we're the one getting the benefit.

Relief From Suffering
All sentient creatures suffer in one way or another. Simply being human means that we will suffer from hunger, want, pain, disease and ultimately death. Relief from suffering is as universal a desire as we can imagine.

Avoid Taking Life
Does it not seems logical that no one wants to be killed by another? Tribal ethics almost universally condemn the taking of life within the tribal community, except where allowed by the laws of the tribe and after due process. Can this be extended to not taking the life of other sentient creatures? Most assuredly, but it's rarely the case.

Avoid Sexual Misconduct
Can any of us honestly conclude that being raped, groped, touched or in some way exposed to unwanted sexual attention, is good? We discuss this in greater detail in the section below (Chapter 3.2) - Item 3 of the Five Precepts.

Reverence For Place - Protect the Environment
For the common good, having a clean environment in which to live would seem preferable to having one which is polluted. Ask any individual if they'd prefer clean air, clean water and protected wilderness environments, over polluted air, dirty water and spoiled wilderness, and almost everyone would respond in the affirmative.

Still, as with all of these universal responsibility suggestions, there is always a matter of 'how clean' or 'how unpolluted?' If we want oil to fuel our cars or natural gas to heat our homes, we need to decide the price we are willing to pay for those benefits, since there will be costs to the environment.

Leave a Positive Legacy
What we leave behind for our children, family and tribe matters. It sets things up for the next generation. Leaving them a clean environment, a good name, a solid education and a good upbringing all matter to the next generation. No child wants to inherit a bad name or bad circumstances.

Build Trust
All communities must operate within some rules and regulations laid down by the community at large. Trusting in those rules and what they mean allows for all members of a community to trust other members of the community.

Willful Compliance With the Law
When we all obey the laws of our community, the community, as a whole, benefits. This is part of the common good. Of course there will be times when laws and rules need to be rewritten or deleted altogether and then peaceful (or sometimes not so peaceful) civil action may be required. No one wants to obey laws simply because they are threatened with reprisal, rather, they'd prefer laws that are just, make sense for the times, are applied fairly, equitably and in a timely manner.

Concerning Divine Wisdom

How, if at all, are we to concern ourselves with 'divine' wisdom? That is to say, that wisdom that has reportedly been passed down to us mere humans from on high? With religion it becomes even tougher to suss out the source, since the very nature (or supposed nature) of the source is, by its "divine" nature, beyond the comprehension of mortals. Yet we are constantly pummelled by divine wisdom, supposedly passed down to yogis, priests, popes, fakirs, bishops, kings, queens and television preachers to pester and perturb mankind - always pitting one tribe against the other.

In Buddhism, we are not asked to blindly accept dogma, scripture or 'divine' wisdom. Instead we are urged to use our mind, our observations and our direct, personal experience to prove to ourselves what is wise and what is not – what works and what does not. The question of the divine is rarely a point of contention in any discussions of Buddhism.

Wisdom, for Buddhists, is thinking, speaking and acting in a manner that helps us, as individuals, relive suffering, not only for ourselves, but for others. As a side benefit (or as the main event, depending on how you approach Buddhism) these same actions move us towards enlightenment and Nirvana.

The Four Cardinal Virtues Proposed by Aristotle

1. Prudence; The habit of choosing a good livelihood to achieve noble ends

2. Justice; The habit of ensuring the rights and liberties of others

3. Temperance; The habit of moderation in sensual pleasures

4. Fortitude; The habit of restraining fear or rash behaviour in the face of danger or adversity.

3.2 Wisdom and The Five Precepts

We've danced around it a bit, but we can't go much further in our discussion about wisdom and its place in Buddhism until we discuss the Five Precepts. From the perspective of a practicing Buddhist, these are five, seemingly simple rules that provide guidance when it comes to developing personal values, making moral choices and enacting ethical behaviour.

These precepts are general guidelines by which we might conduct our lives and a set of values upon which wisdom might arise. They are not commandments or immutable laws that are handed down from some higher authority with threat of punishment if not obeyed. They are not dictates or laws. They are not undertaken as a matter of legal necessity or as a matter of rite, (although in some locales they may be one or both) rather they are practiced as a matter of conscious, a matter of direct experience of life and the recognition that they are useful behaviours by which one might live in society with others.

The precepts will already be largely familiar, as we've already discussed them - albeit briefly, in the section above. In this section we discuss them at greater length and with a Buddhist point of view.

The Five Precepts

1. Abstain from taking life
2. Abstain from stealing
3. Abstain from inappropriate sexual relations
4. Abstain from telling lies
5. Abstain from intoxicants.

1) Do Not Kill
The idea of not killing, seems pretty self explanatory. Certainly we don't want to kill one another, but we want to avoid killing other sentient features as well.

One violates the first of the five precepts where the following conditions exist;

- First, there exists a living, sentient being. This is to say that the being possesses consciousness and breath. This includes humans, all other mammals, fish and insects. It does not include plants. (While some plants may exhibit an elementary response to their environment, they seem to lack essential self awareness.)
- Secondly, one needs to be cognitive or aware that this sentient being exists
- Third, there needs to be an *intention* to carry out the killing
- Fourth, the act of killing is carried out
- Finally, the being ceases to live.

It's critical to understand that the violation of the precept arises in the mind, when we recognize the existences of the being and the wilful intent to kill it. When we then carry out the act and the creature dies, then it's a further impact on our karma.

In one episode of *Doc Martin*, (a BBC Television production) the village GP very much dislikes his neighbours little dog and this is well known to many in the community. One day, he backs out of his driveway on the way to an urgent house-call, and he runs over the dog. It was an accident, but the rest of the episode is spent sorting through the fallout, in a morosely comedic manner. The criteria outlined above were not met - especially around intention so, if the doctor was a Buddhist, he would not have violated the precept.

Asking, coercing or ordering another to do the killing is the same as doing it yourself and does not absolve you of the violation. Knowingly withholding words or actions that would prevent the killing also has karmic consequences.

Remember that thinking, words and acts all have karmic consequences.

Does this suggest we not eat meat? The logic seems to leads us there. What If we go to a friends house and they serve roast chicken? Do we decline the food? Do we eat it, and console ourselves that we didn't kill the chicken with our own hands, nor ask another to do it for us? If we were a Tibetan monk, out on our daily rounds to get food offerings, do we not eat chicken wings if some well-intentioned householder places them in our bowl? Even the Dahlia Lama recognizes that eating meat may be necessary for some health reasons. He himself is not a strict vegetarian.*

Setting aside the health discussion of eating meat, we must then consider the pain of the sentient creature that we kill to eat. If we, as Buddhists, are concerned about ending the suffering of all sentient creatures, how then do we justify killing them for food? The long and short of it is, we can't. But, as complex thinking creatures ourselves, we are, curiously, able to hold, and validate, two mutually exclusive ideas at the same time.

We could have a discussion about the value of a rabbit's life vs. that of a cow. Both are sentient creatures who do not want to die. Both are cute enough, in their own way. Both are domesticated, to one degree or another. Both creatures are raised for food, depending on where you live, culture, etc. A rabbit may feed three or four people, while a cow may feed dozens of people. Is it better to kill a cow as it will benefit dozens of people? Is there more or less karmic consequence to killing one or the other?

2) Abstain From Stealing
This is relatively simple. It's an injunction not to take things which neither belong to you or are not freely offered. This has nothing to do with "the law" or what's "legal." It has everything to do with not harming others or depriving them of property that rightfully belongs to them, in the same way we would not want someone to deprive us of our rightfully obtained property.

---

* Rick Westhead - Toronto Star, staff reporter. Sat. Oct. 16, 2010

This goes a little further than simply not stealing. It also involves giving something back which you possess, to the person you know to be the rightful owner.

What if you were hiking in a national park and knelt to take a close up photo of flower and felt your knee strike something hard amongst the leaves. You investigate and discover it's a little Swiss Army knife. You take it home and after a bit of oil and a thorough cleaning, it was good as new. You didn't steal it or come to possess it in any way that could be described as questionable. There was no way you could reasonably determine to whom the knife belonged. It wasn't engraved with any name or identifying marks. It was found in a public park. Keeping it not going to cause any further suffering by the person who had originally lost it.

Sometimes things just come our way, we have no way of knowing to whom these things belong, so we can keep them with little or no karmic disturbance. If you wanted to get a little more mileage out of finding something, you might donate it to a good cause, for performing acts of merit would seem to be good karma.

The karmic consequences of taking things that don't belong to you seem to vary, when we engage in some moral gymnastics. For example, if one ran into the AGO and grabbed a Matisse off the wall, the karma effects would be significant. First, you'd likely get caught before you got out of the building and charged with theft and who knows what else, but as importantly, one's karma would suffer from the act. The painting clearly belongs to someone else and it was not freely offered. Decamping with it causes pain to another or, in this case, to many other art lovers. So, major impact on the karma.

On the other hand, if you ran into a building where stolen art was being stored and stole a painting from there, it seems your karmic consequences might be less. If you had the intention of returning the painting to the original owner, the consequences may be less still, perhaps, even positive. You might even be called a "hero."

This then, brings up the question of how karma might be affected by our mental state or by our 'intent.' If you steal a previously stolen painting, with the intent of returning it to the original owner and don't seek any accolades for the effort, you would seem to have had a good karmic event. On the other hand, if you stole the previously stolen painting, but after you got it home, decided to keep it for yourself even when you knew who the rightful owner was, you would have a different karmic outcome. If you felt good or bad about keeping it, that would affect your karma too.

Intention, deed and subsequent feelings all seem to have varying affects on karma. Whether or not the intention was to *actually* perform a deed has consequences. Leaving a coffee shop, having simply *forgotten* to pay, would not negatively affect our karma as much as *knowingly*, leaving the coffee shop without paying. In either case, going back next day to pay them seems to offset or at least minimize any original, negative intent.

Feeling some guilt about an intentionally negative deed and then doing or at least saying something about that would seem to have some beneficial effect on negative karma.

Astaya (Asteya)
Aside from simply not taking 'things,' there is also recognition that we can 'steal' a person's, time, energy or concentration.

We all know people who seem to be an energetic drain on us - *energy vampires*. They tend to be;

- Unable to 'read' their audience
- Overly critical
- Overly negative
- Melodramatic
- Always making mountains out of molehills
- Chronically complaining
- Always exaggerating
- Unable to take 'no' for an answer
- Always finding the worst in people or situations
- Resistant to letting others speak.

These people will talk and talk, long after their audience has lost interest in the subject or the subject itself is exhausted. They then go back over the same material, in excruciating detail, seemingly oblivious to the fact that they've lost their audience or that their cause simply isn't your cause. They insist their cause is righteous and, surely, you (being a reasonable person) must agree with them.

Of course, these energy vampires don't know what they're doing. They might just think, "This person seems to find my antics interesting and engaging, so I'll carry on." Being unaware and so *unable* to moderate their behaviours or attitudes, it really comes down to you to set boundaries.

Identify
These energy vampires don't always easily identify as such when you first encounter them. They may seem interesting, engaging, well informed, etc. Their flair for the dramatic may seem entertaining, but you may soon feel something is wrong. If you come away from an encounter feeling; restless, irritable, unheard, tired, headachy, confused or sad, you may have just met an energy vampire.

Limit Exposure
Once you've identified a person like this, maybe a family member, a co-worker, a person at the gym or local club, limit your engagement with them. The more time you spend in their company, the greater the likelihood that you're going to come away drained. Start the conversation with a polite, but firm, "I have to be somewhere in a few minutes, so let's make this short." Then, when the time comes, firmly and politely disengage.

Self Care
You're never going to 'fix' their problems, for they will keep coming up with more tales of woe to suck you in and try to infect you with their negativity. Usually the best course of action is to simply express your confidence in their ability to find their own solution and start heading for the doors. You don't want to be rude about it, but neither do you want to stand around and engage, for you're never going to get a handle on their sorrows and their negativity will only start bringing you down. You must look after yourself. Our positive

energy is a precious resource and we have to be careful not to squander it where it cannot flourish.

The Wisdom Gleaned From The Energy Vampire

On the other side, be aware of your own opinions and how you present yourself to people and take care not be an energy vampire yourself, stealing positive energy and time from others. Remember that we have two ears for listening and only one mouth for speaking - so listen more than you speak.

"A wise old owl sat on an oak.

The more she saw, the less she spoke.

The less she spoke, the more she heard.

Why can't we be like that wise old bird?"

~ An English language nursery rhyme
    of unknown origin

---

3) Abstain From Inappropriate Sexual Relations

For the purposes of this discussion, from a Buddhist perspective, it's fairly simple and straightforward;

1. Avoid sexual encounters with those who are under age
2. Avoid sexual encounters with engaged or married people
3. Avoid non-consensual sex

It should be clear that this still leaves a lot of room for personal preferences, proclivities, sexual orientation, kinks and fetishes. So long as we're talking about consenting adults, Buddhism has very little to say about who you do and how you do it. There is no concern about same sex coupling or multiple partners, pre-marital sex, BDSM or whatever you're into.

Once again, we are not looking at this from a "legal" point of view. In-so-far as we don't want to harm others, it's wise to follow these rules. While laws may be in place around certain sexual acts, in certain countries, states or counties, Buddhism itself has very few injunctions.

In the case of abstaining from sex with engaged or married people, even if they are both consenting, there is a third party involved who may be harmed – namely the spouse or intended spouse of one or both of the partners. Where families with children are involved, they could also be harmed if the parents were to split up over sexual misconduct.

It would be unwise for a supervisor to engage in sexual relations with his or her employees – even though it may be consenting. It may put the employee in a difficult or compromised position and cause harm, however unintended it may be. Ask Bill Clinton about that. Many companies, provinces and states have strict, if not always enforced, rules around supervisors not putting employees into such positions. Any person in power or authority must abstain from inappropriate sexual contact with any one whose lives, careers, jobs or pay may be adversely affected.

Harvey Weinstein

In October 2017, investigative reporter, Jodi Kantor broke a story in the New York Times about Hollywood producer, and film industry mogul, Harvey Weinstein. Her well-researched and documented story puts Weinstein right in the middle of multiple allegations around sexual harassment and inappropriate sexual contact with a number of actresses and those who worked for him. Most of the allegations seem to be about using his position of authority to coerce women into having sex with him. There are even allegations being put forward regarding sexual assault and rape.

The Weinstein story isn't about just this one man who has allegedly been acting in a manner that is not only inappropriate, but illegal, it's about almost everyone around him knowing about it, then turning a blind eye.

Since this story first broke, dozens of his friends and acquaintances have maneuvered to distance themselves from any relationship they had with him. Many have expressed their shock and distaste for his actions. He has publicly disgraced and humiliated himself, lost his status and even livelihood within the film industry.

On March 11, 2020 Weinstein was taken to Wende Correctional Facility, near Buffalo, New York to begin his 23 year jail term after being convicted of rape and sexual assault. Through his inappropriate, immoral and illegal sexual relations, he has done irreparable damage to those he coerced and abused.

Weinstein *could* have demonstrated both wisdom and compassion when dealing with these women. He *could* have been a mentor, an aide or an invaluable ally as these women worked their way through their acting careers. In the end, they might have stood and sung his praises for the invaluable support they received from Weinstein, as they accepted their Oscar. But this is not how it's going to end, for he *unwisely*, chose to cause harm, *unwisely* chose to demean others and *unwisely* chose to deny, deflect and deceive when found out – typical D4 behaviour.

Noah Levine

Closer to home, we have Noah Levine, founder and dharma teacher at Against the Stream [Buddhist] Meditation Centres. In mid-2018, he was named in sexual misconduct allegations that have brought discredit to himself and the organization he served. He's no longer on the ATS board and his conduct has brought financial hardship to ATS which has resulted in the shutting down of some of their centres, leaving that Buddhist sangha confused, betrayed and unsupported.

A signed statement by the ATS's Board of Directors, Grievance Council and Teachers Council, reads [in part] as follows;

"The standard for evaluating a Buddhist teacher's actions are not the same as the criminal or even the civil standards of proof. Spiritual leaders are held to a higher ethical standard than the public at large and higher than other community leaders,"

So, while Levine has not been found 'guilty' in any civil or criminal proceedings, he is being held accountable for his actions by his spiritual community and the very organization which he helped found. It's been reported that he violated, "the Third Precept of the Teacher's Code of Ethics, namely, 'to avoid creating harm through sexuality." *

While we're on the topic of sexual misconduct, we can't leave out the Catholic Church and the unfolding story in Pennsylvania.** Allegations have been levelled at the Archdiocese of Pennsylvania, regarding ongoing sexual abuse by clergy against members of the congregation. Documentation has shown that the Vatican knew of these abuses and made efforts to cover them up. Voices calling for major reforms have been growing. One parishioner, in Atlanta, Naka Nathaniel, interrupted a Sunday sermon in order to question his priest about how the Church was handling all this.

"[The priest] turned to me and he said, 'You and I have no influence.' It was crushing to hear that..."†

According to BishopAccountability.org (a non-profit that tracks allegations of abuse in the Catholic Church) some US$3.8 billion has been paid out by the Catholic Church and its insurance carriers regarding more than 8,600 survivors who were allegedly sexually abused by an undisclosed number of clergy since the 1950s.

Jeffrey Epstein

Fast forward to September, 2019 and Jeffrey Epstein, convicted sex offender and American financier is in the news. Long story short, his well documented history of sexual misconduct has caught up with

---

* Mathew Abrahams, Tricycle Magazine, Aug, 27, 2018.
Also, Sean Elder, for Los Angeles Magazine, July 10, 2019.

** Holly Yan for CNN, August 28, 2018. 'The accusation comes two weeks after the release of a grand jury report saying hundreds of "predator priests" had abused children in six Pennsylvania dioceses over the past seven decades."

† CBCs *The Current* interview. Connie Walker with Naka Nathaniel, by phone on August 29, 2018.

him. Epstein has been in and out of prison, and has some 11 criminal charges outstanding against him.

On August 10, 2019, while awaiting sex trafficking charges in the Metropolitan Correctional Centre, NYC, he was found dead in his cell - apparently suicide by hanging.

Preliminary investigation has revealed a lot of things going wrong prior to his body being found at 6:30 that morning. He was *supposed* to be on suicide watch, he was *supposed* to have a cell mate, he was *supposed* to be checked on every 30 minutes, the camera in front of his cell malfunctioned earlier, etc. There are a lot of questions about his death, not the least of which being, was he murdered for what he knew about whom? He was, after all, allegedly procuring women and under-aged girls for wealthy and/or well-connected political persons. Unsubstantiated allegations have been made that some high-flying politico had him killed. Epstein's lawyers said that the evidence concerning Epstein's death was "far more consistent" with murder than suicide. ††

As we near the end of this section of the book, we don't want to leave the reader with a sense that one must abstain, avoid, run from or be fearful of having sex with anyone. We are human and the urge to merge is deep and powerful. The drive to couple and reproduce is biological and not easily set aside. It is pleasurable, therapeutic, comforting and with the right partner, loving. It has an honoured place in our psychology and physiology that is millions of years old. Without it, we would not be here.

For monastic purposes, at least in Buddhism, we are told sexual contact is widely discouraged. Sexual and sensual pleasures are viewed

---

†† Azi Paybarah for The New York Times, Oct. 30, 2019. "A forensic pathologist hired by Jeffrey Epstein's brother disputed the official finding in the autopsy of his death, claiming on Wednesday that the evidence suggested that he did not take his own life but may have been strangled." - Benjamin Weiser, Michael Gold contributed reporting

as a distraction for those who are seriously on the spiritual path. The passion to which it can give rise is one of The Three Fires of the human mind that must be dealt with before approaching Nirvana, that of passion. Further, what if the union resulted in a child? How can a monastic look after a child when they've taken a vow of poverty? Where does the child fit into the practice? Is the laity expected to offer alms to support the child? Some difficult questions, to be sure, hence the principle of monks abstaining from sexual relations. For the average Buddhist on the street, the so-called "householder," this prohibition is not applicable.

4) Do Not Lie

People lie every day—literally—every day. From political debates to who took my lunch out of the staff fridge. Bill Clinton *did* have, an "inappropriate relationship," with Monica Lewinski. Richard Nixon *was* a crook despite his denials.* Ted *lied* about Chappaquiddick.** Flynn *lied* to the FBI,† Michael Cohen *lied* about the Russian tower deal.†† It's all the rage, this lying business.

Lies, deceptions and misdirections are done for a lot reasons, not the least of which is to avoid shame, loss, pain or censure. As noted earlier, avoidance of these circumstances drives a lot of human behaviour. But we also lie for the exact opposite reasons; to seek or obtain fame, gain, pleasure or praise. We discuss these eight worldly concerns in Chapter 8 – *THE EIGHT VICISSITUDES*

Not telling the truth and not offering the *full* truth is usually harmful to someone and doing no harm is one of Buddhism's first principles.

---

* Nov. 17, 1973 "And I think, too, that I could say that in my years of public life, that I welcome this kind of examination, because people have got to know whether or not their President is a crook. Well, I am not a crook. I have earned everything I have got." Richard M. Nixon speaking to reporters at the Annual Convention of the Associated Press Managing Editors Association, Orlando, Florida.

** May 19, 1970 issue of the National Review.

† In 2017, Flynn pleaded guilty, in the District of Columbia's U.S. District Court, to lying to the FBI about contacts with Russia's ambassador to the US - Sergey Kislyak.

†† November 29, 2018, Cohen pleaded guilty about lying to the Senate and House Intelligence Committees about Trump Tower, Moscow.

Is there a time when a lie, an outright bald-faced lie, might be beneficial? Is there a time when simply avoiding the truth could be helpful? Were the lies told by Miep Gies as she hid Anne Frank and her family from the Nazis in the annex above her father's business, 'good lies?' An extreme example perhaps, but demonstrative of the ethical choices that need to be made when one grapples with how, or if, to tell the truth.

"Truthfulness has never been counted among the political virtues, and lies have always been regarded as justifiable tools in political dealings. Whoever reflects on these matters can only be surprised by how little attention has been paid, in our tradition of philosophical and political thought, to their significance, on the one hand for the nature of action and, on the other, for the nature of our ability to deny in thought and word whatever happens to be the case. This active, aggressive capability is clearly different from our passive susceptibility to falling prey to error, illusion, the distortions of memory, and to whatever else can be blamed on the failings of our sensual and mental apparatus."

~ *Lying in Politics* - 1971 - Hannah Arendt.

Lets set aside the Anne Frank question and just talk about daily life, life in our jobs or out with friends. Telling lies, omitting or 'skirting' the truth and twisted truths should all be avoided if and when it is being driven by a desire to;

- aggrandize oneself
- put another down
- divide people, groups or families
- avoid uncomfortable social or legal circumstances or
- take credit for something you didn't do.

One can certainly imagine circumstances where a 'white' lie might be better than the truth. Situations in which a person might be deeply offended, disadvantaged, or harmed might warrant a bit of 'soft' truth telling. Perhaps not an outright lie, but truth told in a way that eases the blow.

We could split a lot of hairs here, but suffice it to say that avoiding lies, deception, twisted truth, duplicity, double-dealing, malpractice and misdirecting is best avoided in our daily lives. These actions tend to hurt others and make them look bad, while inflating our own ego and sense of worth.

In her book, *Standing on the Edge*, Roshi Joan Halifax takes a look at lying in the chapter titled Five Gatekeepers of Speech. She writes that The Buddha suggested practicing these five disciplines before we open our mouths. We should consider:

- Is it true?
- Is it kind?
- Is it beneficial?
- Is it necessary?
- Is it the right time?

"Among the calamities of war may be jointly numbered the diminution of the love of truth, by the falsehoods which interest dictates and credulity encourages."

~ Samuel Johnson *

Truth is the first casualty of war and politics. What one person finds 'true' may be a fabrication to another.

Take for example, the needs of the government to protect its citizens, borders and general way of life. *Arcana imperii* or 'mysteries of the government,' are falsehoods, deceptions, misinformation or misdirections that mislead or misinform the citizenry in order to protect it.

Of course, those misdirections extend to foreign consumption as well. One such misdirection would be not letting your enemy know the full extent of your military capability. Obviously, in order to keep this a secret from your potential enemies, you also need to keep it a secret from your citizens. This type of misinformation might include an over-statement of military personnel, budget, weaponry, deployment capability and misdirection around the location of troops and other military assets.

---

*Samuel Johnson, The Idler, #30. Corruption of News Writers. November 11, 1758. *"In a time of war the nation is always of one mind, eager to hear something good of themselves and ill of the enemy. At this time the task of news-writers is easy: they have nothing to do but to tell that a battle is expected, and afterwards that a battle has been fought, in which we and our friends, whether conquering or conquered, did all, and our enemies did nothing.*

"Scarcely any thing awakens attention like a tale of cruelty. The writer of news never fails in the intermission of action to tell how the enemies murdered children and ravished virgins ....

"Among the calamities of war may be justly numbered the diminution of the love of truth, by the falsehoods which interest dictates, and credulity encourages. A peace will equally leave the warriour [sic] and relater of wars destitute of employment; and I know not whether more is to be dreaded from streets filled with soldiers accustomed to plunder, or from garrets filled with scribblers accustomed to lie."

Other examples of *arcana imperii* might be what happened in a foreign land around casualties, property destruction or non-combatant fatalities. This usually takes the form of under-reporting the facts, putting a positive spin on the facts, or aligning the facts in a certain order or association to make it more palatable for domestic consumption. The fog of war is always quick to descend.

How you hear these 'truths' is largely dependent upon whether you're a 'dove' or a 'hawk.' A hawk, or someone in favour of the military action, might accept 1,000 military casualties as the price to pay for engaging the enemy, while a 'dove' might find even 10 dead soldiers too high a price to pay and be disappointed that peace talks were not fully explored and foreign policy is an utter failure, etc.

In 2020 we are facing a similar discussion in our 'war' against the novel coronavirus, COVID-19. At the time of this writing, we have the unvarnished truth of over 130,000 US citizens dead from this new virus – and that, since March 6th, 2020, only 4 months. For that reason, in order to limit the spread, most US states (in fact most countries, including Canada) had 'locked down' their citizens, issued 'stay at home' orders and/or dramatically curtailed their travel and mobility freedoms. Businesses and organizations all across the country have been shuttered. The economy has taken an unprecedented blow. In the US, some 36 million people have lost their jobs. Unemployment, in some regions, is approaching 20% which is the worst it's been since the Great Depression. The Liberal Canadian government has been forced to offer the Canadian Emergency Relief Benefit (CERB) in the form of cash payments to the multitudes who have lost their jobs.

After 30 to 90 days of 'lock down' a lot of people are willing to say, 'Screw this, I have to get back to work. I can't afford to take off any more time without a paycheque." The truth of our pain and suffering is undeniable. Then Donald Trump encourages state governors to re-open their economies —by Easter—as if the virus is on some sort of schedule and one can simply hurry it along.

Contrast that to the CDC, NIAID, WHO, and literally every health department of every state across the country strongly recommending that any re-opening of the economy be done slowly, in a measured, calculated manner, based on the testing results and related numbers, or run the risk of doubling or even tripling the mortality rate of this deadly virus. The truth of their statistics is also undeniable.

So, what do you do? Sacrifice more people to this virus or stay home and possibly, default on your mortgage, miss a couple credit card payments, ruin you credit score, jeopardize your home, keep the kids out of school, not get your university degree, etc? Tough choice.

Other 'truths' might be based on verifiable facts, such as, "It's raining." One puts ones head out the window and you know whether it's raining or not. But what if you're on the phone with a friend across town and he says, "Wow, look at that rain!" and you can't see any rain out *your* window? How do you know it's raining at his end? You can't verify it. You have to take him at his word.

Two people might be standing outside, side-by-side and water starts falling from a cloudy sky, one might say, it's 'pouring' while the other might say, 'drizzling.' In both cases, water is falling from the sky, but we have two different interpretations of what it looks like or what it even means. These might not be lies, *per se*, but they are different interpretations of the same event and both contain a kernel of truth - water falling from the sky.

Sometimes out senses don't give us the right information. These might not be lies, but the truth is in question. How often have we seen a friend across the room, then approach him or her to find they aren't the person we thought at all? How often have we mis-heard something on the radio? Have you ever heard the lyrics of a song incorrectly and only been corrected years later? How often have our eyes been 'fooled by the light?' The senses we possess are not perfect instruments and thus, how we perceive the world cannot be perfect.

Is It Kind?

There is wisdom in taking a breath, counting to ten and cooling off before we speak. If what we are about to say is divisive, mean-spirited, intended to harm or dismiss someone, then we ought to hold onto our thoughts.

> Is there room for criticizing someone? Of course, but it must be done from a cool head in as kindly a manner as we can muster.

We should try to use our words to build people up, bolster their confidence and strengthen relationships. Words that do not do this, should be avoided. When we have good intentions, our words will naturally be kinder and less harsh.

Is It Beneficial?

It may be beneficial for you to blow your top and yell at someone, but was it beneficial for them? Probably not. No one wants to hear bad news delivered in a harsh manner, complete with vitriol and anger. There may be truth in the words and the anger justified, but is it *truly* benefiting the recipient? Take a moment to think how your words can benefit the individual before sounding off.

Does your husband really need to know he laughs too loud at parties? How will he benefit from that knowledge? Will he now stifle his enthusiasm and no longer see joy in being with his friends at a gathering? Will he watch his every word and every nuance of a smile in order to avoid laughing and offending your sensibilities? Will he stop going to parties? Who knows?

> Be sure to check your thinking before criticizing people and make sure you know there will be benefit to the recipient, in your speaking.

Is It Necessary?

There will be plenty of times where it becomes necessary to correct people. You can't sit back and watch as a supervisor at work sexually harasses an employee. The supervisor needs to hear, loud and clear, that his/her behaviour is not appropriate and is likely illegal.

> Not letting people hurt others is a very good reason to speak up. But even in these circumstances, the intent should not be to embarrass or demean the offender, but rather to correct them. Bet-

> ter to get them alone and express your concerns in calm, non-judgemental manner. Let them know that their words or actions are hurting others.

Mind you, like the 'whistle blower' noted back in Chapter 3, you may be out of a job. Some people like to wield their power in a ruthless manner. There is always risk to speaking up when you see such predatory behaviour. It's up to you to decide if you can live with the consequences of protecting another individual.

5) *Do Not Take Intoxicants*

Intoxicants have been with humanity for a very long time; caffeine, tobacco, peyote, alcohol, hallucinogenic mushrooms, cocaine, marijuana, etc. Why is this so? Why have so many intoxicants been used by even our earliest, ancient ancestors? Why has humanity spent so much time and energy seeking them out?

It might simply be that life as a human being is very hard. We suffer in one form or another almost every day. Modern man suffers from work stress, family stress, urban stress, financial stress, looking after ageing parents stress, etc. It's very stressful and we almost always want to be doing something else, feeling something else or feel like we are someone else. Our brain drives us crazy thinking of ways to be anywhere, other than in the here and now. The brain works its way back to the past and rushes ahead to the future, but it just can't stay in the present moment without a lot of work, for the present moment may be too stressful.

> Intoxicants give us the *illusion* of escaping to another, better place. Another time or another state. They often, but not always, numb our feelings and our emotions, making the stress of everyday living *seemingly* easier to take.

They can also be a social undertaking, in the same way that some people gather for a meal, others gather to take intoxicants. "Grabbing a beer," after work is so common that bars will often have a "happy hour" to entice regular customers to consume alcohol at their premisses. In Venice, they have their *cicchetti* bar crawl (shadow walk, turning of the shadow or *giro d'ombra*) for workers on their way home. They stop in a number of these bars, eat tasty morsels from toothpicks and wash it down with a glass of wine.

In North America, some high school students will gather after hours, out behind the school at 4:20 to smoke/consume marijuana before their extracurricular school activities or before going home.*

Intoxicants, while offering the promise of escape, rarely present any real or lasting benefit to the user. Intoxicants muddle the mind and make thinking less clear. When thinking is not clear, we may more easily say unskillful words or enact unskillful deeds. We may drive our car dangerously. We may insult people. We may perform silly or embarrassing acts that we will have to apologize for next day. We may harm people or assault them while under the influence of intoxicants. This inability to think straight, brought about through the use of intoxicants, means that real wisdom is suppressed and the *Johnny Walker* wisdom (noted in the song *Closing Time*, by Leonard Cohen) comes to the fore.

In January 2018, two Toronto police officers were in the news over intoxicants. Having intentionally eaten marijuana chocolate bars (which they found at a crime scene), they began hallucinating and had to call for backup. When the backup officers arrived, one of them slipped and fell on ice, injuring her head, requiring an ambulance and hospitalization. One officer (Vittorio Dominelli) has lost his job, been charged with evidence tampering and received a nine-month conditional sentence, six months of it to be served under house arrest. Taking intoxicants is not likely to lead to wisdom.

Taking intoxicants to 'escape' has dangers beyond simply muddled thinking and embarrassing behaviour. There are real risks that can lead to a dependency and addiction. Addiction can lead to major

---

* Back in 1971 a few students from a San Rafael, California high school used to meet after school, by a wall, off school property. They then planned their search for a reported abandoned marijuana crop in the area. After numerous attempts to find the crop, they gave up and just smoked weed when they met at 4:20pm.

health problems and even death. Tragically, overdoses among addicts are all too common.

For the Buddhist monastic intoxicants are to be avoided for all the reasons listed above. When on the spiritual path, as part of a monastic community, one wants the mind clear, the thinking precise and leaving no room for doubt. Intoxicants would only negatively influence that mental clarity.

But what might this mean for the householder or lay person. Is it wrong or unwise to have a glass of wine or a beer with an evening meal? Is it inconsistent with Buddhist values to have a drink after work? These are questions that need to be grappled with, not just "in theory," but in practice. Here in Ontario, Canada, marijuana is now a legal product with little with little restrictions placed on it's acquisition or possession, although its use generally falls under the same guidelines as alcohol or other intoxicants, esp. around legal age, driving and operating machinery and probably enforced by the Alcohol and Gaming Commission of Ontario.

Like most of the Buddhist doctrine, householders are not held to the same standard as monastics. While Buddhist monks are to avoid sexual contact, such is not the case for householders. Where meat is generally not eaten by Buddhist monks, lay persons are free to decided for themselves what to do. It seems to be the same with intoxicants - or at least alcohol. Having a glass of wine with your meal does not seem to bend, too greatly, any exhortations against consuming intoxicants.

> The wisdom in avoiding intoxicants is that we are left with clear and concise thinking. However it feels, intoxicants will only ever lessen our wisdom and increase our risk of exposure to long term mental and physical harm.

3.3 Wisdom and The Paramitas

In the various schools of Buddhism, there is the idea that some people will, over the fullness of time and over many lifetimes of practice, work their way along a path that will take them to *BUDDHAHOOD*.

These Buddhas-in-training are generally called Bodhisattvas. The work they do is decidedly non-egocentric which is to say, their efforts are put forward not for themselves (or not exclusively) but for the benefit of humans and *all* living creatures.

They have taken a vow to come back lifetime after lifetime until their efforts have resulted in relieving all creatures from suffering. Lofty goals to be sure, and their efforts are aided by the practice and application of the Paramitas - the Perfections - and depending on which school of Buddhism you follow there are either typically six or ten paramitas.

Borrowing from the Mahayana tradition they are;

It's easy enough to see how one can practice the first five as they are all actions, aided by good intention, a clear mind, meditation, etc. But what about wisdom? It's not really an action item. Like so many things in Buddhism, each of the paramitas is not a stand-alone set, to be practiced in order 1 through 6. Think of the paramitas as a holographic set, with each one containing all the elements of the other five - each supporting the others and in turn being supported.

Wisdom, as it relates to the Bodhisattva, is generally expressed as seeing and understanding the true nature of the phenomenal world – that environment which we, as human beings, are able to discern with our senses – and recognizing all things are impermanent and empty of any inherent meaning. It also means having deep insight and understanding of the Four Noble Truths.

> When we practice the first five paramitas and apply them in our daily life, then we begin to sense a coalescence of the sixth paramita - wisdom.

When we wake up in the morning, we might think, "I'm going to practice generosity today," and we would have a good idea of what that's going to look like. We might give money to the poor, help a homeless person, donate to a food bank or similar. We could say the same of all the paramitas—except wisdom. What do we imagine when we say, "I'm going to practice wisdom today?" It can't really arise just through dint of will. It's not a real action item, for it depends upon so many other practices, coming first. It needs something upon which to arise. It needs a foundation and the paramitas are a major aspect of that foundation.

1. Generosity *(dāna)*
2. Morality *(śīla)*
3. Patience *(kṣānti)*
4. Vigour *(vīrya)*
5. Concentration *(dhyāna)*
6. Wisdom *(prajñā)*

In a sense, much of the remainder of this book looks at the many different ways that the paramitas can be practiced and how that practice aids the development of wisdom.

Key Points Summary – Universal Responsibility

Peace and Peaceful Coexistence	• The preference for peace over war, harmony over conflict and geniality over acrimony
Honesty	• Arcana imperii, notwithstanding, nobody wants to be lied to
Satisfy Obligations	• If we expect others to fulfil their commitments, then we must honour ours
Act with Good Intention	• Hidden agendas are not well received by others.
Equal Rights For All	• Equal treatment under the law • Equal pay for similar work • Equal access to credit/capital
Reverence for Place	• Respect for the fact that others share our environment • Right to clean air and water
Built Trust	• All communities have rules for the benefit of those living in the community. Have trust in the rules and trust that others will abide by them • With the community at large, rewrite rules when they no longer have relevance
Willful Compliance with the Law	• Where laws are fair and equitable, we obey them. Where they are not, we work peacefully, but energetically, to change them
Practice the Paramitas	• Generosity - Morality - Patience - Vigour - Concentration - Wisdom

Key Points Summary – Values

Mastery of Our Values and Understanding those of Others	• The greater our understanding of our own, personal values and understanding that values held by others, the greater will be our ability to make a wise choices around any situation • Values vary over time and place and from person to person
1st Precept **Do Not Kill**	• Killing deprives sentient being of their life and causes suffering
2nd Precept **Do Not Steal**	• Taking from others, that which has not been freely offered, deprives that individual of their rightful property causing suffering • Stealing produces karma that may have a negative effect on your later life or next life • Avoid 'stealing' the time and energy of other people.
3rd Precept **Avoid Inappropriate Sexual Relations**	• Avoid relations with underage children, married or engaged persons or with persons against their will. • Be cautious of relations with those over whom you hold power and/or authority
4th Precept **Do Not Lie**	• Speaking untruth or twisted truth is sure to harm others and reflect poorly upon the speaker. • Where a 'white lie' may be beneficial, think carefully before saying anything
5th Precept **Avoid Intoxicants**	• Consuming intoxicants, such as alcohol, marijuana, cocaine or any other intoxicating substance, robs us of a clear mind, muddles our thinking, causes us to think, say and do things we may later regret • An addled mind is not conductive to the development of wisdom

4. Humility and Humour

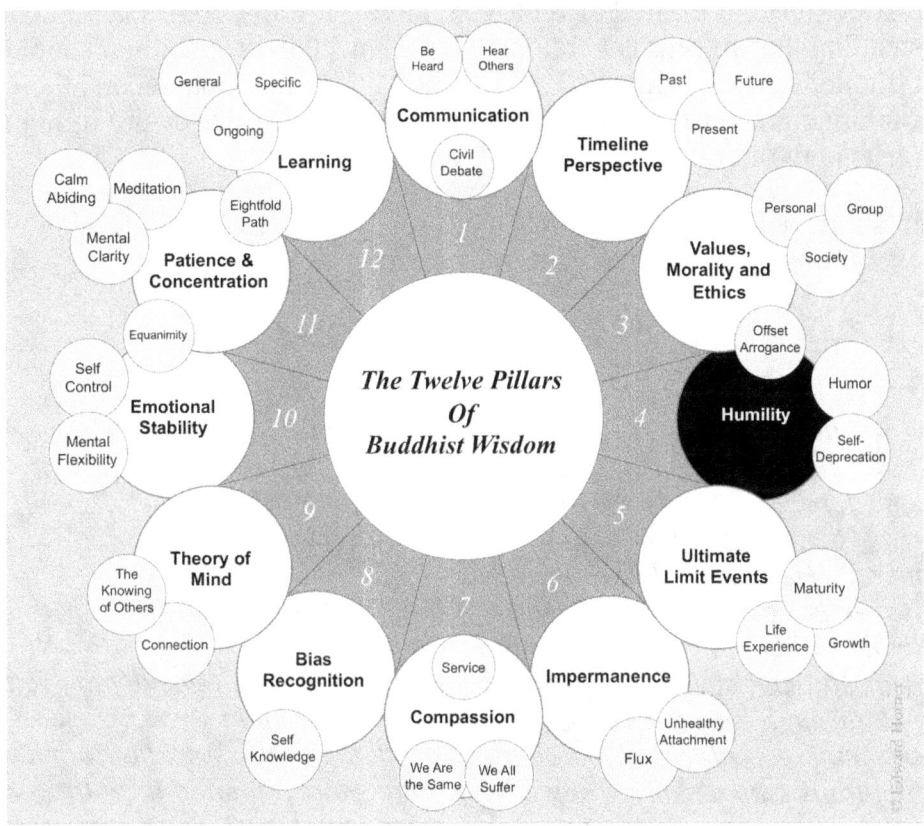

A SENSE OF HUMILITY OR SELF-DEPRECATION is considered key to spiritual progress and development of wisdom. Why is this so?

The opposites of humility are arrogance and pride. Both pride and arrogance are considered to be distractions on the path to higher spiritual attainment, largely because they limit the ability to hear, have an open mind, accept new ideas and learn from one's spiritual master, teacher, or guru. As such, arrogance is limiting to spiritual progress. Understanding that you don't know, and often *can't* know, everything about a topic helps put context around what we think say and do.

Taken further, a sense of humility leads to a sense of no-self or no separation between 'me' and 'you' or 'us' and 'them." When such distinctions are limited or removed, there naturally comes an understanding that all sentient creatures are connected through their shared afflictions of pain and suffering. When this realization occurs, there can arise greater compassion for others and a greater desire to help raise them out of suffering.

In short, being humble allows us to recognize that we do not know everything and that there is more to learn.

Raikva the Cart Driver

There was, once upon a time, a great king named Janasruti Pautrayana, who lorded over his vast lands with generosity, kindness and mercy. He was well known and respected by almost everyone living in his kingdom. He built beautiful parks for the people, put through smooth roads, set up market places, installed fountains and ensured a well-funded infrastructure so that the people in land thrived and were well looked after. He erected statues of himself, carved his name into the fonts and named lakes and rivers after various members of his royal family. From his advisors and scientists he gained the benefits of a good education and a wide range of knowledge. From his doctors he maintained good health. From his teachers he gained wisdom and knowledge. King Janasruti was pleased with himself and filled with pride for all that he had done for his kingdom and all that he, himself, had become.

One day king Janasruti heard about a man, living within his lands, who was considered even more wise than the king, more giving of his spiritual advice and more abundant with his time for others. King Janasruti thought that he, himself, was the most generous and wisest in the land. "I must meet this fellow and see for myself how he comes to eclipse me." So, he sent out his aides to scour the kingdom for this man named Raikva.

They looked in the darkest of caves where it was known that wise men dwelled. They searched along the canals and by the riversides. They sought him in the cool forests and in the rugged mountains. They searched in the dry plains and the fertile farmlands, but he was not to be found.

After months of searching, the kings aides were exhausted and dispirited. They thought they might never find Raikva and began even to doubt his very existence. They did not relish returning to their king with disappointing news.

On the way back to deliver their final report to the king, they made a stop in a market about a two hour walk from the palace, hoping to refresh themselves before standing before the king.

The market place was all bustle, bursting at the seams with fresh produce, baked goods, vendors making cool chai drinks, men and women cooking delectable food over open fires. The heat of the day was oppressive and the kings representatives sat down under a shade tree with the intention of having a refreshing drink. As they sat, they noticed a poor man sitting under a cart not far off. His clothes were overly worn and his sandals in poor repair, yet, as he sat in the shade he seemed calm and cool as he scratched himself, seemingly disregarding everything around him. An aura of peace and tranquility seemed to radiate from the man.

"That man looks a lot like Rishi, the great Indian seer. Maybe he can help us find Raikva," suggested one of the aides, and so they went to speak with the man they believed to be Rishi.

"Are you Rishi, the famous Indian seer?" they asked.

"I am not. I am Raikva, the cart driver."

The aides were at first shocked, then awed and finally overjoyed, for here, almost within the shadow of the palace sat the very man they long sought. They ran back to King Janasruti with the good news.

The king, in turn, was overjoyed to hear that Raikva had been found. With haste, he caused to be assembled an entourage of mighty elephants, strong soldiers and grand chariots and led them all through the city to meet with Raikva.

As King Janasruti rode through the city, seated in his sedan, the citizens shouted to him, "Jai

Raja! Hail our king! Peace to him and long life." Soon he arrived in the market. In his turn he placed his hand upon his heart and bowed his head to his well-wishers. As he stepped down from his sedan, the citizens met him with garlands of flowers, flurries of trumpeting, the beating of drums and much glorious shouting. The king gratefully acknowledged the regard of his subjects, but in a moment, he held up his hand for silence and the crowd obeyed. He proudly walked towards Raikva. A servant, a few steps behind, bearing in his arms garlands of jasmine and marigold.

"Are you Raikva the cart driver?" asked the king.

Peering out from beneath his cart, "I am," responded Raikva.

"Greetings, reverend Raikva. I am your lord and king, Janasruti Pautrayana. Our royal court smiles upon you this day. I bring you good fortune and blessings. I bestow upon you these garlands of flowers, a golden necklace, chests of the finest and rarest species from the furthest reaches of the land, silver bells made by my own skilled artisans, plus six cows from the royal heard. All this comes to you today as a result of your kings generosity and good intentions. All I ask in return is that you teach me your wisdom."

The king stood, thumbs hitched onto his wide belt, pleased with himself, arrogant, chest out, chin up, taking in the warmth and adoration of the crowd. The king, and indeed almost everyone in the crowd, knew that Raikva would be overwhelmed with gratitude and eagerly acquiesce to the kings request and take him on as a student.

Raikva, continuing to peer out from beneath his cart, looked not at all upon the gifts being held by the kings servants. He did not see the garlands of scented flowers, nor the golden necklace, not the rare spices nor the silver bells. His eyes were fixed upon the face of King Janasruti Pautrayana.

"I do not wish to have your gifts, king of mine. I ask that you give them to others who need them. Please leave me in peace."

Everyone within earshot was shocked and there arose a gasp

from the assembled. Few could believe that anyone would insult the king by not accepting his gifts. What might this mean? What would happen to Raikva?

The king said nothing. He stood motionless for a moment, brow furrowed. Then he turned and walked to his sedan and was carried back to the palace. Once there, he told everyone to leave him in peace as he retired to his private, marble covered terrace. He wanted to think upon what just happened. He wanted to understand why Raikva did not accept his gifts. Was he not generous? Was he not benevolent? Did he not act with good intentions?

Perhaps he had not offered enough! Yes, that was it. He was, after all, wealthy beyond words and he offered but a tiny percentage of his wealth to Raikva. "I am so wealthy that I should have offered more for his teachings," he thought. "I clearly undervalued the worth of the man's teachings and so insulted him."

The very next day, King Janasruti again caused his entourage to be assembled, but this time he included greater gifts, 60 cows from the royal heard, gold enough for the needs of a modest town and even one of his own daughters for Raikva to marry, providing the wise man with royal lineage.

Again there was a procession through the city. Again the citizens yelled, "Jai Raja! Hail our king! Peace to him and long life." Again the king stepped down from his sedan and again he offered his gifts (now ten times what he had previously taken) to Raikva. Again he stood, proudly, chest out, chin up, absorbing the warmth and adoration of the crowd.

"Revered Raikva, cart driver. All this bounty is yours to keep or give away as you desire," said Janasruti with the wave of an arm. "Do what you deem best with this bounty. The choice is yours. Should you and my daughter decide to marry, we will grant you freedom to live in our palace for the rest of your days, should you both so desire. We ask only that you accept me as a student that I might learn your wisdom."

Again Raikva peered out from beneath the cool and shady spot beneath his cart, looked directly into the eyes of the king and said, "I do not wish to have your gifts, king of mine. Allow your daughter to marry whom she pleases. I ask that you leave me in peace."

Like the previous day, King Janasruti did not outwardly take offence, but simply returned to his sedan and was carried back to the palace.

Once again he sat alone in the evening mulling over why Raikva would not accept his gifts.

The next day, King Janasruti left the palace in the hours before dawn, under the light of a waxing moon, and walked, alone and empty-handed towards the market place in the city. He was dressed in a simple manner without any trappings of power or any symbol that would identify his royal family.

As he walked the dark streets he was aware of people lurking in the dark and he felt fear. He quickened his pace to get away from these people. He tripped over a dead dog laying in the road, fell into a vile puddle and hurt his knee, causing him to limp and to bleed. He heard shouting from humble abodes as men and women argued. He heard the cries of young children who were sick or hungry and had little relief. He hurried though the dark streets, running now even with his aching knee, exhausted, sweating and bleeding with a terrible thirst and worsening fear.

By the time he arrived at the market, the sun was just beginning to peek over the horizon. He fell to his knees and held onto a table being set up by a stall owner, as he tried regained his breath. "Begone beggar! Get away!" shouted the merchant and he was shooed away and caned like a cur.

He stumbled across the square and sat down by a fountain (a fountain that he, himself had caused to be built and even bore his name) and drank deeply as he recovered from his exertions.

Before long, somewhat disoriented, he shuffled along the edges of the market square and, like the previous days, he found Raikva sitting quietly and peacefully beneath his cart, but this time he seemed deep in meditation.

The king sat down quietly upon the cobbled pavement of the

square in front of Raikva and waited.

As he lingered, other men and women quietly arrived at various intervals and sat down near him. Soon there were a dozen or so people sitting around him, in silence, waiting for Raikva to end his session of meditation and give them his wise words and spiritual teachings.

Raikva uttered a final word or two of gratitude and opened his eyes and immediately fixed upon King Janasruti, whom he recognized even without the king's usual trappings and fine raiments.

A man, seemingly familiar with Raikva, went to his side and spoke quietly to him for a moment. Eventually Raikva nodded and set his hand upon the man's shoulder and the man withdrew.

"So, king of mine. You have come without gifts, without entourage and without pomp. You have dressed as your subjects dress and walked the streets as your subjects have walked the streets and seen what they have seen, heard what they have heard and experienced the fear that they have experienced. Why have you come from your palace in this way? What do you want from me?"

"Only that you allow me to be your student, your disciple and learn what I can from you. I see now that offering gifts to one who has all that he needs, is wrong. I know now that all I own is marble and gems, all that I have given or offered was done with wrong intent. I now see that you possess inner peace and spiritual knowledge. What you have I cannot buy, but with diligence and your guidance I might be able to learn. With all my heart, I desire that you allow me to become your student. I humbly asked that you keep any or all of the gifts I had previously offered to the benefit of whomever you deem suitable and to keep them whether or not you take me as a student."

And with that, King Janasruti, in front of all the people, leaned forward and touched his forehead to the ground.

After a long pause, Raikva began, "Do not bow to me King, but hear this, your first lesson. It is good that you like to give, but do not give with pride or improper intent. Give without expectation of return. Give with-

out expecting gratitude from others. Give without expecting applause. Instead, give because you recognize need and want in others. Give because you have had direct experience of their suffering and wish, with the same ardor that you wish me to give you my teachings, that you can help relieve their suffering.

"While it is good to give such items as you have, such material goods as may be useful to others, give also of your time. Give people the benefit of your knowledge and give them benefit of your spiritual awareness. People do not only suffer from lack of food and water, but from lack of moral guidance and spiritual enlightenment. Look after their spiritual welfare in the same way you would look after their hunger.

"Remember this lesson."

Raikva, now seeing King Janasruti had surrendered his pride and recognized his limitations, agreed to accept some of his gifts, with one hand, on behalf of those in need, and he agreed to have him as a student.

King Janasruti learned to meditate each morning at dawn and each evening at sunset. He became peaceful, less agitated. He learned how to be content. He wanted this for all the subjects of his lands and so he ordered that meditation centres be set up and anyone who wanted to attend, would be allowed.

Janasruti became known as a spiritual king or Maharaja who found fulfilment within himself and was able to transmit that fulfilment to his people.

So, we have two ends of a spectrum. At one end is the well developed self-pleased, self-centred individual filled with pride. At the other end is ultimate humility, no-self and being one with all sentient creatures. Like so many things in Buddhism, there is usually a seeking of the middle way and so it is here.

In the early stages of practice, one may come to recognize their pride or arrogance, but as one progresses, that pride will naturally fall away as we learn that we don't know everything.

But can we really be humble? We all know someone who is smarter than us, more talented and more skilled at some pastime. Perhaps they are a university professor with published books that they refer to as, "My clumsy efforts," when in fact they are brilliant, well respected works, perhaps used in universities across the country. We've all been to dinner at a friend's house which was sumptuous, well prepared, well presented and exquisite in both flavour and form, but when we express our gratitude, we are usually met with, "Oh, you're being too kind," and refer to their efforts as 'plain,' or 'inept,' but deep down, they may feel their efforts were outstanding.

We are often encouraged to be self-deprecating and use language that implies humility, but it is really only a well codified secret language that we all know, but don't discuss. Essentially they are ceremonial courtesies that allow us to speak of our works, but not take too much credit for them. Perhaps it's a simple matter of semantics. Perhaps it's a matter of avoiding extremes. Maybe we should simply;

- Avoid arrogant words, attitudes and behaviours
- Respect and appreciate the efforts and works of others
- Know that we may have talents in one area, but be sorely lacking in others
- Avoid being too hard on ourselves or overly critical of our own efforts.

If we behaved in such a way, then we would be practicing humility and maybe we could call ourselves humble and be open to new learning, new ideas and new experiences.

4.1 Humour

The Buddha, in speaking of old age, pain, disease, injury and death was right that there was, and still is, little to laugh about. He was also right when he observed that, ultimately, life is unsatisfactory. But what he didn't say was that life was *nothing* but suffering and *completely* unsatisfactory. He said it is *ultimately* unsatisfactory.

A lot of things in life are funny, ironic, curious, laughable and downright hilarious. Anyone who has watched Harpo Marx, Woody Allan's Bananas, or Planes, Trains and Automobiles knows that *some* things are funny. Even if you didn't find those films funny, you at least recognize that you think something is funny, by way of comparison.

When we do silly things, and get called on it, we can either become defensive or we can laugh at ourselves. When we are young, we may become defensive easily, but as we age, a lot of what we do is just plain funny and we've to learned laugh about it, rather than get defensive. How long do men do the 'comb-over' with their hair until they finally throw up their hands and say, "Looks like I'm going bald," and simply laugh at their antics.

In short, humour allows us to find the light in situations or conversation. Sure, not everything is funny all the time, but our day is almost always punctuated by someone doing or saying something funny that gets a laugh or two. If we were serious all the time, we might fall into depression - worrying about all the things that are wrong or could go wrong.

A group of monks were meditating together when a Buddhist deity appeared before them. The deity addresses one monk in particular and says, "Your meditation is so pure that it has been noticed in all of the Pure Lands of The Buddha. It has been decided to award you with a choice of Buddha's wisdom, or wealth even beyond that of King Pautrayana."

With little hesitation, the particular monk chooses wisdom.

"So be it," said the deity and then disappeared.

The monk sits for some time, saying nothing. Eventually a sad shadow crosses his face. Finally one of the other monks couldn't stand it anymore. "Say something! You have the wisdom of Buddha!" he pleaded.

The blessed monk sighs, stands up, dusts himself off as he walks to the open window. He looks down into the verdant valley to the houses and farms far below. He clasps his hands behind his back and hangs his head. He turns to the other monks, "It turns out I should have taken the money."

The point of all this, of course, is to emphasize the fact that not every moment in our lives is serious. There are things to laugh at and laugh about ... especially ourselves if we can lighten up and see how we behave or listen to the things we say. When we can laugh at ourselves, we begin to develop a sense of humility and take ourselves less seriously. We may enjoy life a little more, see things in a different light and forgive or admit to our errors. After all, when we learn to forgive ourselves it becomes easier to forgive others.

Humour makes hard times, easier to bear and helps defuse conflict. When we cultivate humour and practice laughing at ourselves, we make it easier to let go of harmful emotions such as hatred, envy, anger or resentment.

To be sure, the medical community walks a narrow path around humour as a treatment. Essentially every paper I've read on the topic of treating physical or mental illness with a good dose of humour concludes that since there are no serious/identifiable side effects, there is no reason not to use humour as part of a comprehensive program for an individual to return to health.*

It's no surprise that the medical community has a hard time reaching a definitive conclusion, for what is funny to one person isn't to another. How do you do a clinical trial on the benefits? Do you expose one group to Seinfeld and another to George Carlin, then measure how long/hard they laugh? There are too many variables around societal norms, changing times, cohorts and political leanings.

---

* For example – Suzanne M. Skevington & Alison White (1998) Is laughter the best medicine?, Psychology & Health, 13:1, 157-169, DOI: 10.1080/08870449808406139

> As we cultivate humour, we must not laugh at others, make them feel uncomfortable, ignored, humiliated or less valued. Humour, therefore, is best directed at ourselves and our shortcomings as it sheds light on our inconsistencies, foibles and programmed thinking.

Using humour wisely means that our intention is to bring people together, lessen our differences, ease discomfort, recognize our personal shortcomings, all the better to understand ourselves, others and the human condition.

As Osho said, as he passed through this realm;

"One should simply laugh of one's own accord, and one should not wait for reasons to laugh. That too is absurd. Why wait for reasons? Life, as it is, should be enough of a reason to laugh. It is so absurd, it is so ridiculous. It is so beautiful, so wonderful. It is all sorts of things together. It is a great cosmic joke."

Perhaps the joke he's referring to is the fact that all things that we aspire to are already within us and that recognizing the transient nature of our short lives makes violence, hatred, jealousy - all our negative emotions - obsolete. That ought to give us something to smile about.

4.2 The Five Remembrances

To help us look more fully at the nature of human existence, and exercise our humility, we can think upon the Five Remembrances. This is an exercise in which we look at ourselves and think deeply about our nature. This is not a matter of being sullen, but a matter of being true to our nature and gaining some appreciation for the life we have been given. We are what we are and there is no escaping it. When we see that, and gain understanding into it, then we will soon find we suffer less.

Take a few moments and think about what each of the Five Remembrances means to you as a sentient being.

I Am Of The Nature To Grow Old
Everyone and everything ages and grows old. It is inescapable. Perhaps think about your ageing parents or grandparents. Understand that they had their times of youth, as you've had yours. Their ageing minds and bodies are little different from what your mind and body will become.

I Am Of The Nature To Become Ill
Illness, disease, sickness and accidents are part of everyone's life. Some may suffer a bit less and others more, but illness comes to us all and we all suffer from it.

I Am Of The Nature To Die
Death comes to everyone, not because we have been abandoned by some god or have not kept up a good health regime, but because we are human and our birth guarantees our death. It's sobering to understand that one hundred years from now, essentially the entire population of todays world, will be dead and buried.

I Am of the Nature to Change
Everything that we have ever known, loved, hated or otherwise, will change. To believe in permanent nature is to be deluded. Look around you, change is everywhere. Deep understanding of that brings one closer to better understanding our human nature as we transit this life.

I Am of the Nature to Own My Karma
What we think, do and say has a direct and intimate relationship to our karma. We need to own our words and actions and recognize that there is no escaping consequences. What we have thought, said and done in the past, has a direct and sometimes unintended impact on what we have become and will become in the future.

"It is a curious fact that ... people are never so trivial as when they take themselves seriously."

–Oscar Wilde, *The Pall Mall Gazette, The Story of the Cross*

Key Points Summary - Humility and Humour

Mastery of Humility	• When we fully understand that many things in our lives can and should be laughed at, we begin to lighten up and see that a lot of suffering is self-inflicted.
Humility Our Shortcomings	• Humility is the recognition that we might not know everything there is to know about any given circumstance.
Humility Helps Us Recognize We Are Not That Different From Each Other	• Humility helps us towards the realizations that there is little separation between 'me' and 'you' • When we recognize we are all prone to error, embarrassment, shame and aversion to blame, then we are closer to understanding that we are all really the same.
Use Humour to Build Relationships	• Our humour is best directed at ourselves and our own shortcomings • Avoid laughing at others and making them feel bad • Avoid using humour to cause division among people, cause harm or demean them.
The Five Remembrances	• When we think upon the fleeting nature of our lives, and what it's like to be human, then we gain a real sense of perspective and an appreciation for our life. • Knowing that we will soon pass away, we gain a sense of humility.

4.3 Wisdom and The Three Mental Defilements

In Theravada Buddhism, there is considerable emphasis on purifying the mind of it's 'defilements,' namely; ignorance, greed and hatred.

- Until we get a handle on the fact that we have been conditioned to see the world in a certain way (ignorance/delusion) we can't profess to genuine wisdom
- Until we understand that an unending desire for 'things' and 'novel experience' runs us ragged and taints how we see the world, we will not understand why we behave as we do, and wisdom will elude us
- And, until we see that we have aversion to many things and circumstances and that those aversions drive us in any number of directions, then we can't think, speak or act in a wise manner.

In Chapter 3, (Values, Morality, Ethics and their role in Wisdom) we discussed the Five Precepts and their relationship to Buddhist wisdom, but simply adhering to them, doesn't make one wise. Those precepts are mostly about behaviours that encourage the conditions for wisdom to arise and paint a picture of what Buddhist 'morality' might look like. Further, the Five Precepts are simply good rules to practice in order to be welcome in a community. People who practice not to take life, not steal, speak kindly, avoid intoxicants and sexual misconduct would certainly be more welcome into a community than someone who does not practice those precepts. When it comes to the Three Defilements of the mind, we get into root causes that allow us to lose track of the importance of the Five Precepts in our daily lives.

The Three Mental Defilements are like clouds that continually circle our head. When we need to make a judgment about something, one, two or three of the clouds descend and we see the situation through that fog. We can't see clearly what is in front of us, because the mental clouds form and obscure, distort, flavour, twist and bend the situation to best suit our subjective experiences or our needs at any particular time.

4.4 Ignorance, the First Mental Defilement

In Buddhism, we might define ignorance as a wrong or misunderstood view of the world.

When we do not understand how the world works, or how we operate within the world at large, then we are ignorant. For example, if I thought that my relationship with my partner would last until "death do us part,' then I would not recognize the nature of impermanence and I might be inclined to think that we really will be together for the rest of our lives. Yet, it is very unlikely that any couple would stay together throughout their lives. It happens, of course, but the odds of that happening makes it unlikely. My partner might leave me, fall in love with someone else or simply die. My relationship has ended or at the very least it has altered dramatically. It was not permanent, despite my believing it may have been so. This is ignorance.

If one believed they drove a car well, but in reality, based on any given analysis of an expert, they actually drove poorly, then that person would be *delusional* about how they drove. They would be ignorant of the reality of the situation. Even after a driving expert informed them that they were a poor driver, explained where they were going wrong and what problems they were causing on the road, they may continue to drive as they always because their ego might not want to take in the reality of their driving skills. Mental clouds descend and twist their view of the situation to best protect their ego and their distorted view of the world. They might begin to attack the instructor's personality, their intellect or parentage - anything that might give a foothold into the developing delusion that he or she must not really be an expert and that they, themselves, knew better.

When we do not recognize that all things come to an end; relationships, business dealings, present situations and even our own life and the lives of our loved ones, we are ignorant. Impermanence and change is the central theme to all our lives and is inescapable. To believe otherwise is to court ignorance.

More specifically, as it applies to Buddhism, we say we are ignorant when we fail to understand the fundamental nature of human existence. As we will discuss in the chapter on The Four Noble Truths, the common experience of human existence is suffering, but we will save that for a bit.

Denialism

It's one thing, by dint of being misled or fooled, into a misunderstanding of how the world works, or to place complete confidence in one's imperfect sense organs to determine 'reality,' but quite another to actively and knowingly create a whole new way of seeing the world and to combine this new vision with others of a similar mind in order to create a collective delusion - an accomplishment known as 'denialism.'

As we discussed in Chapter 3.2- *Do Not Lie*, we lie to ourselves and to others all the time and for lots of good reasons. Telling a particular truth might result in suffering or pain for ourselves or others. The truth might put us into a difficult or untenable spot. We want to avoid shame or blame. We don't want to be accountable for the results of our poor decisions, etc. For the most part, these choices are personal and pragmatic. We seek to avoid an unpleasant situation for ourselves or ones we love or perhaps depend upon.

There are certain social conventions that we have learned to adhere to if we have any aspirations about getting along with others in our tribe. We learn, fairly early in our lives, that calling out the fact that the Emperor has no clothes is not generally conductive to good social standing within the tribe or acceptance into the good graces of the Emperor. Telling truth to power, while sometimes necessary, is not generally going to end well for the teller.

Another reason we might be in denial of the ways of the world is that we honestly want to create a better vision of what the world might be, if only enough people bought into our collective vision. We might ignore obvious truths, conclusions or best practices in order to put into place some dogma that will lead us to a new utopia.

Of course the obverse side of that coin is also true; we might not be able to accept the horrors of this world and will create an alternate view, any alternative view—even if it's delusional—in order to 'break' from this world and maintain some semblance of sanity. Perhaps the world is so untenable to us that it becomes necessary to escape into a fantasy land that we build, brick by brick using, fake news, pseudo science, flawed logic and fundamental ignorance of the world.

Sometimes denialism is driven by financial gain. For years, the tobacco companies denied that there was any link between their product and lung cancer (or any number of other cardiovascular diseases) because to accept the science would have been to accept the financial consequences of the damage their product has done to millions of people. They were correct of course, at least about the financial link, and eventually had to pay staggering amounts to survivors of their product.* They then suffered the indignity of having government put restrictions on their products, health warning, graphic pictures, loss of advertising opportunities, etc. Their denialism was primarily, and perhaps exclusively, motivated by money.

The *users* of tobacco also tend to be denialist in nature. Quitting the very addictive habit has proven almost impossible, so, rather than make the effort, people may deny the reality of the situation.

- "I only smoke 'light' cigarettes"
- "I don't inhale"
- "I'm not really addicted. I can quit any time"
- "I only smoke when I drink with friends"
- "My father lived to 90 and he smoked a pack-a-day"
- "It's not a lung problem, I just have a cold."

Literally any excuse, or denialist reality, other than the actual fact that smoking cigarettes causes lung cancer, for to admit that would mean that some action needs to be taken and the user will be found

---

* These payouts are generally summed up, or perhaps best exemplified, in the Tobacco Master Settlement Agreement (MSA) of 1998. Essentially, the tobacco 'majors' had to pay 46 US states substantial sums to off-set health care costs related to smoking. Further, the 'majors' pay an annual sum, in perpetuity, to the various states as part of their health care cost recovery.

wanting in will or determination. It might also mean that you have to come up with a rationale that can hold both the truth of cancer and the truth of still smoking, such as, "I know it's bad for me, but I like smoking." You know better, but you just like smoking, ergo, you accept the well known health risks for the sake of a little pleasure.

—We can also be denialist around political affiliation. If I want to be a good Republican then I have to believe in any number of policies or made up views of the world - same for Democrats. If we want to belong, we need to swallow whole the party ideology - even where it disagrees with our own conclusions and personal experiences in the world. We might need to accept the stories around universal health care being 'too expensive' or that building a wall to keep out Mexican migrants is 'good,' a 'terrific job' was done in Puerto Rico after Hurricane Maria or more guns would mean 'safer' schools, etc. Even where obvious, clear evidence to the contrary exists, we must, by a need to associate with a political party, accept a flawed narrative and become denialist - defending what we profess to believe ... even if we don't really believe it.

—Of course the same can be said for religion. The desire to be 'saved' and live a life eternal in heaven can only be attained by 'believing' and having faith - even when to do so makes no sense to us. We will turn a blind eye to sexual abuse in the church because to call it out would mean we are not good members of whatever faith or practice we follow. We might be ostracized, outcast and discredited. We want to belong, so we accept whatever sham story is being told in order to do so. We become deniers of what is really going on, even where our own personal experience and observations see through the false narrative. This isn't intended to discredit religion for religion can bring a lot of comfort to a lot of people - the point is that we will turn a blind eye and actively take up denialist thinking, if we think there is something to be gained.

—A mother who knows her child is being sexually abused by a member of the immediate or extended family and doesn't call out the perpetrator, is practicing denialism. The need to, 'hold the family together' at the expense of a safe environment for the child is not only denialist, flawed logic and poor conduct, but failure to report such activity is almost certainly a breach of child care law. Some unidentified, misplaced need for acceptance or belonging overrides all other considerations, at the expense of the traumatized child.

—Denialist behaviour around medical practice is quite common. People who 'believe' that vaccinations are a 'Big-Pharma' program to control and pervert the will of individuals might turn to an outlier report about someone who had a bad reaction to a vaccination as evidence that *all* vaccinations are bad. Reasoning from the specific to the general is false reasoning, yet there are a lot of people who have concluded that *all* vaccinations are bad for *all* people, *all* the time, based on a limited data set.

Perhaps they haven't seen the results of polio or been hospitalized themselves due to tetanus or watched their child convulse and gasp for breath from whooping cough or watched a friend or relative die from a particularly virulent form of influenza - all ailments for which there is a useful, effective, preventative vaccination.

> There is a tendency for denialists to string together outlier stories, outright lies, half-truths and misunderstandings, into a story that best suits their own view of the world. Anyone who tries to correct the facts or point out inconvenient truths is simply viewed a part of the problem.

Denialists also tend to seek the scientific community's blessing - the very community which they are trying to discredit. Deniers will often try to string together a lot of facts, from varying reports, to make their cause look 'scientific.' They may take one report, questioning the conclusions around global warming, (maybe an outlier year in which sea ice coverage actually *increased* over the previous year) add to it their personal observations of their local weather being unusually cool and conclude global warming is a falsehood and then attribute all manner of conspiracies as to why the scientific community is trying to hoodwink us into believing the Earth's atmosphere is getting warmer.

Providing denialists with contrary evidence only tends to fuel their denialism and feeds into the conspiracy narrative - simply, *you* become part of the conspiracy (always without you realizing it), providing further proof that they were right all along.

If you're a denialist, you're not going to be convinced in these pages. Of course, if you were a denialist, you couldn't identify as such. Really, all that is asked here is that you take time to look at conclusions, examine why you deny evidence around particular issues and give thought to your conclusions.

> In the end, unless we come to know, and fully understand, that our world is viewed through distorting clouds, then it seems almost impossible to raise wisdom in thought, words or actions.

"No one is wise by birth, for wisdom results from one's own efforts."

~ T. Krishnamacharya The Yoganjalisaram

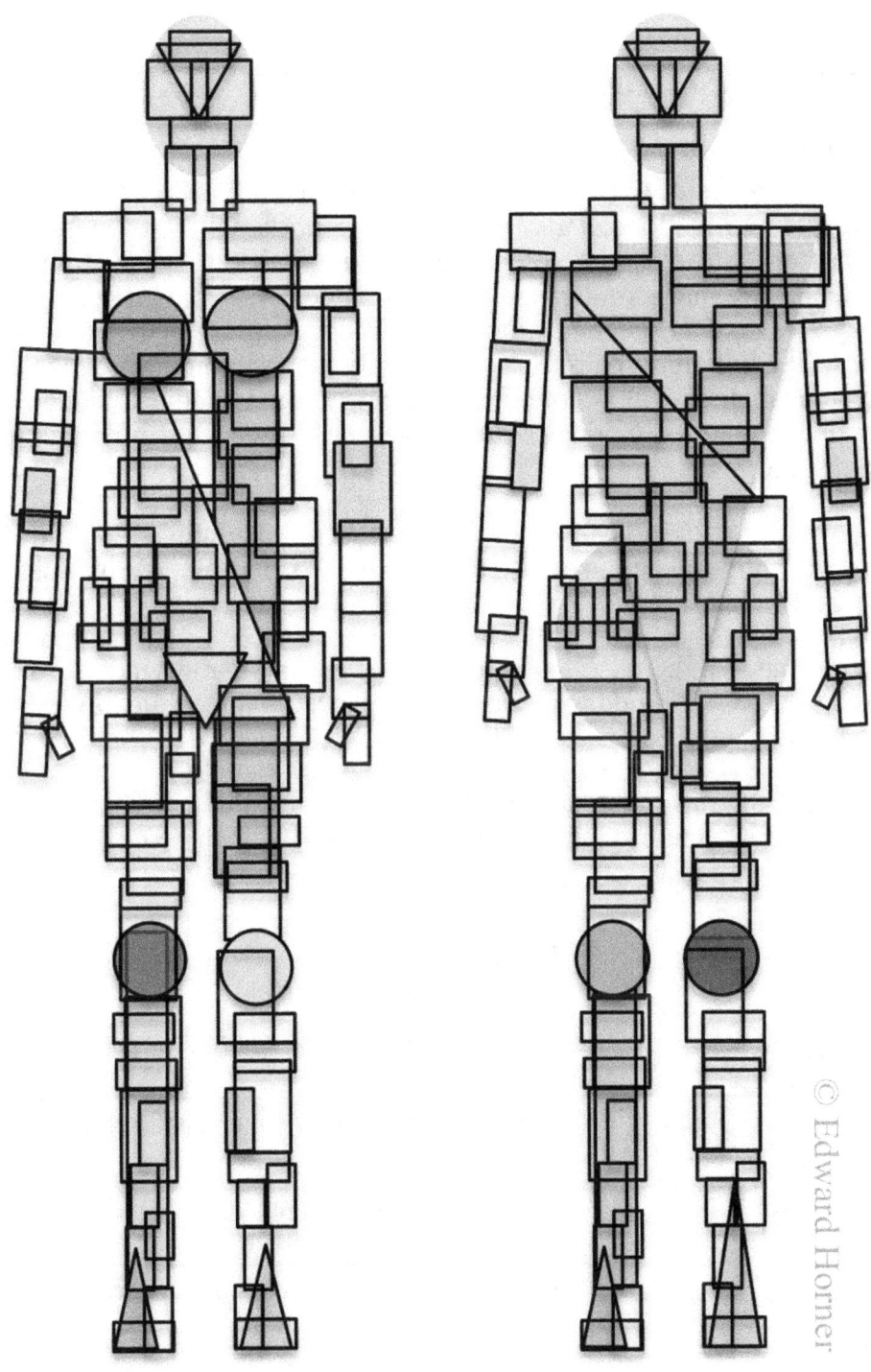

4.5 Overcoming Ignorance

Recognize Your Ego

Somewhere inside our head, the mind is hard at work telling the body to breath, pump blood, walk, run, find food, drink, talk to friends, go for a run, hold onto the pole in the moving subway, balance on a skateboard and tens of thousands of commands every day to keep the body alive and so keep the mind alive. Of course some of these functions, like breathing and heart beating, are autonomous, which is to say, they happen without our even thinking about it. Others, like going out for a drink, calling friends or getting exercise, are more conscious, thoughts.

So, what is the mind up to? Why is the mind running the body ragged trying to keep itself alive? What is its purpose? Why does it exist? Where is it?

It turns out that there is a specific part of the mind that we identify as "us," or "me." In Buddhist terms it's known as anatta, while in Western terms it's called ego.

The ego contains the code for what and who we think we are. For Buddhists it's the product of the *Five Skandhas* or the *Five Aggregates*, which consist of;

Form	• The body and all the sense organs (ears, eyes, tongue, touch, smell)
Sensation	• Feeling an object or situation as being good, bad or neutral
Perception	• Being able to determine the existence of, say, a tree
Mental Formations	• Thoughts, opinions, mental habits, preferences, aversions, etc.
Consciousness	• That part of which discerns or supports all experience

Through the five skandhas we are aware of ourselves and our surroundings. Largely, it's how we recognize ourselves.

> Our ego is an ever changing pool of information, experience, mood, desire, pain, pleasure and a hundred other experiences that have come to us through our six senses, filtered by the five skandhas. By looking into the pool, we see who we think we are.

Of course "who we are" changes over time. It changes with life experience. One day we were a son or daughter, then another day we find ourselves a parent. One day we are an employee, earning a wage and the next we are a business owner. Almost overnight we might go from being single to being partnered, then perhaps back again.

> Who we think we are – how the ego identifies us as ourselves – is the manifold permutations of our ever changing experiences and thought processes. Our ego is an illusion that changes with time and experience.

Ego, illusion or not, has been doing a pretty good job keeping us alive. Any time something, an idea or a person, threatens us with actual physical danger, or just danger to our sense of self, then ego jumps to defend. It's races to ward off any threat to the self, any threat to *itself*. When difficult ideas arise, ego jumps up with, "Nope, couldn't be. Not possible. We're doing fine here. We know what we're doing. We like things just as they are, thank you."

Persist

Overcoming ignorance is not a one-time thing. One may even suggest that overcoming ignorance is more of a process than a goal. Both the world and ourselves change with time, necessitating the need for constant re-evaluation and revision of our conclusions. Understanding the world in 2008 is not the same as understanding the world - and our relationship to it - in 2020, for both have changed.

Meditate

Ego is a major impediment to our properly understanding the nature of the world for it pits 'us' against 'them.' It creates an adversarial situation in almost every instance of every day, making us believe that we must *always* be in conflict with those around us. Unchecked, it will build a world of 'scarcity' believing in a zero sum environment in which anything someone else has received is at the expense of what I have *not* received.

We will look at this in greater detail in Chapter 11 - Meditation, Concentration and Patience, but for now, recognize that sitting quietly, with all the background distractions turned off, as far as that is possible, and looking deeply into the workings of our mind, will go a long way to developing the mental discipline that will assist in overcoming the delusions we've developed about how the world operates. Meditation helps us loosen ego's hold over our mind.

"Enlightenment for Gautama [the Buddha] felt as though a prison which had confined him for thousands of lifetimes had broken open. Ignorance had been the jailkeeper. Because of ignorance, his mind had been obscured, just like the moon and stars hidden by the storm clouds. Clouded by endless waves of deluded thoughts, the mind had falsely divided reality into subject and object, self and others, existence and non-existence, birth and death, and from these discriminations arose wrong views—the prisons of feelings, craving, grasping, and becoming. The suffering of birth, old age, sickness, and death only made the prison walls thicker. The only thing to do was to seize the jailkeeper and see his true face. The jailkeeper was ignorance. . . . Once the jailkeeper was gone, the jail would disappear and never be rebuilt again."

~ Thich Nhat Hanh, *Old Path, White Clouds*

4.6 Greed, the Second of the Mental Defilements

Sometimes, and seemingly without any particular reason, things or circumstances just seem desirable. There may seem to be no reason at all, but you just want something. We become obsessed with having the item or circumstance and can't let it alone. We may be compelled to save money to obtain it. We may be pressed to spend less on other things in order to have it. We may put it on our credit card and buy it with money we don't have. When all else fails, we may even beg, borrow or steal that which has attracted our attention.

We may believe that we have a perfectly good reason for possessing this item and that we are deserving of it. We may rationalize needing it for some personal reason. We may even fabricate a need to defend the irrational desire to own a particular item.

The marketing industry has become very good at creating a need around any particular product or service. The need may be improved looks, better health, greater wealth, more comfort, greater knowledge, better safety, faster travel, etc. The list of "needs" goes on and on. The marketers have their greatest success when they cause you to believe that you invented the need yourself. They might point out the poor qualities of the item you may already possess, present their item, then let you put two and two together. Voila! They didn't even have to tell you to buy their product, you decided all by yourself!

Simply possessing things that have been earned, found or received as gifts, is not a defilement. The defilement comes when we no longer recognize that we are being driven, primarily by our ego, to desire more than we need, almost always at the expense of others, and this, of course, is where the 'morality' of a situation comes into play.

When we seek wisdom, greed takes the mind off course. When greed dominates the mind, other things fall off the mental map and we no longer take time to adequately consider them. When greed takes over, it excludes humanity, humour, compassion and concentrates only on obtaining what is desired by the individual. Its morality, excludes the concept of the common good, inflames the mind with its charge to secure the desired object or situation, at any cost.

When greed enters the mind, it discounts, devalues or dismisses altogether, the Five Precepts;

- Do not kill
- Do not take what is not freely offered
- Do not lie
- Do not engage in inappropriate sexual relations
- Do not take intoxicants

Desire, in our western society, seems not to be a negative trait. Desire might be viewed at one end of the 'want' spectrum. It's quaint, almost romantic, essentially a wish. Greed, on the other hand, is something less than savoury and might be found at the other end of the spectrum. It's an undisciplined aspect of our mind. A mental aberration or abhorrent character flaw that, even in western culture, is considered distasteful.*

In Buddhism, the difference between 'desire' and 'greed' is somewhat artificial, for to passionately 'want' any object or situation, deserved or not, is a mental obstruction and hindrance to mental discipline and is a cloud that must be lifted, or at the very least seen and understood, if one is to proceed along the path to wisdom.

> Greed, then, is an impediment to wisdom, for it clouds the mind, ignores reason and will too often harm, demean or disadvantage others to get what it needs.

---

* Notwithstanding Gordon Gekko's well crafted speech to his audience in the 1987 film *Wall Street*. "The point is, ladies and gentleman, that greed, for lack of a better word, is good. Greed is right, greed works. Greed clarifies, cuts through, and captures the essence of the evolutionary spirit. Greed, in all of its forms; greed for life, for money, for love, knowledge has marked the upward surge of mankind." But don't forget how the movie ends; Gekko gets *too* greedy and begins to hurt others with his methods. The SEC/FBI charge him with insider trading and get him on tape admitting to it. We learn, in the 2010 sequel, *Wall Street, Money Never Sleeps*, Gekko did some time behind bars.

4.7 Hatred, the Third Mental Defilement

Hate arises from ignorance of the world and denies everything and everyone is interconnected. We come to think of ourselves as standing apart or separate from the world and judge everything and everyone by some internal standard that we may not even recognize or understand. When those people, things or circumstances that we judge are found *wanting* in some way, we begin to develop negative feelings towards them. It takes many forms and can be described in many ways; abhorrence, disgust, detestation, intolerance and loathing, to name a few.

This judging is most destructive and causes the rising of hatred and its many manifestations, such as; prejudice, racism, religious intolerance, homophobia, ill-will, animosity, sexual assault, murder, war or genocide.

When we look at our hatreds we almost always find they are, in fact, conditions imposed on us by others, often our parents, teachers, peers, government or religious organizations. According to Silva Dutchevici, LCSW, president and founder of the Critical Therapy Center, *"We live in a war culture that promotes violence, in which competition is a way of life. We fear connecting because it requires us to reveal something about ourselves. We are taught to hate the enemy—meaning anyone different than us—which leaves little room for vulnerability and an exploration of hate through empathic discourse and understanding. In our current society, one is more ready to fight than to resolve conflict. Peace is seldom the option."*

In the late Nelson Mandela's book, *Long Walk to Freedom*, (1994) we read, *"No one is born hating another person because of the colour of his skin, or his background, or his religion. People must learn to hate, and if they can learn to hate, they can be taught to love, for love comes more naturally to the human heart than its opposite."*

Essentially we obtain our hatreds, at least at an early age, from forces and influences from outside agents.

For some time, The Buddha was visiting a sangha in a small town. Many people came to visit the sangha, meet The Buddha, spend some time in his presence and learn some of his teachings. In attendance throughout at least a few hours of each day, were two sons of a local businessman. Like most others, they simply came to sit in silent contemplation, then hear The Buddha's teaching and maybe ask a few questions.

Their father, a local businessman, thought this wrong. He believed his sons should be with him, tending to the family business, making more money and not sitting with some fellow for hours each day, eyes closed and doing nothing. The more the man thought about this, the more he became agitated.

His agitation soon turned to a distaste for The Buddha and this gnawed away at him for days. Before long he began to hate The Buddha and his followers and anything that had anything to do with the dreadful man who was taking away the attention and labour of his sons.

One day he stormed down to the sangha and confronted Buddha. His face was red, his eyes threatened to bulge out of their sockets. The only thing he could hear was the blood rushing in his ears as his body prepared for a fight. He had, quite literally, lost control of his voice and could not utter even one word of what he wanted to say to The Buddha. All he could do was spit in the face of The Buddha.

This shocked everyone in attendance and angered them, (in the same manner it would anger us) but as they were in the presence of The Buddha, they did not respond, but waited to take their cue from Buddha himself.

Contrary to what we, ourselves, might have done, The Buddha simply smiled, wiped his face with a sleeve. His eyes expressed compassion and understanding of why the man might be angry. The businessman, having at least expressed his contempt for The Buddha, turned on his heel and strode out of the meeting.

That evening, the businessman could not sleep. He tossed and *turned all night. The memory of how he treated another person kept coming back to him and he felt guilt and remorse. He had never treated another person as he had done today, not even his most competitive business rivals. He felt as though his entire body had turned against him. His world felt turned upside down.*

The next day, the businessman returned to The Buddha and, in front of the assembled sangha, threw himself at the feet of The Buddha and told him how sorry he was. He told The Buddha he was not himself and begged The Buddha to forgive him.

"I cannot forgive you," responded The Buddha.

The businessman and even the followers of The Buddha were shocked that The Buddha would not forgive the man.

In response to the surprised and hurt look on the face of the businessman, The Buddha explained. "I cannot forgive you, for the man who stood here yesterday, and upon whom you spat, no longer exists. If I see that man, I shall tell him of your apology. To the person who stands here before you today, you have done no wrong."

Of course we all experience anger and hatred in our minds from time to time. We rail when things are not going our way and may learn to 'hate' working late on Fridays or having to come back early from a vacation. We usually let these go quickly enough and they don't consume us.

There will always be 'others' for us to hate. If not a race, then a religion or culture or sports team or school or country or politician. We expend a vast amount of energy on this hatred. What have we gained by holding onto and acting out on these negative emotions? Nothing. We have only managed to pollute our minds, hurt others and even ourselves. We diminish the world around us through an infantile view of 'how things ought to be,' but never will be. We live a life of constant disappointment, sadness, regret and disenchantment – in short, suffering. We can never be happy, because there will always be something or someone for us to hate. This is *Dukkha*.

On the up side, if you want to be angry about something, you can use that anger to combat racism, poverty, disease or any number of afflictions that plague humanity. You can use that negative energy towards improving the state of the environment or the state of a local river, park or wetland.

Negative energy and negative emotions can be transformative, but you must learn to let go of the things that originally made you angry. The only way that we can truly let go is to practice loving kindness towards others - even when we don't want to. When we do it enough, it becomes second nature. Each time we help someone in need, it becomes easier to help a second time, or a third and a fourth. Eventually it becomes second nature. Hatred *can* be un-learned, but it's not an easy job.

> When we hate people, things or circumstances, we rob ourselves of wisdom. Our mind becomes inflamed and cannot be quenched. When we are angry or full of ill-will, we no longer think straight. Wisdom eludes us since we are ruled, not by our rational thoughts, but by conditions imposed on us by outside forces. Our rational, logical mind is held hostage to the negative emotions of hatred, acrimony and revulsion. We literally are not in control of our mind and until we recognize that, wisdom cannot arise.

In order for us to lay the ground work for the raising of wisdom, we need to get a handle on our ignorance, greed and hatred. When we are consumed with any or all of these mental afflictions, our head will be in a fog, unable to see the true nature of our condition and the condition of all others. We will be pushed and pulled by our ego, our programmed hatreds and our irrational desire for things. When and where these three conditions exist in our mind, a common good cannot be seen, a desire to help others out of their suffering cannot arise and so wisdom is stunted and withered.

"Conquer the hateful man with love; conquer the bad man with goodness; conquer the miser with generosity; conquer the liar with truth."

– Dhammapada, quotes attributed to The Buddha

4.8 The Five Stages of Wisdom

Siddhartha Gautama, the man who would ultimately become *The Buddha* (Enlightened One) left the protected comfort of his fathers palace complex. He left behind his family, riches and power and set out to discover why there was so much suffering in the world and why the gods of India would not help or intervene. He sought a way for all sentient beings to be free of suffering.

He sought out experts in meditation, yoga and other masters in mental and physical disciplines. He studied long and hard. He learned whatever he could from the masters and moved on, accumulating a great amount of knowledge and understanding of the world. He sat often and thought long and hard about why people continued to suffer and why there seemed to be little in the way of relief.

After years of seeking out knowledge and experience, he finally sat down under a bodhi tree in deep contemplation, set aside his ignorance, hatred and greed, put together everything he had seen, heard and learned until he realized the four essential truths that caused people to suffer and how they might end that suffering. This realization, this wisdom, is discussed in some detail beginning in Chapter 11.1 The Four Noble Truths and The Eightfold Path. For now, we can simply note that there were five distinct stages of progress towards his ultimate wisdom and we briefly dissect them here.

Hearing or Learning
It's clear that we cannot be brilliant at everything. It's unlikely that anyone is going to be a first rate rocket scientist, brain surgeon, Grey Cup champion, Nobel Peace Prize winner, Poet Laureate for the state of California and Artist in Residence at the New Broadview Hotel all at the same time. We might be over-joyed to be only one of those or be an expert at almost anything else. Having specialized knowledge is a starting point on the way to becoming an expert in a given field, but being an expert, by itself, doesn't make one wise.

Knowing how to build houses, without the understanding of transportation systems, electrical grids, topography, threat to property from climate change, cultural preferences, etc. means that one only has a grasp of one concept and has not or cannot make wise choices involving a multitude of disciplines.

The more we learn beyond our chosen field, the better and wiser our decisions become.

Begin with silence. Become a curious fool. Listen to what is being said and taught. Quiet the hubbub and silence the distractions. Clear the mind of 'us' and 'them.' Allow the mind to let go of its dogma and pre-conceived ideas and biases. Listen deeply to your teachers to gain understanding - even when you don't fully agree with them.

Clarification and Interpretation
After we become aware of something or some situation, we need to sit down, think about it and how it relates to what we already know. In the example of building houses, it might be critical to think about how a house will fit into the landscape, neighbourhood or city. It might be important to know if a river floods seasonally in order to not build too close to the water or adjust the design so the house is on stilts, or it might float. If we are building in the hills of California, we might need to know that there is a cyclic season of brush fires and could the backyard swimming pool be used for fire suppression, if needed. Sitting and thinking deeply, with concentration and attention is needed to fully understand how the topic at hand fits into the wider world.

Nothing exists alone and all things arise from, and are effected by, other things. All worldly phenomenon have context and not knowing that context, we rob ourselves of wisdom. But this extends beyond mere 'things.' It extends as well to ideas and thoughts, beliefs and values. Even though these exist only in our mind, they too will have arisen from previous ideas and experiences. That which came before and that world in which they arose and now exist, is their context.

> When we think, speak or act without context, to address a common good, we do so without full benefit of wisdom. This isn't to suggest that thoughts, words or actions without full understanding of the situation will always be wrong, for indeed, there is great wisdom in getting out of a burning building, without knowing the cause of the fire.

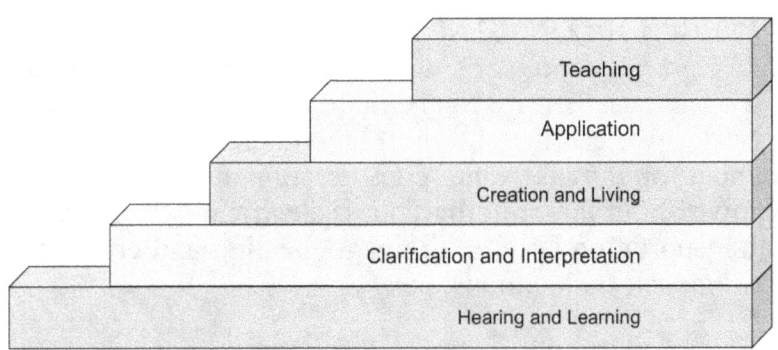

Creation And Living

It's not enough that we listen to our teachers, observe our world and compare it to our understanding. It's not enough that we as ask questions and clarify what we do not understand. We need to build a life based on those understandings. In the case of wisdom, we need to create and live a life which;

- Shuns ignorance, hatred and greed
- Integrates learning, both specific and general
- Adheres to the five precepts or similar set of values
- Incorporates self-deprecating humour

- Includes some form of 'universal responsibility'
- Minimizes the 'us versus them' paradigm.

> In short you want to live a life that avoids all those things which we have so far discussed as being limiting to the development of wisdom. From waking up in the morning to going to bed at night, we need to encourage those conditions that help give rise to wisdom.

But be careful. We need to remember, as we will discuss later in this book, that we cannot allow our thinking to go unchallenged. We cannot allow ourselves to be locked into a mental position when new information comes our way. We must not allow our thinking and wisdom to be clouded by pre-conceived notions and a 'locked in' position.

Application In The Real World

Once we *grok* the topic or situation and how it will affect us and the world around us, then we can begin to apply our understanding in the real world. We can begin to build the house, knowing that we have accounted for and taken into consideration all that could reasonably be known about the building codes, electrical standards, flood control, transportation system, drainage, heating and cooling, environmental impact, trade unions, etc.

After the house is built and the owners move in, we do follow ups to see how happy they are with the design. We go back to see how the heating is working and how the house performs in the flood season or rainy season, etc.

> We don't just build a house and walk away, but rather look back and examine our thinking and how it turns out in the real world. Where errors were made, how can they be corrected and what caused them? How can our thinking change to accommodate being wrong?

Teaching

Earlier, we discussed that wisdom, whatever it may be, can't be locked up in your mind - it needs airing - it needs to be examined and found fit for purpose. It needs to be put to use to help with a common good. Hoarding your wisdom is no wisdom at all.

> Teaching others is the ultimate crystallization of learned knowledge and wisdom. It forces us to fully understand a topic in order that we may impart that knowledge and understanding to others. We need to have answers and explanations ready and at hand when difficult questions come up.

We need to deeply understand what we are teaching, but again, we cannot lock ourselves into a position. We need to keep a flexible mind that is able to incorporate new ideas and ways of doing things.

In the case of The Buddha, once the man came to understand the nature of human suffering and how it might be alleviated, (his 'enlightenment') he sat for some days wondering how, or even *if*, he might impart this knowledge to others. It seems he was very reluctant to start talking about his realization for he believed no one would listen to him. He was 35 years of age.

In one story, Brahma, King of the Gods, appears and persuades him to spread his knowledge by saying that some people only have a little dirt in their eyes and might be awakened if only they could hear his story. So, he makes his way to Sarnath, India, where he meets up with five companions that he associated with earlier in his life. There, in a deer park, he is said to have given his first sermon, which was called the *Dhammacakkappavattana Sutta* or "Setting of the Wheel of Teaching in Motion."

For the next 45 years, The Buddha was a teacher and focused on two things - the nature of human suffering and its relief.

Key Points Summary

Wisdom rarely strikes, like a lightening bolt, from the sky. Rather it is the intentional application of various mental disciplines

Hear and Learn	• Quiet the mind, listen to and deeply understand your teachers
Clarification and Interpretation	• Nothing exists alone • We must put what we've learned into context against what we observe and experience in the real world
Creation and Living	• Build a life that incorporates those elements which give rise to wisdom
Application	• Put what we have learned into practice
Teaching	• Wisdom, untested and not applied to a common good, is no wisdom at all • Like The Buddha, spread your knowledge to the world at large.

5. Ultimate Limit Events
Life Experience

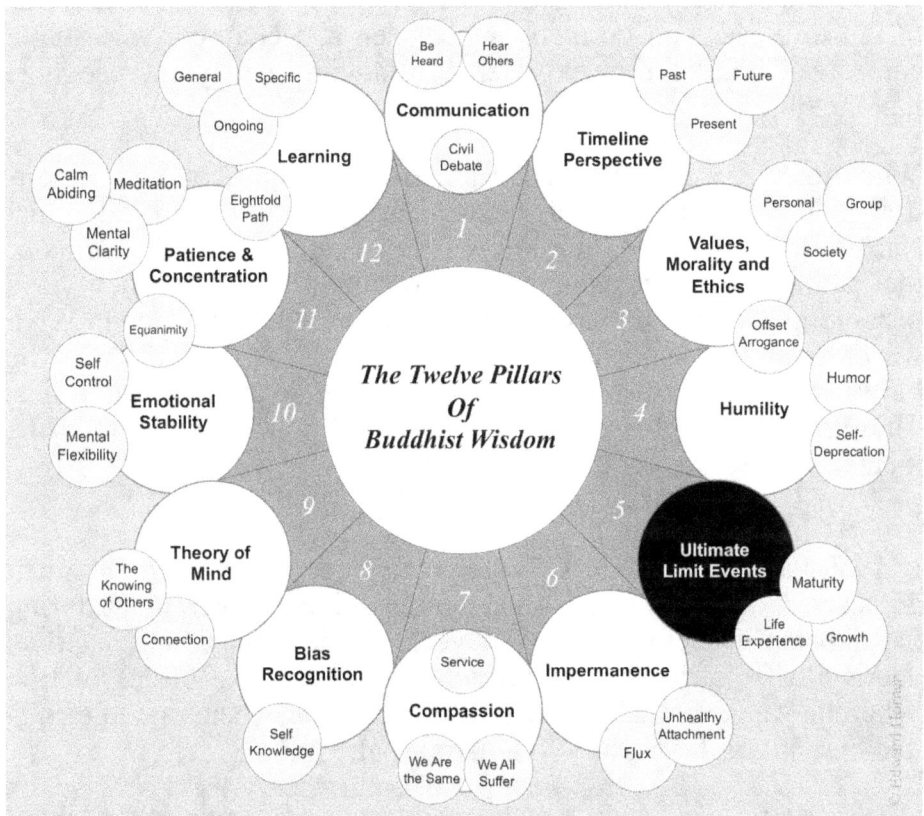

SITUATIONS THAT PUSH US, as individuals or groups, to the breaking point, stress our coping skills, overwork our mental and physical abilities or test our spiritual resolve are known collectively as Ultimate Limit Events or Ultimate Limit Experiences (ULEs). These events are significant because they show us our performance envelope around any given stressful experience. We learn how far we can go and still get back. We get wrenched away from what we perceive as 'normal' and are placed in a situation that we believe we are not able to withstand.

The late French philosopher, Michel Foucault, would call this, "The point of life which lies as close as possible to the impossibility of living, which lies at the limit or the extreme." We learn that adversity, in and of itself, is not going to kill us—*necessarily*—or cause us to fall to pieces and go mad. Once seen and endured, we usually come away better for the experience, although we may not recognize it at the time.

Where the ULE is met with awareness, skill and courage there is tremendous opportunity for personal growth. When an individual can 'walk the edge' of their known reality and explore the limits of their abilities, new facets of their personality may emerge, new ways of looking at things and assessing situations will be revealed. What we originally thought of as our 'upper limit' of potential may be blown completely away to reveal new and exciting possibilities. These are the benefits of a ULE *if* the individual can summon the mental fortitude and courage to see that.

In 1959 Palden Gyatso (1933-2018), a Tibetan Buddhist monk, then 26 years of age, was imprisoned by the Chinese government during the Tibetan Rebellion. For 33 years Gyatso was held captive, deprived of his liberty and provided with only the basics of life. When he was eventually released, in 1992, the Tibetan people spirited him out of the country to Dharmashala, India.

Since that time, Gyatso has been interviewed and written about extensively. In his book, *Fire Under the Snow*, (1997 Harvill Press) he recounts his 33 years in prison. One of the main takeaways from this book is that Gyatso was able to hold compassion for his tormenters year after year. He knew their actions were a result of their ignorance and they were products of the system that created them and he had compassion for them. This isn't to imply that he never hated them for the suffering they inflicted on his mind and body, but he was always able to raise compassion after the fact. I'm not suggesting that Gyatso wasn't changed during his 33 years of imprisonment, but he is an example of someone who has been through a ULE of unusual severity, and come out with his beliefs and values still in tact. He continued, until his death, to be a practicing Buddhist Monk and had become an outspoken champion of human rights in Tibet and around the world.

Now, to be clear, not everyone is going to come away a stronger, smarter, wiser person. Some people may, indeed, fall to pieces. For some people, the ULE may cause them to 'break' from their reality and fall into a depression, malaise or long-lasting funk that may stick with them for a lifetime, affecting everything they think, say or do. Without help, these people may suffer developmental challenges that could hold them back from better jobs, new relationships, challenging and rewarding careers, etc. They may, unwisely, turn to drug and/or alcohol abuse to help ease the pain. Some may even contemplate suicide. This *POST-TRAUMATIC STRESS* (PTS) may stay with them for a lifetime if not professionally addressed.

Examples of Ultimate Limit Events

- Near death experience
- Imprisonment
- War
- Job loss
- Death of loved ones
- Loss of (religious) faith
- Physical abuse
- Financial ruin
- Loss of limb
- False accusations
- Sexual abuse
- Mental abuse
- Divorce
- Betrayal
- Loss of health
- Public shame
- Chronic pain
- Major failure
- Abandonment
- Crushing poverty

We all know someone who has suffered through one of more of these Ultimate Limit Experiences and noted how they came out the other end. Some will have endured the trial and come through with a new sense of what they are capable of, having seen new upper limits and discovered new aspects to their personality. Others, may not emerge so lucky and spend the rest of their life rocking back and forth on a park bench wondering what the hell happened to them. You never know how it's going to end, but having an open mind, a resilient mind, a mind willing to accept new ideas and new situations, understanding the nature of impermanence, seems to be a key element of emerging with minimal damage. *

> Adversity, in and of itself, is not going to kill us – necessarily – or cause us to fall to pieces and go mad. Once seen and endured, we usually come away better for the experience, although we may not recognize it at the time.

Wisdom, particularly as it applies to Buddhism, starts with the understanding and acceptance of some basic Buddhist ideology such as; The Four Noble Truths, the nature of impermanence, dependent origination, the nature of ego, endless desire and such. It's not even about accepting and understanding them but the process of taking them from the intellectual, book-learned lessons to the personally felt and directly experienced manifestation of these ideas in ones life. Largely this is done through the development and cultivation of the mind and we discuss this further in Chapter 11.7 the section on meditation.

But this is where the first cautionary note comes in; We cannot blindly "believe" what we are told, no matter *who* told us. Even The Buddha, made it clear to his followers that blind faith is a dangerous game. We must educate ourselves, make observations, examine history, analyze our own biases and cultural mores before we agree with conclusions being presented to us. We must not simply 'believe' for the sake of believing.

As we will discuss in Chapter 11, simply reading about the Four Noble Truths is not wisdom. Memorizing the Eightfold path is not

---

* Juan Pascual-Leone - Mental Attention, Consciousness, and the Progressive Emergence of Wisdom - Journal of Adult Development, Vol. 7, No. 4, 2000. "Every experience of enduring in the context of hard effort and fear of failure, functionally approaches a limit situation; this is so for as long as the person does not succumb or give up. For this reason life's hardships that are endured with existential awareness lead to remarkable grown in the self. But ultimate limit situations that cannot be undone and are nonetheless faced with consciousness and resolve - situations like, death, illness, aging, irremediable oppression or loss, extreme poverty, rightful resistance or rebellion, guilt, absolute failure, danger, uncontrollable fear, etc. lead to the natural emergence of a transcendental self, if they do not destroy the person first.

wisdom. The wisdom comes in learning them, understanding them, experiencing them, interpreting them and going on to apply their lessons and observations to our every day lives.

> Buddhist wisdom then, is not simply hearing and learning. It is about seeing and experiencing, in your daily life, the truth of the learning. No one is asking you to 'believe' anything.

Perhaps this is why the language of 'seeing' is so often used in Buddhism when speaking of the attainment of or searching for wisdom. We speak of 'seeing' the truth of suffering or 'seeing' the truth of impermanence or 'observing' our mind as we meditate, etc.

We Are What Our Mind Believes

We are almost always more interested in what we already know, than in examining the world. It is a rare individual who is otherwise. Examining the world is difficult. It means we may have to give it some thought. We may have to turn off the TV and sit, in contemplation, and worry over an idea. We may have to examine two polar concepts and work towards a middle ground. We might have to change our view, or almost as bad, come to the realization that someone else may have a valid view. Worse still, we may even have to learn to *like* the middle ground and *talk* about the middle ground and *walk* in the middle ground and *think* in the middle ground.

Walking that middle ground seems to be an almost impossible task for the vast majority of people, yet that middle path is where Buddhist wisdom is nurtured. Notwithstanding that things are rarely black and white, people seem, almost without exception, to gravitate to one extreme or another on almost any topic. After-all, being in the grey zone, one runs the risk that, without proper explanation, people won't understand you. Speaking from the middle ground, you run the risk of sounding 'weak' or 'uncertain.' You might be accused of being a 'fence-sitter' or 'non-committal.' For sure, one benefit of holding a polarized view is that people know, *exactly* where you stand, even if you're absolutely, completely dead wrong.

When past US president George W. Bush declared, on September 21, 2001, only 10 days after the attack on the World Trade Centre, that;

"... every nation in every region now has a decision to make. Either you are with us or you are with the terrorists ... either you're with us and love freedom and with nations which embrace freedom or you are with the enemy. There's no in-between ... I will continue to make that clear."

Well, we knew where he stood on the issue, but it was, and is still is, a simplified, either/or view of the world. It's dangerous to deal in absolutes. He failed to grasp (or at least failed to demonstrate) that he understood it was more complicated than, " ... with us or against us." It was entirely possible to be with the Americans, but not support their newly minted, "War on terror," and swallow whole the Bush Doctrine. *

It would be next to impossible to find anyone in the "free" world that endorses terrorism, but that's a long way from joining the Americans, as willing combatants, in a war based on dubious intelligence reports and a couple of grainy photos in a land far away, against an 'enemy' who didn't wear a uniform and didn't represent a nation state.

Was there danger? There sure was and that's since been well demonstrated. However, at the time, the source of the danger, its reasons, components and vectors were not fully understood. Yes, action was needed, but what was lacking at the time of 9/11 was *nuanced* thinking, *nuanced* speech and *nuanced* actions. Bush was in shock – America was in shock. The nations pride and an evolving and an-as-yet-not fully understood mission of 'national security' required that a stick be taken to the hornets nest, but it was an all-or-nothing proposition, which rarely works in a world so full of varying stakeholders, different opinions, religions, cultures and political ideals. The one-size-fits-all approach that was being offered by Bush meant that a lot of important allies for his *"Coalition of The Willing"* were

---

* The phrase seems to make it's first appearance in 2001, when Charles Krauthammer used the term in describing the Bush administration's foreign policy, esp. The unilateral withdrawal from the Kyoto Accord and the ABM treaty. Perhaps more relevant and more important, it came to refer to the new view from Washington that America had the right to protect itself from any foreign power that harboured terrorists and that 'right' included, among other things, pre-emptive military strikes.

left on the sidelines, unable to go along with his approach when it came to Iraq.** This is but one lesson from history.

This isn't meant to be a rattling of GW's cage, but it is a reminder that things are not always as they seem. It's a reminder that knee-jerk reactions are rarely 'wise' and can too easily set one down on the wrong side of history. Wisdom is aided by patience, a calm mind and concentration – three attributes that seemed lacking at that time.

We return to Thomas Merton. In the same letter quoted earlier;

What was on TV? I have watched TV twice in my life. I am frankly not terribly interested in TV anyway. Certainly I do not pretend that by simply refusing to keep up with the latest news I am therefore unaffected by what goes on, or free of it all. Certainly events happen and they affect me as they do other people. It is important for me to know about them too; but I refrain from trying to know them in their fresh conditions 'news.' When they reach me they have become slightly stale. I eat the same tragedies as others, but in the form of tasteless crusts. The news reaches me in the long run through books and magazines, and no longer as a stimulant. Living without news is like living without cigarettes (another peculiarity of the monastic life). The need for this habitual indulgence quickly disappears. So, when you hear news with the 'need' to hear it, it treats you differently. And you treat it differently too.

Remember, that letter was written in 1968, way before Twitter, Facebook, Snapchat and other high velocity, high frequency social media variants. Even then, Merton was concerned about his impulse to respond to every newspaper or TV article - it has only gotten worse for a lot of us today.

** The countries included, to varying degrees of participation, in the 'Coalition of The willing' included; Afghanistan, Albania, Australia, Azerbaijan, Bulgaria, Columbia, the Czech Republic, Denmark, El Salvador, Eritrea, Estonia, Ethiopia, Georgia, Hungary, Italy, Japan, South Korea, Latvia, Lithuania, Macedonia, the Netherlands, Nicaragua, the Philippines, Poland, Romania, Slovakia, Spain, Turkey, United Kingdom and Uzbekistan.

"A fool is excited by every word."

~ Heraclitus of Ephesus (535–475 BCE)

Where, once, we may have read newspapers or listened to the radio as a matter of civic duty, as if it were homework, today we are ready and willing to receive an update on everything from sister Mary's check-in at the iHop, to the shaking of the *Pax Americana* due to some frantic tweet from Trump.

Merton was not far off the mark when he suggested that we approach the news from a distance, in a manner where we can receive the updates, but not feel any sense of urgency around them.

> Knee-jerk reactions are rarely 'wise' and can easily set one down on the wrong side of history. Wisdom is aided by patience, a calm mind and concentration.

Do Not Believe Everything You Are Told

Wisdom, to a large extent, is learning to see the world, not as we are told it is, but to see it as it *actually* behaves. We need to think about the world, make observations and compare those with our personal, first hand experiences. Without trying to sound too much like Garry Kasparov, the point of 'propaganda' these days seems not only to misinform, confuse, create uncertainty or push an agenda, but also to tax, pressure and exhaust our critical thinking, to annihilate reality and make it as difficult as possible for us to see the truth. The 'dissolution' of reality makes it much easier for us to be lead-by-the-nose by the first charismatic leader who comes along.

5.1 Fake News and Post-Truth

Oxford Dictionaries define "post-truth" as "relating to or denoting circumstances in which objective facts are less influential in shaping public opinion than appeals to emotion and personal belief."

On February 10, 2020, president Donald Trump stood before a large crowd of his supporters in New Hampshire and, on the topic of the novel coronavirus (COVID-19) said the following, "And by the way, the virus, they're working hard. Looks like by April, in theory when it gets a little warmer, it miraculously goes away." His supporters cheered wildly. He offered not a shred of scientific proof to back up his statement. He simply said something his supporters wanted to hear – *a miracle is on the way* – post-truth at it's finest.

Exactly one month after that statement, 26 Americans were dead from COVID-19. One month after that, 16,690 were dead. By July 4th, 145 days after Trump's initial post-truth, miracle proclamation, 130,000 American citizens had been wasted. That's an average of 896 American deaths each and every day since Feb 10, 2020. Contrary to the White House spin, the virus was not under control then and it's not under control as this book goes to print. The 'miracle' never arrived.

Look Beyond The Headline
We've become terrible consumers of news. We believe almost anything, if it's a headline. Take the time to read the story. Does the story make any sense, given your observations of the world and your direct, personal experience?

Search Other News Outlets To See If The Facts Align
When one news outlet puts out a story, it always wise to check into what other outlets are reporting on that same topic. Are the facts largely agreed upon? Are the dates right? Are the people involved the same in both stories, etc.

Question The News Source
It's a rare news outlet that isn't biased. When CNN reports on something Trump did, it will assuredly provide a Democratic/Liberal viewpoint. The same story from FOX will represent a Republican/Conservative view. Simply reporting on something with a biased viewpoint is not, necessarily, fake news. Just check their angle.

Check The Times, Dates
Fake news stories are too often poorly researched and documented. They get tripped up with dates and times quite frequently. In short, they are often sloppy.

Look For The Author On A Search Engine To Help Determine His or Her Credibility
You can find out a lot about news writers on the internet. Has this author been a solid reporter, respected and accurate? Perhaps they've been accused of sketchy, journalistic practices by publishing false stories in the past. Maybe they've plagiarized the work of others in the past or been found guilty of academic misconduct or playing fast and loose with the facts. Has the author written on the topic before?

What Is The Credibility Of The News Outlet That Published The Story?
Can we believe Agent K (MIB) when he 'checks the hot sheets' and asserts that "tabloids are the best investigative reporting on the planet?" *

Check The Links And Other Sources Used In The Story
A lot of links in 'fake news' stories are either dead or send you to conspiracy theory websites that support whatever the author is writing about. Does the story contain adequate footnotes to back up or explain assertions?

Question Photos and Quotes
Just because we see a photo of the Pope lifting weights, doesn't mean the Pope actually lifts weights. *Does the photo make sense?*

When a quote is linked to a photo, do the dates match up? Would the person in the photo actually be saying what they're reported to be saying?

Are we looking at another Third Vatican Council story? **

Be Aware Of Your Own Confirmation Bias -
(see Bias in Decision Making, Chapter 8)
When we believe something, we tend to see truth in anything that supports that view.

Putting One's Head in the Sand
The take-away here isn't about the reality of COVID-19 or the fact that Trump seems not to understand the severity of the situation his country faces, rather it's about how easy it is for anyone to stand up, cross their arms over their chest and just ignore facts and well thought out conclusions of others. Putting one's head in the sand and pretending problems don't exist, do not make the problems go away - the problems only get worse. Ignoring the pandemic and the chaos wrought by the novel coronavirus is not wise as Donald Trump is finding out - to the detriment of both his country and his re-election bid.

False Attribution
Don't fall into the trap that locks us into falsely attributing intention to others. When people don't agree with us we immediately jump to believing they don't have enough information. So, we trot out the facts and figures so they now have the required data. If they still don't agree with us, we then jump to questions about their intellect,

---

* Agent K (born Kevin Brown, also known as Kay, or simply K) is a fictional character in the Men in Black film franchise. Kay is portrayed by Tommy Lee Jones. MIB is a fictional government agency which protects 'regular' humans on Earth from the truth that extraterrestrials live among us.

** In December 2003 a story was making the rounds on the internet that Pope Francis declared "all religions to be true," based on the Third Vatican Council (which was apparently set up to finish the work of the Second Vatican Council). Trouble was, there was no Vatican III and Pope Francis said nothing of the sort. It was a satirical piece, published on the Diversity Chronicle (a WordPress blog). On the landing page of the Diversity Chronicle, it clearly states that most material on the site is satirical in nature and is written, largely, for the amusement of the blogger. It made the rounds for months.

"They're just not smart enough." But what if they've demonstrated their intellect and we see that maybe they actually are at least as smart as us? This can leave only one conclusion - they have a hidden agenda, some nefarious intention that they are not disclosing.

Some of that or all of that may be true, but there are other possibilities;

- They might not be able to agree (party politics, religious affiliation, cultural norms)
- They may only want to agree on their own terms
- They might not *want* to agree (vested interests, too much/rapid change, nationalism)
- Too expensive to agree (need to spend money to fix problem), etc.
- Their need to belong to a particular tribe might be greater than their need to express disagreement with something that the tribe is doing
- Sometimes it's as simple as, "It was good enough for my father and his father, so it's good enough for me."

What appeals to *us*, personally, in a discussion, may not appeal to others. Some people are oriented towards facts and figures, others are not. Trying to convince someone with numbers who is not numbers oriented is a losing cause. Knowing what motivates them, (family, emotions, loyalty, patriotism, money, status, etc.) and then finding some common ground which you both share may prove far more fruitful. We will look at this more closely in Chapter 9 - Theory of Mind.

We have become afraid of learning beyond what we already think we know. We seem so unable to process information and new ideas that it puts us into a state of paralysis, unable to move ahead as we cling to old ideas and old ways - even when they are dangerous and short-sighted.

The rigour and energy required for analytical thinking is often hard to muster. We have so many other things to think about; day-care, taxes, ageing parents, private vs. public schools, medical expenses, retirement planning, automobile repairs, health care plans, vacation plans, relationships, sports for the kids, etc. Being able to sit down and think, *vigorously*, through a major set of premises and synthesizing a meaningful solution or understanding is, at the very least, daunting.

Drop by drop is the water pot filled. Likewise, the wise man, gathering it little by little, fills himself with good.

~ Buddha, Dhammapada.

We are pre-programmed to think in certain ways, along specific lines and are heavily influenced by our parents, teachers, peers and media, even before we are aware of it. We are influenced, even by the language we speak and place in the world.

Betty Birner, professor of linguistics and cognitive science at Northern Illinois University, makes the point that our language/culture effects how we see the world and thus how we interpret and respond to the world. To cite one of her examples, the language spoken by the Guugu Yimithirr people of Far North Queensland, does not include 'left' or 'right,' Their version of our left/right is more east/west or north/south depending on our orientation. This requires that one have a remarkable spacial sense, since every time you wanted to indicate left/right you'd have to orient yourself and the person receiving the message to 'north.' Having such an orientation might mean that we see and respond to the world differently – the Guugu Yimithirr people, unlike us, might not think of themselves as being at the centre of the universe.

We return, once again, to not blithely believing what we are told about something - no matter who is telling us. It's about examining, pondering, extrapolating and making reasonable conclusions, based, not merely on our mental pre-conceptions, but combined with our observations and direct, physical experience. When our conclusions match with our observations of the world, then we are in a good spot to make wise decisions, make wise statements and perform wise acts.

Thoughts on Certainty

Rest assured, sometimes you're going to be wrong. When you're wrong, it hurts. The difficult thing about being wrong, is that it feels *exactly* the same as being right. You feel, clever, righteous, vindicated, honourable, exonerated and smug, just like if you were right. "The moon *is* made of cheese," feels exactly the same as, "the moon is *not* made of cheese," *at least until you learn the truth.*

Our certainty of ideas and actions is created and reinforced by the reality distortion field * that we generate all around us, every day, all day long. Certainty is a trap.

> We spend an inordinate amount of time avoiding even *thinking* about being wrong. It's not enough we are *actually* wrong, but we then get out the duct tape and start taping over the wrongness so that we won't trip over a corner while walking around in the dark!

We know about being wrong. We see other people being wrong all day long. We 'get it,' at least in the abstract. We know humanity can be wrong about so many things. We suppose we *could* be wrong about something, but it just doesn't translate into our everyday thinking – and that's dangerous.

When we're right, it feels so much better than being wrong. Being wrong implies improper thinking, improper logic, improper conclusion-drawing. It suggests lazy thinking or poor homework skills. It invites ridicule, suspicion and shame.

---

* A term widely attributed to Bud Tribble at Apple Inc. in describing Steve Job's charismatic personality and its role in getting projects pushed through, although some claim it also showed up in the Menagerie episode of Star Trek.

In an earlier chapbook, *Certainty in Buddhism*, I take my reader back to when I was in grade nine. It was my first year in high school and one of my first math tests. I got such a bad mark. Algebra simply eluded me. I just didn't understand. It was so embarrassing. The teacher actually pointed out how wrong I was by calling me out—by name—putting the question(s) up on the chalkboard, then making me try to figure it out again - in front of the class - while standing, chalk in hand - at the blackboard. I stood there looking stupid, powerless to do anything. I might as well have had my pants around my ankles — that's how exposed I felt. Fellow students in the front row were whispering to me what to put up, but it didn't help. I still didn't have the answer - how the hell could I? I only just got the paper back and didn't know my errors until two minutes earlier.

The lesson learned that day was *not* how to solve math problems, but that being wrong is going to result in embarrassment and false accusations of; laziness, sloth, low intellect, poor reading skills and even some allusions about one's parentage. No sir, being right was *far* better than being wrong. There was no room for error. Alternatively, avoiding having to give an answer was almost as good. That's where I learned the benefits of sitting in the back row.

Avoidance of having others know you are wrong drives a lot of behaviours. Avoidance of shame and blame also drive a lot of our behaviours, as we will learn in Chapter 8; *Bias in Decision Making - The Eight Worldly Concerns.*

In our Western culture, there is scarcely any benefit to being wrong. It's not rewarded and rarely tolerated. You get fired for it. You get criticized for it. You get ostracized for it. You don't get the promotion and you don't get the pay rise.

When we are right, we get accolades, the big grant, the news story, the Pulitzer or Nobel Prize or any number of awards for our good work. No one remembers the number of experiments that ended in inconclusive results before finally hitting upon the right formula, process or methodology for the ultimate success. No one remembers why WD40 has that particular name or why CR49 is the name for the plastic lenses found in most eyewear. *

Failure and uncertainty are hidden away and not unpacked until success is achieved – if ever.

When the late Steve Jobs, then head of Apple Inc., introduced the original iPhone, it was an immediate success. What we didn't hear about, at the time, was that the iPhone demonstration he provided at the key note address in January of 2007, was a hair's width from failure. The infrastructure that had to be set up to demonstrate the simple conference call between himself, Jony Ive and Phil Schiller made the technical sophistication of the Houston Space Command Centre pale in comparison.

Dozens of telephony technicians from AT&T descended on the Moscone Centre to plug, prod, cajole, jerry-rig, cut, copy and paste the in-house switching components to make that call work. They brought in dedicated switching equipment ,just for that day, for the exclusive use of the iPhone. Even with all that support structure in place, it still did not function 100% of the time during rehearsals and everyone was more than a little worried the demo would not work as planned. According to Jobs, as we read in his biography, it almost didn't work and he was very nervous as he made the calls, but no one talked about that at the time.

The eyes of the world were focused on Steve Jobs – live! There was no ten-second delay. There would be no retake - no 'cut-aways.' The audience in the auditorium was not a bunch of actors, paid to cheer on demand. The crowd consisted of employees, fans, share holders, critics, reporters, competitors and technology gurus. There could be no "wardrobe malfunctions," *a la*, Janet Jackson. If he made the

---

* Norm Larsen, founder of the Rocket Chemical Co. Was working on a lubricant and water displacement agent and failed 39 times. Water Displacement formula 40 was his success. Similarly in the 1940s Columbia-Southern Chemical Corp. refined a resin that would be used to coat the inside of the fuel tanks on B17 aircraft. It was the 39th formula that would do the trick, Hence CR39 or Columbia Resin formula 39. After a bit of refinement, it was found to be almost ideal for lenses in eyeglasses.

calls and everything went smoothly then all would be fine. However, if it didn't go well, Apple stood to lose their first-to-market advantage, their status as technology leader and smartphone innovator. They would be seen as a failure and most assuredly, heads would roll.

Of course, it did go well and the rest, as they say, is history. Still, it wasn't until some years later that we learned of the near miss. It was hidden away until enough time had passed that it could be talked about without threat.

> For the most part, being wrong isn't a pretty option in our society and that's why we place so much emphasis on being right or building and protecting the *appearance* of being right. The four things we all want to avoid or at the very least minimize are; pain, shame, blame and loss.

Our Conclusions are Not Immutable

We cannot hold onto our ideas as being immutable. Things change all the time and occasional re-visiting and examination of our conclusions is wise. When we stop asking questions and stop examining our beliefs and stop critically examining our mental constructs, we slip slowly, but relentlessly, towards 'unwise.'

Reflect on the previously discussed Florida hurricane of 1928 - Chapter 2. By the 1930s, Florida legislators did a complete re-think of the flood plans for Lake Okeechobee. More canals, flood control gates and channels were built to better manage the waters of the lake. The dam was reinforced, and enlarged. They didn't just stick to the idea of building a containment dyke, but rather, expanded the thinking to include the alternatives of managing water. They even began limiting settlement on the flood-prone land and putting into place evacuation procedures just in case the worst case scenario played out again.

Fast forward 89 years to early September 2017, Hurricane Irma made landfall in Florida and closely reproduced the conditions of that 1928 storm. This time, however, the more expansive water management plan meant that the storm didn't cause the lake to breach the dams, although Florida did, wisely, issue and mandatory evacuation of the town of Belle Glen, as a precaution.

Collectively, the authorities re-visited their plans and learned more about flood control and water patterns. They were better able to assess the risk factors during these types of storms and ultimately there was no loss of life during hurricane Irma that could reasonably be attributed to Lake Okeechobee, although tragically, state-wide some 75 lives were lost, primarily due coastal flooding, but remember that over 2,000 lives were lost in 1928.

5.2 Our View of the World

When we are young, say, in our 20s, we have a very clear idea of what the world is, how it operates, what is should look like and how people should behave. We may even know what we need to do in order to 'fix' it. These ideas may have come largely from our parents and teachers at school or we may have synthesized them for ourselves. At any rate, we have a very lucid picture of the world and how it operates ... it's almost certainly, wrong, but we have it and it's ours.

By the time we get to our forties, we usually develop a whole new view of the world, equally clear, equally concise. Almost certainly vastly different from the way we thought about the world only twenty years earlier. We have gained experienced, listened to more people, seen other places, read books and viewed films. All of a sudden, the world is very different.

The wisdom comes in recognizing that both the world and ourselves change and we therefore need to evolve new ideas and ways of thinking about that changing world.

Read Widely - Ignorance is Not a Virtue
We discuss this a little further on in the book, Chapter 12 - Learning, but a quick note here is in order. To some degree, we've already looked at this under the heading Do Not Believe Everything You Are Told, but beyond that, we need to read divergent opinions on issues

that have a hold over humanity and it's suffering. Reading and educating oneself about climate change, geopolitical conflict, international law, urban renewal, human rights law, public transportation, etc. provides us with greater understanding of how the world works. That understanding can better help us understand how people suffer and how we can help relieve that suffering. I cannot think of a single practical application where lack of knowledge is an asset.

5.3 Wisdom in Ageing

" ... it is our duty, my young friends, to resist old age; to compensate for its defects by a watchful care; to fight against it as we would fight against disease; to adopt a regimen of health; to practise moderate exercise; and to take just enough of food and drink to restore our strength and not overburden it. Nor, indeed, are we to give our attention solely to the body; much greater care is due to the mind and soul; for they, too, like lamps, grow dim with time, unless we keep them supplied with oil."*

It's well documented that as we age, cognitive functions are usually impaired or diminished. Problem solving skills are less sharp, reasoning not always up to snuff and memory tends to fade, but there is some good news.

The late Dr. Freda Blanchard-Fields and her team at the Georgia Institute of Technology did many studies and experiments that compared how younger and older people responded to situations of stress in a social environment. Her conclusions, in short, were that older people (60s to 80s) were able to use their life experience, emotional regulation and strategic thinking (or situational awareness) to successfully solve problems, better than young adults between the ages of 18 and 27. **

---

* Cicero. De senectute, De amicitia, De divinatione - an essay on Ageing - 44CE. English translation by William Armistead Falconer. London, W. Heinemann; Harvard University Press, 1964.

** Everyday Problem Solving and Emotion; An Adult Developmental Perspective, 2007 Blanchard-Fields

"... older adults (a) tailor their strategies to the contextual features of the problem and (b) effectively use a combination of instrumental and emotion-regulation strategies. I identify factors of problem-solving contexts that affect what types of problem-solving strategies will be effective." *

What this seems to demonstrate is a kind of balancing act in ageing adults with the gradually declining cognitive skills on the one hand and the wisdom gained through life experience, emotional intelligence and situational awareness on the other. Rejoice, for there is some truth to the adage that wisdom comes with age.

" ... therefore, who allege that old age is devoid of useful activity adduce nothing to the purpose, and are like those who would say that the pilot does nothing in the sailing of the ship, because, while others are climbing the masts, or running about the gangways, or working at the pumps, he sits quietly in the stern and simply holds the tiller. He may not be doing what younger members of the crew are doing, but what he does is better and much more important. It is not by muscle, speed, or physical dexterity that great things are achieved, but by reflection, force of character, and judgement; in these qualities old age is usually not only not poorer, but is even richer." **

Even though there is some hope that wisdom arises as we age, and Dr. Freda Blanchard-Fields' study and Cicero, notwithstanding, it's not all that rosy. In general terms, there is little evidence that ageing, in and of itself, will give rise to any greater wisdom. In fact, the opposite is generally true; as we age, there tends to be fewer and

---

* Ardelt M. Age, experience and the beginning of wisdom. In: Dannefer D. Phillipson, editors. The Sage Handbook of Social Gerontology. London: Sage; 2010.

** Cicero, as on previous page.

fewer occasions where slower cognitive functions give rise to greater levels of wisdom.

Meditation helps slow cognitive decline and improve concentration in ageing adults

One 2017 study by *Marco Sperduti*, et al.* looking into the benefits of meditation on cognitive function and ageing, concluded, among other things, the following;

- *Meditative practices, built on the training of attentional capacities, have proven effective in promoting neurocognitive plasticity.*

- *The practice of meditation could thus prove to be a promising tool in the prevention and remediation of cognitive decline linked to aging.*

Another study, by Brefczynski-Lewis et al,** discovered that the number of accumulated hours of meditation, in particular, samatha meditation, are directly related to one's ability to hold concentration and filter out distracting inputs. Simply, the more you meditate the greater your ability to concentrate. We will examine this further in Chapter 10.

In a 2014 study funded by Harvard University and the Department of Veterans Affairs Clinical Science Research and Development, lead by Drs. Francesca Fortenbaugh, Joe DeGutis, and Michael Esterman, it was concluded that;

- *A persons ability to sustain attention is greatest around age 43*

- *Activities such as spending more time outdoors, exercise, cognitive training and meditation are ways in which people at any age, can enhance their ability to concentrate.*

---

* Marco Sperduti, Dominique Makowski, Philippe Blondé, Pascale Piolino. Meditate to age well? The possible benefits of meditative practices on age-related cognitive decline. Geriatrics and Psychology Neuropsychiatry of Aging. 2017; 15 (2): 205-213. doi: 10.1684 / pnv.2017.0672

** Neural Correlates of Attentional Expertise in Long Term Meditation Practitioners. Brefczynski-Lewis, Lutz, Schaefer, Levinson and Davidson.

It seems that there is a general agreement that the ageing brain can be retrained to improve cognitive function - at least to some degree. This is good news indeed as the population of Canada and the US ages at a pace that is unprecedented.*

Wisdom In The Age Of The Internet

One aspect of wisdom, that of 'sharing' with the upcoming generation to help them along with their *travails* has, historically, been of considerable value. Mothers and fathers passed down choice pieces of of information, methodology or wisdom as their mothers and fathers did for them. Building present day wisdom on knowledge passed down from earlier generations has been a tried and true method of learning from past mistakes and successes. Not that the lessons were always taken to heart ... Not that the lessons were always wise. But in this age of instant historical research on the internet, vast quantities of (sometime dubious) information and videos on how to do everything from duplicating and distributing fence posts in SketchUp to breeding zebras in captivity, what is the value of wisdom from the elders?

There seems two obvious reasons why the younger generation *might* turn to the older generation for advice or some form of wisdom; It's natural and the current crop of 70-80 somethings have a unique life experience.

In the first case, given that humankind has been around for some 1.5 million years, it's natural for a younger person to turn to an older person for advice. Information about how to track animals, hunt them or grow food has, for millennium, been passed down from one generation to the next. One might even imagine that without transmission of such knowledge, the younger generation would perish or deplete. Their very survival may well have depended upon advice from elders. How does a farmer survive a drought? How does a gatherer know which mushrooms are poisonous and which are good to eat? Why is MS-DOS running under Windows? Why should I bother with C++? Why was Albert Einstein wrong about Lambda?

* An Ageing Population, Canada Year Book, online catalogue 11-402-X

Trial and error by each new generation seems a terrible waste of resources, time and energy. Better to get the goods from the older generation and not bother to re-invent the wheel. In this way, simple 'knowledge,' supports the drive to wisdom.

It's until only recently (say 400 years or so) that any alternative source of information was even available. Until Gutenberg came up with the movable print, printing press and was able to disseminate information more widely, only a few books hoarded by the church or state and the earlier generation were all that was available for reference. Even then, when print was first introduced, few people knew how to read. It took another hundred or so years before books were both widely available and widely read – the Library at Alexandria, notwithstanding. Prior to widely available printed reference material, the community elders were the repository of all knowledge that could help the community survive and in that way, they were almost immortal - their knowledge lived on long after they were gone.

In the second instance, our current crop of 70 to 80 somethings have lived a life that is, in the experience of those Canadians or Americans who represent the generation prior to the Baby Boomers, unique or nearly so. Surely there are lessons to be learned from someone who had lived through the economic crisis of the 1929 Great Depression or the tragic events of the Second World War. In these cases, the elders have a unique view, possess unique skills and information that younger people cannot - for few have lived through or experienced such ULEs.

One can only imagine what store of knowledge and what lessons will be learned from this generation, as it navigates the current pandemic.

Directing Energy
All our reading, researching, investigating, experimenting and philosophizing is raw material which can be used in various ways. We could, for example, take our scientific knowledge gained through mathematics, experimentation and research to built a destructive nuclear bomb or, using that same information, we could build machines and develop techniques in nuclear medicine to help detect

and cure illness and disease. Of course, the two, are not mutually exclusive.

When we direct our energy and mental faculties to the benefit of humanity, and not its destruction, we are practicing wisdom. When we seek to help others escape or lessen their suffering, we are acting in a wise manner.

To Conclude This Section

We return again and again to addressing the common good and relieving the suffering of ourselves and others. Life experience and what we learn from it can help us in that quest.

Ultimate Limit Events, if endured and survived with an open mind and compassion, have the ability to help us raise wisdom. As we age, we typically experience more ULEs, accumulate more life experiences and have a chance to reflect on our lives. As we mature, we have the ability (if not always the inclination) to see how our experiences have formed our thought processes and thus our opinions on everything from politics to choice of pie.

Better knowing ourselves, and understanding how we became what we are today, is another aspect that promotes wisdom. Knowing that our senses are imperfect and our language and culture shape how we see things, clears the way for wisdom to arise.

When we take the time to consider news stories and look beyond the headlines, we are blazing a trail upon which wisdom might walk. Taking time to deeply consider our thoughts and our relationship to the world, while sometimes painful, can allow wisdom to rise. Thinking less ego-centrically and more about our fellow humans and how we might ease their suffering, is wisdom.

Key Points Summary - Ultimate Limit Events

Ultimate Limit Events	• Circumstances beyond our control that push us to our limits, and sometimes beyond, can radically alter how we see ourselves and the world • Handled properly, these events can be, transformative catalysts for positive change in how we think
Do Not Believe Everything You are Told	• Examine everything for yourself and come to your own conclusions • Learn to suss out 'fake' news stories
Be Aware of Your 'Absolutes'	• The world is rarely black or white • Be aware of thinking that sets you down in one camp or another • The reality of the world is that it largely operates within the grey zone
False Attribution	• Be careful that you don't fall into attributing false motives to people around you • Examine the words and actions of others, bearing in mind that they have differing experiences from yours
Open Your Mind to Alternatives	• Seek other sources of information and dissenting opinions
Read Widely	• Educate yourself widely to avoid 'narrow band' thinking • Solutions often come from divergent disciplines
Be aware of Your 'Certainties'	• Re-evaluate your conclusions regularly • What you think you know, changes
Benefit of Meditation	• Many studies conclude that meditation, especially Vipassana, helps to slow decline in cognitive function and improves concentration, as we age
Wisdom and Ageing	• While it is true that there is rarely any cognitive improvement as we age, there is benefit in knowing that Emotional Stability, Life Experience and Situational Awareness help offset cognitive decline

6. The Illusion of Permanency

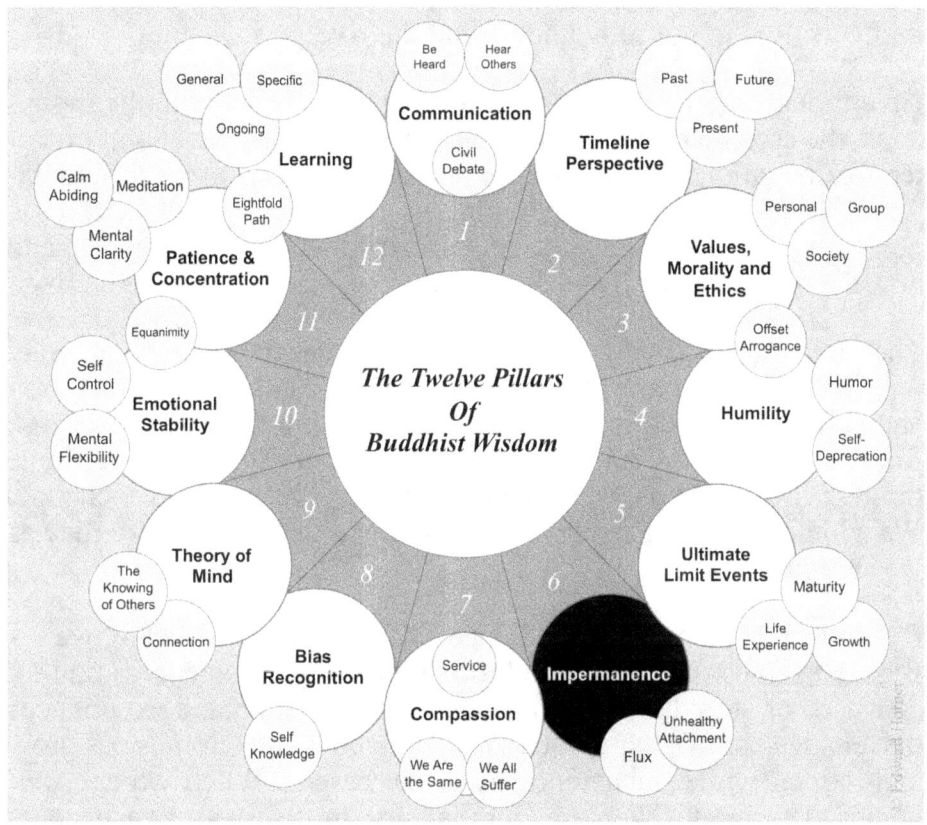

"No man ever steps in the same river twice, for it's not the same river and he's not the same man."

~Heraclitus of Ephesus (535–475 BCE)

HERACLITUS OBSERVES that even if the river looks the same, feels the same and appears to be in the same place, it's only an illusion. The river changes course constantly, the water ebbs and floods throughout the seasons. The water may run clear one day then murky the next. Fish may run and fish may die. The river is in constant flux. It is never the same from moment to moment. There is no permanence to the river. It may last for thousands of years, but it will run dry, or go underground or change course and go through someone else's backyard. It is not a permanent fixture. To think of 'the river' without thinking of the things which affect it, or those things which it affects, it is to not fully understand the river or its nature.

Give thought to the rains which fall, the melting snow in the mountains, the erosion of the land, the digging of canals, the taking of water for irrigation, the re-channeling for transportation, the undulations of the land and the damming of the waters for hydroelectric power, etc. Without knowing the place of the river in the world and how everything else effects the river, you can't really know the river.

The same must be said for the man. One who steps in the river today will be different tomorrow or next week or next year. Motivation and skills change daily. So it is with strength and resolve. These four forces that so dominate mankind are inconstant. As we move through life - even as we move through any given day - we change. We will not be the same person who stepped in the river yesterday as we are today.

Even our bodies constantly change. Molecule by molecule, we refresh ourselves. We consume food that is turned into energy and either used or stored. Our minds absorb information and experiences that change us. We work out at the health club and our muscles grow and harden while our endurance is increased. When we age, our bodies deteriorate, we lose our balance more easily, we become winded just walking up a hill and we may begin to forget things.

We are constant change and yet we seem to act like it isn't happening. We become very attached to our bodies and believe them to be permanent. The younger we are, the more we believe this, but as we age and near death, it becomes clear to us that the permanence of our bodies is pure fantasy - an illusion.

"Many have died; you also will die. The drum of death is being beaten. The world has fallen in love with a dream. Only sayings of the wise will remain."

— Kabir, The Bijak of Kabir

When we recognize this impermanence we quickly realize the power and influence we have over the little time remaining. Believing that you will last forever often causes us to put things 'on the back burner' to deal with at a later date. We think there is always time to do it tomorrow or next week. We will get around to writing that book when the NFL has played its final championship game of the season or I'll get to work on that sculpture I've been working on after just a couple more episodes of Outlanders on Netflix, but time is fleeting and what few years are allotted are too often wasted.

The Gods Dissolve

When the Greeks built temples to Zeus or Athena, they were utterly convinced in the permanence of these gods and goddesses. They believed, fervently, that their gods would be around for ever to help them in their daily lives. When the ancient Romans built the Jupiter Optimus Maximus on the Capitoline hill, they had no doubt that Jupiter was infinite and permanent. Yet where are these gods today? A mere 2500 years has passed and the gods have fallen out of favour and been left to the history books. The same happened with Minerva, Isis, Ra and Inana to name only a few.

The same will happen to the gods we call upon today. As hard as it will be for some people to swallow, It's very likely that 2,000 years from now, our descendants will only come across Vishnu, Krishna, Mahavira and maybe, (although never a god) even Buddha in dusty history books, having been replaced by gods or religions that will have greater relevance to the people of that future time.

That's the way it is. Religious practices always reflect the needs of the society, culture and times in which they were created. Of course not all gods are invented out of thin air. Some gods we know today are reincarnations of previously known gods. For example, the Titans precede the Olympians, Apsu and Tiamat precede Marduk and Enki. Many of the gods we know today have some ancient equivalent and are thus a recycled version of a previous deity.

"What we think is 'everlasting, permanent and timeless' is anything but."

~Heraclitus of Ephesus (535–475 BCE)

One pre-Socratic philosopher, Heraclitus of Ephesus (535–475 BCE), had an interesting idea about the nature of the universe. Like the early Greeks, he concluded the universe consisted of, and was controlled by, the interactions of earth, water, fire and air, further energized though the interaction of sets of opposites; wet/dry, hot/cold, up/down, high/low etc. Heraclitus seemed to know that everything around him, both seen and unseen, was in constant change. He even notes;

"The same thing is both living and dead and the waking and sleeping and the young and the old for those things transformed, are those and those transformed back again."

Clearly, Heraclitus recognized the constant change of the world and it's cyclical nature.

Central to Buddhism is the recognition of the impermanent nature of the world as well as it's cyclical nature. Both Heraclitus and Buddha managed to develop similar views of the world and, even though they were contemporaries, there is no evidence that they ever met or could have been influence by each other - it seems Buddha never traveled more than 100 kilometres from where he was born. While The Buddha sought to help mankind ultimately escape suffering, it's unclear what Heraclitus had in mind, for much of his thinking and conclusions are lost to history.

To see the world as permanent is folly, a misconception. It is ignorance of the first order. Failure to recognize the end of all things will bring unavoidable suffering, discontent, sadness, disillusion and depression. While we suffer over many other things, not understanding impermanence is a major impediment to our peace.

There is considerable wisdom in knowing that everything is passing, perhaps not on a relative scale, but on the absolute. In relative terms, the sun is all but certainly going to shine for the lifetime of anyone reading this book, but on an absolute scale, the sun will burn itself out eventually.

As painful as it may be, change and impermanence are the central theme of all our lives. Everything that ever was or ever will be, eventually comes to an end, falls to dust and is blown away in the winds of time.

Meditation on Impermanence

Sit quietly in an area where you will not be easily disturbed. Sit comfortably, with your back straight, shoulders relaxed. Eyes open or closed as you prefer. Bring your mind to the intake and exhalation of your breath - in, out. Think only of your breath and let go of past and present thoughts. Try to be in the moment.

Once you've settled down, bring your mind, once again, to your breath and it's impermanent nature. Each breath, may, on the face of it, seem the same as any other, but think more deeply on this. Notice that not every breath is the exact same length. Notice too that the air circulates differently for every inhalation. Sometimes you can feel the coolness of the air as it enters the nostrils, other times not. Sometimes you inhale with awareness of your diaphragm working and other times not. Each breath, on the surface is the same, but upon examination each is unique.

Think then upon each part of your body as you sit quietly. Be aware of your head; how it is positioned, chin up or slightly down. Can you feel a breeze in your hair. Is there stress or strain in your neck? Does it the muscle tension come and go? Bring awareness to you mouth, tongue and teeth. Notice that they are constantly changing from one moment to the next. Become aware of your shoulders; are they raised in stress and discomfort or have they fallen in comfort and ease? Their position will alter in every session and rarely remain the same. Everything about your body is changing and in a state of flux at all times - even as we sleep.

Bring your mind to the sounds of your environment. Can you hear bird song? Perhaps you hear traffic noise or an ambulance siren. The sounds are constantly changing; far away, near, moving towards or moving away. Some sounds are loud while others are less so. Some cause pain while others allow us to rest easy. Sound is constantly changing.

Are you looking at a forest scene? Or perhaps a cloud drifting through a blue sky. Everything you see is constantly changing. Things come into focus and vie for your attention, while others recede and are overlooked.

Bring attention to your mind. What is it doing right now? Is it calm and rested, or are you upset and on edge. Notice that these states come and go day after day. A 'bad' mood may be upon us one day but not the next. We may begin our meditation feeling ill at ease, but finish with composure and calmness. The opposite may be true. The mind is especially susceptible to change and impermanence. It can flip from a bright inclusive mood with thoughts of generosity and equanimity to a mind of darkness, distrust and fear within moments.

Everything that we think and feel, comes and goes - second to second, moment to moment and day to day. Our mind is in constant motion and we are rarely even aware of it, unless we sit down and think about the situation.

Now bring your mind to your house or workplace. Recognize that things change there constantly. People come and go at work, the lawn at home needs trimming, the flowers need planting and the dishes need washing. We sometimes feel like one day is just like the one before, but that's not the case. Every day is different.

Office towers are built, renovated, torn down. Our old house is sold to a developer and torn down to make room for a new house. Trees grow, die and are cut down - perhaps within our own lifetime.

The Earth we inhabit is constant change. Tectonic plates shifting and crashing into one another, causing devastating earthquakes, landslides and even tsunamis. The oceans rise and fall, rivers change course, glaciers melt and the atmosphere heats up. Nothing is for ever.

In the distant reaches of our galaxy, stars are forming while others are blinking out of existence as they collapse upon themselves. Everything changes and for us to think that our situation is immutable or unchanging, is delusion.

Many of us have this idea that impermanence is to to be routed, overcome, or in some way vanquished, but in the end it may be much better to embraced change, get to know it, live with it and appreciate its unending nature.

Key Points Summary - Impermanence

Everything Changes	• A great deal of human suffering happens because humanity rarely recognizes that everything is in flux • Change and impermanence is the central theme of all our lives
We are Not Who We Were	• As we go through life and gain experiences, we change, take on new roles and enter different circumstances • How we view the world changes
The World is Not What it Was	• The world around us is in constant change and how we respond to it also changes • What we take for granted today is most certainly going to change tomorrow
Meditate Upon Impermanence	• Everything about our body is change • Our mind changes constantly • Our environment is in constant flux • On a galactic scale, nothing is at rest and all is constant motion and change from stars to molecules. To believe otherwise is delusion

7. Compassion and its Role in Wisdom

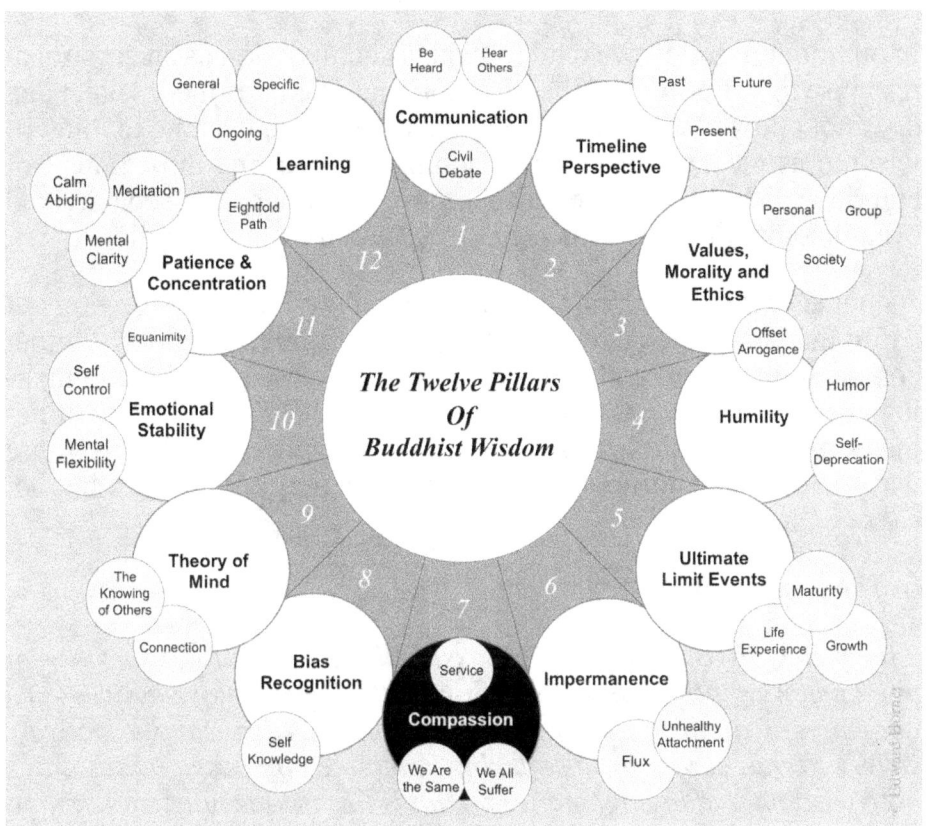

What is Compassion?

IN BUDDHIST TERMS, IT'S THE WILLINGNESS AND CAPACITY to hear and bear the pain and suffering of others while developing a state of mind wherein one desires to help and takes action to do so, in whatever capacity one can.

One of the central teachings of Buddhism is to aid in the relief of suffering, wherever and however it appears. When we develop compassion and give rise to the conditions that encourage compassion, when we understand and know from direct personal experience the suffering of others, and we are better able to help in the relief of suffering.

In our modern times, we tend to think of compassion as an emotional response to suffering and, being emotional, it clouds the intellect and does not allow clear thinking. On the other hand, we tend to think of wisdom as clear, disciplined reasoning, without the impediment of emotions. There is the belief that these two things are separate and even incompatible, but this is not the Buddhist understanding.

As noted earlier, wisdom and compassion are like the two wings of a bird that allow the creature to fly its true course. Wisdom, without compassion, is cold and analytical, perhaps blasé and given to making choices that do not fully account for the fact that all sentient beings suffer. On the other hand, compassion without wisdom is a sure way to emotional burnout since compassion may not address the root cause of suffering.

In *The Essence of the Heart Sutra*, the Dalai Lama writes;

"According to Buddhism, compassion is an aspiration, a state of mind, wanting others to be free from suffering. It's not passive -- it's not empathy alone -- but rather an empathetic altruism that actively strives to free others from suffering. Genuine compassion must have both wisdom and lovingkindness. That is to say, one must understand the nature of the suffering from which we wish to free others (this is wisdom), and one must experience deep intimacy and empathy with other sentient beings (this is lovingkindness)."

How to Raise Compassion for Others

The Practice of Tonglen
Tonglen is part of a larger meditation practice discussed in greater detail in Chapter 11, but for now, we can simply say that Tonglen is the meditative practice of raising BODHICITTA or compassion for ourselves and to connect with the suffering of others.

One sits quietly, and focuses on the breath. During inhalations, one imagines taking in the suffering and pain of someone else and freeing them from that discomfort. On the out breath, we imagine light and kindness going out to that person. It's a slow, thoughtful process that brings to our awareness the difficulties of others and raises compassion within us. This compassion or connection with others allows us to see into their lives and gives us greater understanding to help our wisdom arise.

When done as part of a daily practice, tonglen helps to reverse the age old condition of selfishness and we begin to feel compassion for others and even for ourselves. It allows us a chance to see the world differently, in a less self-centred way.

Tonglen can also be done separate from a daily meditation practice. Walking down the street, seeing a homeless person or someone suffering from a debilitating mental illness, we can take a moment and take in their pain and send them whatever we believe would help them with relief. We can do it for the ill or the dying. We can send relief to those we know and those we don't. From our desk, we can pause, close our eyes, concentrate on the breath and send positive thoughts out to those we know who are suffering.

Whether or not the person feels relief as a result of our efforts is not really the point. The importance of the practice is that *we* change. When undertaken with an open mind and good intent, tonglen will begin to change *us* and we become more compassionate towards our fellow humans. This upping of our compassion and a greater ability to see and understand the suffering of others, helps us with our wisdom. It helps us know that we are all part of this life, suffering almost daily, stuck here on Earth, with one another.

"The quality of mercy is not strained.
It droppeth as the gentle rain from heaven
Upon the place beneath. It is twice blest:
It blesseth him that gives and him that takes.
'Tis mightiest in the mightiest; it becomes
The thronèd monarch better than his crown.

His sceptre shows the force of temporal power,
The attribute to awe and majesty
Wherein doth sit the dread and fear of kings;
But mercy is above this sceptered sway.
It is enthronèd in the hearts of kings;
It is an attribute to God Himself;
And earthly power doth then show likest God's
When mercy seasons justice. Therefore, Jew,
Though justice be thy plea, consider this:
That in the course of justice none of us
Should see salvation. We do pray for mercy,
And that same prayer doth teach us all to render
The deeds of mercy. I have spoke thus much
To mitigate the justice of thy plea,
Which, if thou follow, this strict court of Venice
Must needs give sentence 'gainst the merchant there."

> — Portia, in William Shakespeare's
> The Merchant of Venice, Act 4, Scene 1

Get Unstuck

Occasionally we might not easily raise bodhicitta. On those occasions, where we are stuck, try thinking of your own pain. If you are feeling inadequate, breathe in that negative feeling then exhale confidence, ability and strength, or whatever eases the pain. Do this for a few moments, then do it for anyone who may feel this way. Soon, compassion will rise.

Expand Your Compassion

When we practice tonglen, we usually start with ourselves or a friend or member of the family. That's good, but with a bit of practice we can easily expand our compassion to co-workers, the postman, neighbours and anyone we can think of. Soon you'll be able to practice tonglen for the benefit of those who you do not even know, or have done you harm or have harmed others.

Tonglen can expand infinitely. As you continue your practice, it will come more easily and more naturally. You may come to see that things are not as set in stone as you may have imagined, and that, while we are individuals, we are also part of a collective and we share the same pain, often over the same things. Again, whether or not the person feels relief as a result of our tonglen practice, is not really the point. The importance of the practice is that *we* change.

"Poor naked wretches, whereso'er you are,
That bide the pelting of this pitiless storm,
How shall your houseless heads and unfed sides,
Your looped and windowed raggedness, defend you
From seasons such as these? Oh, I have ta'en
Too little care of this! Take physic, pomp.
Expose thyself to feel what wretches feel,
That thou mayst shake the superflux to them
And show the heavens more just."

– William Shakespeare , King Lear Act 3, Scene 4

A Story of Compassion

A story is told in the Jataka Tales of a land ruled by King Benares, in which a beautiful deer that is born with an unusual golden fur, silver antlers and eyes as bright as sparkling jewels. As this deer matured, there gathered around him a large herd and he became known as King Banyan Deer.

At the same time, in a distant part of Benares, another buck was born, equally splendid and as he grew up, a large herd gathered around him and he became known as Branch Deer.

The King of Benares was fond of eating venison and he regularly hundred and killed the deer on his land. When he hunted, he would go to the various villages and recruit the villagers to assist him. They would be told to drive the deer in one direction or another, until, eventually one of the deer would be unfortunate enough to suffer a deadly arrow from King Benares. These efforts drew the villagers away from their other duties and it became onerous over the years, for they set aside their farming, irrigating, grinding, family duties and whatever else to help their king.

After some time the villagers gathered and agreed to make a deer park for the King of Benares, in which he and a few of his servants could hunt alone, without their help. And so the park was built. A large area of land was fenced in and the deer from the two herds were driven into the park and the gate closed and locked behind them.

When the deer settled down, the villagers called on the King and told them of their efforts and the King was pleased. He could see the vast herds of deer and could now hunt without dragging all the villagers along.

As he surveyed the herds before him, he caught sight of the two beautiful bucks, King Banyan Deer and Branch Deer. The King thought them so beautiful that he decreed no one should *harm or kill them. They were to live a protected life within his new park.*

Still, once a day, the King would go hunting and kill a deer for his table that evening. Occasionally, the King was too busy, so he sent out his cook to hunt and butcher the deer, reminding him not to harm King Banyan Deer or Branch Deer.

Whenever the deer saw the King or the cook coming into the park with their bows and arrows, they panicked. They knew what was coming. They'd run and panic, trampling each other, tripping over each other and causing much harm to themselves - some suffering great pain.

Seeing all this King Banyan Deer called to Branch Deer and arranged a meeting of the herds. He began, "Death is inescapable for any of us. In the end, all things cease. All things die. So it will be with us, either from an arrow, old age or misadventure. However, this needless suffering from our own panic and resultant injuries can be avoided.

The King only wants one deer each day, so we should choose for ourselves which deer will go to the chopping block and all other injuries can be prevented. One day we shall choose a deer from among my herd and the next day a deer from the herd of Branch Deer. After considerable discussion, Branch Deer agreed.

From that day on, one deer, alternating back and forth between herds, one deer came forward and put his or her neck on the chopping block. The cook simply took the life of the waiting victim and prepared the venison for the King.

One day, by chance, the turn fell to a doe who was pregnant in Branch Deer's herd. She went to Branch Deer and asked that she be excused from her sacrifice, at least until her fawn was delivered. Branch Deer replied, "No. We can't change the rules and put your turn upon another." With that the doe left.

The distraught doe, having failed with Branch Deer, took her argument to King Banyan Deer. He replied, "Go in peace and I will change the rules and put another in your place. With that, King Banyan Deer went himself to the executioner's chopping block and laid down his own neck upon it. Silence fell upon the deer park.

Soon the cook came to kill the willing victim, but drew up short when he saw it was one of the deer that his King had forbidden him to harm. He was afraid to kill him, so he returned to King Benares and told him what he saw.

The amazed king could not believe his ears and went himself to the deer park. He said to King Banyan Deer, "I promised not to take your life. Why have you come here like the others?"

"A pregnant doe was unlucky this day to be the one to die. She asked me to spare her, for the sake of her unborn baby. I could not help but feel sorry and could feel her pain so I took her place to ease her suffering, for I could not ask anyone else to take her place.

King Benares was overcome and tears welled up in his eye. "Even among humans I have not seen such compassion. To offer to share the suffering as you do. Such generosity to give your life for another. Arise! Neither you nor the doe and her unborn baby will be harmed."

"Are we the only ones to be spared, great king? What of the other deer in this park, our friends and our kin? Will they not also be spared?"

"Having seen such a compassionate act, I cannot refuse your request. To your friends and kin in the park I grant their safety and their freedom," replied King Benares.

"What of my kin beyond the park, out on your land? Will they be killed?

"No. They will not be killed. I will spare the lives of all the deer anywhere within my kingdom.

Still King Banyan Deer did not raise his head from the chopping block. "It is good that the deer will be saved, but what of

> *the other four-footed creatures. Will they too be saved?"*
>
> *"They too shall be spared."*
>
> *"What of the birds, fish and other animals that dwell within your kingdom? Will they also be spared?"*
>
> *"Yes. They too shall all be spared."*
>
> *Having pled for the lives of all creatures, and having received amnesty, King Banyan Deer arose and returned to his herd to live out a long and natural life.*
>
> *For his part, King Benares ordered his military to open the gates of the deer park and the fences taken down so that no creature should be hemmed in and could enjoy freedom and safety within his lands.*

To Conclude This Section

From a Buddhist perspective, true compassion, is not merely an emotional response to a troubling situation or a simple outpouring of heartfelt sympathy. Rather, it's a firm commitment founded on rational thought and sound reasoning. When we recognize and deeply understand that we are all humans, with the same pain and suffering, we can more easily make room for compassion for others and make efforts to help them.

True compassion does not waver, even when the person to whom compassion is being extended, behaves badly. But compassion isn't an invitation for others to walk all over you. When wrong is done to you, you can still express indignation, displeasure and censure towards the offender - just do it compassionately, with understanding and skill.

Key Points Summary - Compassion

What is Compassion?	• A willingness and capacity to hear and bear the pain and suffering of others while developing a state of mind wherein one desires to help and takes action to do so, in whatever capacity one can
How to Raise Compassion	• The practice of *tonglen* helps raise compassion in the individual. In Buddhist terms, this compassion is known as *Bodhicitta*
We Are All The Same	• Our ego likes to divide the world into 'us vs. them,' yet we are all the same; we suffer from ignorance, greed and hatred, we cry and laugh, love and hate. These experiences are what make us collectively 'human.' Once this is seen and understood, compassion can arise more easily
True Compassion Does Not Waver	• From the Buddhist perspective, compassion isn't just an emotional upwelling, but a desire and commitment to help, even where we don't like the person who needs it
Wisdom and Compassion Depend Upon Each Other	• Wisdom, without compassion is cold and calculating, perhaps lacking consideration that all creatures suffer, while compassion without wisdom is a sure road to emotional burnout

8. Bias in Wise Decision Making

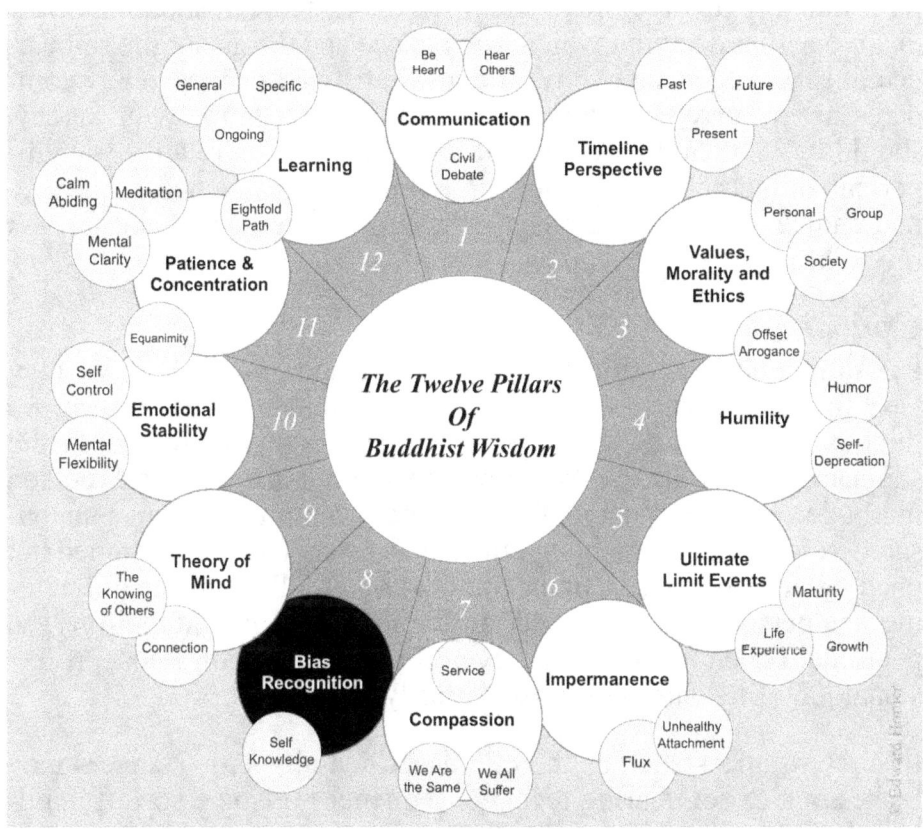

AT THE HEART OF WISDOM is 'good' decision making and 'good' advice giving. Anything that stands as an impediment to that end is best identified and dealt with. As we learned in Chapter 4.1 the Three Mental Defilements, we are often not even aware of forces that may have dramatic impacts on how we think, speak and act. Another set of forces which we may be unaware of, yet is constantly affecting our thinking, is bias.

8.1 The Decision, Unpacked

Not every decision we need to make or every piece of advice we offer is going to involve life or death. In the extreme, it should be clear to anyone that deciding which films to see at TIFF is not the same as deciding which house to buy, or that what style of shoes to buy compares in any way to deciding which retirement home your parents should be in. The first choice of both examples is relatively unimportant and largely reversible with minimal consequences. The second choice of these examples are far more complicated and far *less* reversible.

Critical

In a situation that is critical to life and limb and time is short, we may have to make a decision where little data available. We do what we think best, at the time, given what we know and what resources and skills are then available. We do what we think a 'reasonable' person might do. Is it 'reasonable' for someone to attempt CPR on a unconscious swimmer - even though the rescuer may have been trained but once - many years ago - in the application of CPR? If one did nothing, the person would most certainly die, but if one did their best to resuscitate, then he might live, even if the rescuer didn't do a professional job of it. The choice seems fairly obvious.

In circumstances such as the one described above, bystanders may be hesitant to act, fearing legal consequences or some sort of liability. It is for this very reason that most countries/provinces/states, have Good Samaritan laws. These laws provide legal protection for those who come to the assistance of those in need, injured, incapacitated, etc. in-so-far as they act in good faith, without expectation of compensation, etc.

Urgent

Some decisions need to be made immediately and without delay, but may not be critical. If your driver's licence about to expire, it would be an urgent matter to have it renewed - but it wouldn't be critical. Your health and safety are not immediately dependent upon having your driver's license. It's urgent that you act by the appointed date, but it' unlikely life or limb are in jeopardy if you don't.

Important/Not Important

Whether we order a cup of Café Verona or the Thanksgiving blend from Starbucks just doesn't matter. Our preference might be the Café Verona, but a Thanksgiving blend is fine too. These are preferences, not deal breakers. Sometimes, we seem to make decisions like this, far more important that they really are. We seem to want to add some story to the transaction that goes beyond getting a cup of coffee. There's no need for us to loose our temper with the barista for making our latte with 2% when we specifically asked for 3.5%. None of this is urgent or important in the big scheme of things - we are *making* it important so we can demean someone and feed our ego.

"Sure, just the other day, you bought some incredible single-origin nanolot coffee beans, and that half-pound bag cost as much as two, maybe three avocado toasts. In fact, you bought enough to keep some at home and at work. It's a legit varietal, like Gesha or Bourbon, from a remarkable local roaster who operates quasi-legally out of a sick loft and specializes in light—but not too light!—roasts, a respectful homage to modern Scandinavian coffee that lets you really get a sense of the bean's terroir, down to the GPS coordinates where it was discovered during an expedition into coffee country led by a white man of great taste, and the barista said that the acidity from this coffee is "really wonderful and fruit-forward, like Hawaiian Punch micro-dosed with LSD."

~ Matt Buchanan for eater.com, Jun 8, 2016

Reversible/Not Reversible

Some decisions are, largely, non-reversible. Deciding if you're going to adhere to the wishes of your spouse around 'no resuscitation' is a permanent decision. We are not going to bring back our spouse, once they have died. Deciding to adhere to their wishes is not reversible. Despite the fact that we might have discussed this a dozen times with our spouse, we will still - almost certainly - take more time, once again to think this through. It is, after all, final.

If someone told you that the decision you were about to make would set you on a path for the rest of your life, you'd certainly think long and hard about it. But, if it was reversible, you'd feel a less stress about it and likely make the decision quicker - whatever it may be.

We see evidence of this 'reversible' decision option quite often in stores. Retailers often offer return/refund policies that a) ease the stress of making a choice b) make the choice 'reversible' and c) help build customer loyalty. If we can buy a new backpack for our wife and have the option of returning it within, say, fourteen days for a full refund, then we are *far* more likely to buy the bag than if the store didn't offer those terms. Having the option to 'reverse' a decision - even partially - means that we might spend less time thinking it through.

Complexity
One might decide to write a book. Simple enough, you might think; come up with a compelling plot, do a book outline, start filling out the back stories on the characters, find a 'good' bad guy, decide on the twists, the story arc, the pace, the temper, where to casually drop in a bit of backstory. Should it be told in the first person, the third person or the all-knowing, all-seeing, omnipotent voice? Could the tale be better told through the eyes of dog? So many things to think about, adjust and balance in order to come up with a truly compelling read. Then there's the matter of getting it published, marketed and sold. All very complicated, but all you ever wanted to do was write a book.

In short, the more complex the task, the greater the reluctancy to get it done ... Unless you like that kind of thing.

10/10/10
In their book, *Decisive: How to Make Better Choices in Life and Work* (2013) Chip and Dan Heath bring up another way to parse decision making - the 10/10/10 rule. Essentially, ask yourself what your decision will look/feel like 10 minutes from now, 10 months

from now and 10 years from now. They identified our short-term emotional response as being a major impediment to good decision making. Their 10/10/10 rules helps us get beyond that by looking at the decisions in a longer time frame.

Let's say you're faced with having to put your parents in a long term care facility - a retirement home or similar. When we think ten minutes down the road, we might feel bad about having to do it at all - there's a lot of emotions going on - the child becoming the parent, the parent not wanting to go, loss of independence, etc.

In the short term, our emotions muddle our thinking so we will be uncertain about what to do - emotions are not always the enemy but we sometimes need to put a little distance between the decision and rawness of present emotions. When we think how things will be ten months down the road the situation may seem very different. Our parents will have gotten through their adjustment period and be more comfortable, they might be happier, better cared for, etc. Ten years from now, when they really need close care, perhaps suffering from dementia, they will be in a place where it's available, etc.

According to Heath & Heath;

"Perhaps our worst enemy in resolving these conflicts is short-term emotion, which can be an unreliable adviser. When people share the worst decisions they've made in life, they are often recalling choices made in the grip of visceral emotion: anger, lust, anxiety, greed. Our lives would be very different if we had a dozen "undo" buttons to use in the aftermath of these choices."

Common Good

The next thing we need to understand is the concept of *common good*. Our definition for the purposes of this book, is that of an end state or condition which benefits all or most of the community but is attainable only through the *collective* efforts and/or contributions of the community as a whole, and accrues to all members of the community, balanced against the rights of the individual.

In Canada, we might refer to the universal health care system as a common good, in so far as its benefits accrue to all citizens of Canada and can only be attained and sustained when all members of the citizenry contribute to its upkeep/funding.

Another Canadian example might be Employment Insurance benefits or even the Canadian Pension Plan, both of which benefit any qualifying Canadian citizen, but can only be funded and sustained when all Canadian citizens contribute - primarily through their taxes.

> A common good for humanity, might be relief from suffering, dukkha, that all pervasive feeling that life isn't very satisfying.

Positive Values Reference

Secondly, we need to avoid thinking, speaking and acting in absolutes. Going to one extreme or another is not a balanced, middle way of looking at the world and is almost a sure way of excluding at least half the people from any common good that we have imagined.

We need to use our intelligence, common sense, experience and knowledge to examine questions, referencing some list of shared, positive ethical values and the need to achieve our common good. In the next chapter and beyond, we will look at and examine such a list of Buddhist inspired values.

In the meanwhile, let's reconsider the Five Precepts of Buddhism that was mentioned earlier;

- Do not kill
- Do not lie
- Do not steal
- Avoid inappropriate sexual relations
- Avoid taking intoxicants.

These precepts will be investigated further along in this chapter.

We need to consider our personal interests, the interests of those around us, short term and long term goals while adapting to existing and where possible shifting, future conditions. We need to consider aspirations for ourselves, our aspirations with interpersonal relationships and even the relationship we enjoy with our community, for any effort to achieve a common good cannot operate outside the community which it serves.

Intelligence

Wisdom does not necessarily require high intellect or specialized knowledge, although some intelligence is required to assimilate and assess complex data and specialized knowledge is an asset for decisions around such matters as economic policy, traffic control or municipal planning, for example.

Having the intelligence to completely understand *both* sides of an argument - even to the point of being able to take up and argue the opponents view is an important element of understanding and a plank in the platform upon which wisdom can arise.

"There is a cult of ignorance in the United States, and there has always been. The strain of anti-intellectualism has been a constant thread winding its way through our political and cultural life, nurtured by the false notion that democracy means that my ignorance is just as good as your knowledge."

- Newsweek, *A Cult of Ignorance*
Isaac Asimov, Jan. 21, 1980, p. 19

Our contemporary society - at least in the west - seems to put a lot of stock in measuring and assessing 'intellect,' it's forms, variations and application. Yet, when we look at the major failures of citizens as individuals or citizens as leaders, it's never really about their intelligence. It's almost always about wisdom, or, more to the point, failure to apply wisdom, or even recognize it if were to hit them in the face.

Looking back on failed American leaders, we see Bush, Clinton, Nixon and now Trump. The Italians had Silvio Berlusconi, embroiled in accusations of sexual misconduct, illegal wiretaps and corruption. Toronto endured the emotionally ill-equipped Robert Ford as our Mayor for four, gruelling years. These leaders appear or appeared foolish, out of touch with reality, egocentric, false, overly optimistic about their abilities and morally disengaged when it comes to reasoning and their ability to make decisions. They failed, or are failing, not due to lack of intellect but due to lack of wisdom. They lack that *super suite* of mental faculties we discussed earlier; intellect, deep thought, foresight, humility, humour, learnedness, historical perspective, emotional stability and compassion.

Weighting Criteria

We need to recognize that not every criteria that we take into account needs to be weighted evenly. In fact, it would be unwise to weight everything equally. When it comes to the common good, we need to consider the rights of the individual, but we do not need to weight both the common good and the individuals rights equally. For example, the right of the individual to listen to their own preferred music after 11pm might not have the same weight as the common good of, 'reasonable right to peace and quiet' for the community in which the individual resides.

Another example of unbalanced weighting might include the common good that citizens have clean air to breath against the rights of the coal-burning, electricity producers to pollute said air with carbon dioxide, soot, sulphur or dioxin. In this case we also need to include the common good provided by the electricity plant producing power that the clean air breathing citizens are using to light and power their homes.

The greatest wisdom is found in identifying the common good and convincing others that getting there is a good idea, not only for us, but also for them and most others. Relative weighting might be determined by their potential to bring the greatest result to the articulated common good.

Listed here are only a few of the biases I recognize in myself and they only appear in the order which I think I fall victim in my thinking and decision making. Some pop up every day while others only make themselves known when I actively seek them out. There is a bit of hair splitting, to be sure and some biases are even contrary to some others and yet they can both exist at the same time, such as the my bias to use 'old' technology, while seeing the obvious advantages of the new. We are full of such contradictions.

8.2 Mental Biases

a) Negativity Bias

We seem to be hard-wired to be more influenced by negative stimulus (or loss) than positive stimulus (or gain).

I know that I'd rather *not* lose ten dollars than find ten dollars. For me, losing ten dollars would take me well into the "sad" side of the emotional-neutrality meter, while finding ten dollars would barely nudge me into the "happy" side of the meter. I'm not so sure why this is so. It's almost like the negative feelings are 'sticky' while the positive experiences are 'slick.' The negative experiences seem to hang around longer, affect me more deeply, while the positives seem to be fleeting and less lasting.

In order to 'make up' for losing the ten dollars I think I'd have to find twenty-five dollars in relatively short order. This is just me, but that suggests that 10/25 is a neutral ratio that I'd aim for, at least when it comes to money. Any more losses would result in 'negative' feelings while any more gain would result in 'positive' feelings. Clearly not scientific and I'm sure it's very different for others.

This 'stickiness' seems common for most people. We talk about 'depressive episodes,' 'major depression,' and 'anxiety disorder,' but rarely do we hear that someone benefited from a 'happiness episode' or a 'joy interlude.' Our positive emotional experiences just don't seem to matter very much. It seems to be our nature that we are more attracted to human disasters than we are to our discoveries.*

Negativity in media contributes to our negativity bias of course. We are often bombarded with negative news that is repeated every five minutes on the news channel. When we hear the same story repeated again and again, it worms it's way into our head and we begin to develop negative feelings in general.

In a 2013 study into psychological stress experienced due to the Boston Marathon Bombing (BMB April 15, 2013) it was found, that people in the New York area were negatively affected (due to constant repetition of the bad news cycle) to almost the same extent as were the people who actually experience the traumatic episode in Boston.** Repeated exposure to news stories that are negative, sensational and pessimistic seems to be the norm for anyone trying to keep up with the news.

The Eight Vicissitudes

In Buddhism we recognize that people are driven away from; shame, loss, pain and censure. At the same time we are attracted to and seek out; fame gain, pleasure and praise. These are called the Eight Vicissitudes or the Eight Worldly Concerns. We go to great lengths to avoid circumstances that might cause loss.

So, why is this important to the development of wisdom? In a very real way we become what and how we think. Our minds pay attention to what passes through them and we become what we pay attention to. If negative experiences get more attention than positive ones, then what are we to become?

If we were to always seek out negative experiences, negative thoughts and negative emotions, we become negative. Were we to seek out positive experiences, positive thoughts and positive emotions, we will become positive. The challenge comes in recognizing

---

* Alison Ledgerwood TED talk. TEDxUCDavis | May 2013. Alison is an Associate Professor at the University of California, Davis

**Holman, E Alison et al. "Media's role in broadcasting acute stress following the Boston Marathon bombings." Proceedings of the National Academy of Sciences of the United States of America vol. 111,1 (2014): 93-8. doi:10.1073/pnas.1316265110

that negative experiences are 'sticky' and tend to have far more influence on us that the 'slick' positive experiences.

Imagining that there's some universal rule that gives us a 50/50 change of having either a positive experience or negative experience around any activity or pastime, we are almost doomed to be negative! Even if we were to have many more positive experiences and even throw in a few 'neutral' experiences, it still seems that any negative experiences will have far more influence on us than would reasonably seem to make sense. That one time going skiing, where you hurt yourself, will live in your memory and affect your view of skiing, even when you've subsequently enjoyed 10 other uneventful ski days. It will always be in the back of your mind, reminding you of the possible negative consequences of skiing. Like a sprained ankle that is forever tender.

There's actually been considerable research into identifying the truth of this supposition. In one set of experiments by Dr. John Cacioppo at the Ohio State University it was discovered that there was measurably more electrical brain activity when test subjects were shown a picture known to be disturbing - say, a dead puppy or a badly scared face - than there was when they were shown a pleasant image, such as a pizza or a bowl of ice cream.

One can only guess at why this may be so, but it may simply be that having a bias towards the uncomfortable, negative or even dangerous experiences may have somehow helped us in our earliest development as human beings. Being hyper active around negative experiences may have just kept us safe. Being extra aware of dangerous circumstances may have helped us avoid getting killed or harmed. Having those negative experiences 'stick' with us has likely helped us evolve into the modern human that we are today.

How Can This Negative Bias be Overcome?

Internalize and Act on Positive Experiences

When something 'good' happens to us, we can internalize it, make the brain think about it a little more and maximize its benefit. We become what our brains pay attention to, so pay attention to positive experience, positive emotions and positive body sensations.

In meditation (explored in Chapter 11) there is an exercise in which one thinks about some positive experience, how it arose, who was responsible, where it occurred, etc. We then express gratitude for all the pieces that fell into place in order for us to have that experience. This helps us hold onto the positive experience and reminds us that we have not arisen independently, but because of a lot of circumstances.

Recognize our Own Positive Attitudes

When we recognize a positive attribute in our own mind, we should actively name it and strive to reproduce it, where possible. When we recognize how we felt when we gave to a charity, we should hold onto that feeling for as long as possible. We might think about it, determine if there was a warmth in our chest or a 'glow' in our hearts. We might think about how the recipient felt, gratitude or maybe relief. Hold onto those feelings as well. Allow the positive experience to dwell within the mind for as long as possible in order to maximize its benefit - in order to be as 'sticky' a possible to help counteract the negatives that crop up during the day.

Internalize the Kindness of Others

When someone does something nice for us, we should thank them, internalize the act, feel the warmth and gratitude in our chest, recognize that good body feeling and work to remember how it made us feel.

Reward/Remember Project Completion

When we complete a project at work or home, we should step back, congratulate ourselves for a job well done, think about it and remember it – all to make those experiences as 'sticky' as possible in order to maximize their benefit to our brain. Maybe 'reward' ourselves in some small way; a piece of cake, a trip to the mall or a movie on Netflix. Something to help the brain/body maximize the pleasant experience of 'a job well done.'

Pay attention to the positive and rewarding benefits of emotions and body sensations when something good happens. Stay with it and make it part of your memory. Focusing on the positives in these exchanges releases the chemical dopamine and will strengthen the 'stickiness' of the situation. Dopamine is a neurotransmitter that is associated with mood regulation, especially positive moods and emotions.

The Magic of Five

Turns out that a lot of research has gone into what makes a "happy couple" when it comes to marriages that report to be 'happy.' Among the numerous variables that were identified; race, religion, culture, wealth, age, childhood background, etc, one factor came up again and again. That factor turns out to be repetitive, small kindnesses.

Even when couples argue, it turns out 'happiness' is still reported when the couples reciprocate exhibiting 'kindnesses' in a ratio of five 'positives' to every 'negative.'

What this suggests is the magic number of five positives are needed offset a single negative experience, which seems to support the idea of negative experiences being 'sticky' while positive ones are 'slick.'

When it comes to giving rise to the conditions from which wisdom can arise, we need to recognize the importance that negative bias plays in our emotions and how those emotions might affect our thinking, words and actions.

b) Confirmation Bias

Ignoring information or observations that do not sit well with our pre-defined view of the world, robs us of wisdom. We have a strong tendency to search for, interpret, recall and re-use information that favours our existing ideas or values. We tend to overestimate information when it agrees with our opinions or hypothesis while at the same time, undervalue any information that runs contrary to our pre-held views. We are simply wonderful at interpreting new information in a way that confirms our previous conclusions remain intact. We simply do not perceive situations or data with complete objectivity, but if we can recognize and respond to that bias, then we can at least begin to think, speak and act wisely.

We've touched briefly on confirmation bias earlier in "Thoughts on Certainty," but it's a topic that while largely brushed off by any individual, affects humanity deeply and is deserving of a little more discussion .

There seems to be primarily two reasons why confirmation bias exists.

The first, and perhaps simplest explanation, is that we don't like to be wrong. As we've noted earlier, being wrong is painful. It hurts emotionally and it's embarrassing for most people.

Being wrong in our western society is not well received. When you're wrong in business, it's going to cost time, money and resources and that does not sit well with owners, lenders, investors or shareholders. Being wrong in these circumstances means you're out on a limb and susceptible to censure, damage to reputation and erosion of other's confidence in you. Simply put, we seek to avoid the shame of being wrong.

In my experience, investors in businesses tend to be over-confident and will over-estimate their financial acumen. They tend to research company financial records, not with an open, methodical mind, but with pre-conceived idea of how the company 'ought' to perform, what the company 'ought' to return. When something goes wrong, they could not possibly say, "I didn't have enough information," or "I didn't fully understand," but rather they look to place blame elsewhere; the overall economy, incomplete disclosure, unforeseen market declines, the past president, the current president, malfeasance, changing labour laws or changing SEC regulations. Literally anything but their own failings and confirmation bias.

Prior to the arrival and widespread application of the "scientific method," people in the medical field labeled a treatment 'successful' any time a patient recovered. When a doctor prescribed a course of treatment and the patient recovered, it was deemed a success. No effort was made to determine if the patient had recovered for any other reason or if the patient actually responded to the treatment. Say a patient complained of severe coughing. An early doctor might have suggested rose hip tea with honey. The patient recovers and the doctor thinks, "Ah ha! As I thought, rose hip tea with honey cures coughing." That may be true, but there's also a possibility that the patient coughed up a fly, quit smoking, stopped working in the coal mine, got rid of the cat or started taking a turn in the clear country air. Further, was it the rose hip tea or honey that cause the recovery. perhaps is was the combination of the two. There was no effort to discover other possible reasons for the recovery. Clearly, this confirmation bias would lead to inappropriate treatments for varying conditions.

In the long standing debate around the legalization of marijuana in Canada, the conservative view point might suggest that its use should be strictly controlled or even banned altogether while it ignores or de-values any evidence that the product has proven beneficial to many medical or psychological conditions, where other treatments have been less effective. The liberal view might include the belief that the conservative viewpoint is just a Reefer Madness hangover from less informed times and backward cultural mores. Both sides will tend to select the information and data that best supports their viewpoints while discounting or ignoring altogether any information that is contrary to their view.

To be clear, it's not easy being objective or unbiased around anything. So long as preferences exist, confirmation bias will plague us. However if you can at least name it, you can be aware of its influence in decision making to make wiser decisions.

Wishful Thinking
Simply wishing something to be as we think it ought to be, is delusional.

"It's not that fattening"

"My father smoked until he was 94! Why should I stop?"

"It's only one or two martinis after work. There's no harm"

"I only take cocaine recreationally. I don't *need* it."

When we wish for things to be different from what they are, we are delusional. Wishing ice cream to be non-fattening is delusional. We are delusional when we suggest that smoking is not going to have long term health effects. It's delusional to suggest that one or two martinis a day is somehow good for you. It's delusional to take drugs on a regular basis and pretend that you are not addicted to them.

This self deception, over-confidence and overestimation of abilities is a lot like a drug that numbs you from the realities of the world. This is not to suggest that we abstain from positive thinking, quite the contrary. We need to be positive for our own health, relationships with others and interactions at work, but we need to recognize when our optimism slips into fantasy.

How Can Confirmation Bias Be Overcome?

When we sit down to think about a problem or circumstance or when we need to make a decision about something, we must pull out our list of known and knowable biases and this is especially so when it comes to confirmation bias, for this particular bias suggests that we don't even want to look at our biases for fear that something we don't agree with might come up! Yet we *must* do the challenging work of actively seeking out contrary views and contrary research in order to fully understand the topic at hand from all sides.

In short, strive to understand opposing or dissenting views and opinions - even where (especially where) you don't understand or disagree with them. When we start to think, "That's only an exception," red flags should be popping up and you should start delving deeper into those exceptions, acting as a devil's advocate, until you can truly decided if they were, indeed, aberrations.

c) Early or Anchoring Bias

When we hold a hypothesis and begin to seek information to confirm or deny its validity, there is a strong tendency to believe any early data that tends to confirm our hypotheses. That is to say that we might 'anchor' our evaluation on the early data. The danger is that we don't continue in the search for more information, believing that the early results will be the same as later results. While it may be true that more research may confirm what we've already discovered, it's not a lock.

In the presidential election of 1948, the now famous Chicago Daily Tribune headline which screamed "Dewey Defeats Truman," proved to be embarrassingly wrong. The newspaper, relying on expert opinion from their Washington correspondent Arthur Henning and early results from closed voting stations on the east coast, went to press with the incorrect call for their first edition. The error was corrected in the second edition of the day, but the original was still out there, reminding everyone of the importance of waiting until all the votes were in.

In his book Old Path, White Clouds, Thich Nhat Hanh tells this tale from the life of The Buddha;

"Let me tell you a story about a young widower who lived with his five-year-old son. He cherished his son more than his own life. One day he left his son at home while he went out on business. When he was gone, brigands came and robbed and burned the entire village. They kidnapped his son.

"When the man returned home, he found the charred corpse of a young child laying beside his burned house. He took it to be the body of his own son. He wailed in grief and cremated what was left of the corpse. Because he loved his son so dearly, he put the ashes in a bag which he carried with him everywhere he went.

"Several months later, his son managed to escape from the brigands and make his way home. He arrived in the middle of the night and knocked at the door. At that moment, the father was hugging the bag of ashes and weeping. He refused to open the door even when the

child called out that he was the man's son. He believed that his own son was dead and that the child knocking at the door was some neighbourhood child mocking his grief. Finally, his son had no choice but to wander off on his own."

When we are attracted to one belief and hold onto that belief as if it were true, then we rob ourselves of the ability to see or know reality, even when it comes knocking on our door. In this case, the widower took the first piece of information he found (the unidentified corpse) and clung to the belief that it was his child, even when evidence to the contrary presented itself, so robbing him of a chance to reunite with his son.

How Can Early Or Anchoring Bias Be Overcome?

Be mindful that not all the data has yet been reviewed. Avoid making rash choices where only limited data is available. On the other hand, there are always circumstances where complete data will never be available, or not be available at any reasonable cost, but decisions must still be made. One wants to avoid falling into analysis paralysis, a state in which a decision isn't being made as there may still be more data out there. A pollster might not need to poll each and every American to determine if Americans would like to see more or less gun control legislation. It's a matter of selecting 'representative' populations from all Americans from which to draw out the data, but that gets into a realm that is far beyond the scope of this book.

d) Recency Bias

This is a bias that is almost the opposite of early or anchoring bias. When we hold an idea or speculative thought, and then seek information and data regarding the validity of that idea, we might tend to believe the most *recent* data available.

For example, investors might look to the current state of the stock market and ignore the past ups and downs. If the TSX is sitting at 15,998 today, that information might take precedence or weigh more heavily than the fact that the same index was 7,566 on March 9, 2009.

There is a strong tendency to discount *past* events or data and weigh, more heavily, recent events or data.

How Can Recency Bias Be Overcome?

I once had enough money that I hired a financial consultant who helped me set financial goals for one particular stage in my life. Being a bit of a 'hands on' guy, I couldn't help looking at every up and down of the markets on a daily or weekly basis. I couldn't keep my eyes off the individual Canadian stocks in my portfolio. I'd call up my guy and ask him what I should do. "OMG Pallet Pallet Inc. (PPAL) is down! What should I do? Sell?" He always asked me to return to my "investor profile" and report back to him what my investment goals were. "Long Term, Low Risk, Canadian Investments, etc." The ups and downs were part of the daily life of *his* world, but not mine. He was correct that my goals were over a much longer time span than weeks or months. Going back to my original goals were key to avoiding recency bias. Sticking to my set goals and plans while avoiding 'emotional' reactions help avoid recency bias.

In my first job as a bookkeeper at Directory Advertising Consultants, my boss (a wonderful woman named Gwen Irwin) helped me along at least once a week with her oft repeated phrase, "Plan the work, then work the plan." When the monthly cash flow report or the P&L statements were due, she could see I'd be getting into a panic and she'd just say, "Plan the work, Ed, then execute." It always worked. Thanks Gwen.

Still, recency bias will creep in. If a person experiences an automobile accident in which they are severely injured, the mental and physical trauma they experience can be debilitating and might (without psychological and physical rehabilitation help) keep them out of a car for the rest of their life.

e) Escalation of Commitment Bias

Recently, I went up to Cobbs Breads for a loaf of Cinnamon bread and a couple of apple scones. I arrived, only to find a lineup going out the door and onto Danforth Avenue—everyone practising their social distancing and mask wearing. I dutifully joined the line and waited. After about ten minutes, I was inside the door, but faced what looked to be another ten minutes of waiting. I remember very vividly thinking, "Well I've waited ten minutes already and I don't want to 'give up' my place in the line. I guess I'll wait." All that went on in a few seconds, while at the same time, I knew that the "Dough" bakery just across the street had no line and also carried cinnamon bread and scones. What's a boy to do?

In simple terms, the longer I waited, the more I felt, 'invested' in standing in line.

How Can Escalation Of Commitment Bias Be Overcome?

We need to remind ourselves that the end goal is not without a price. Just because I wanted that loaf of cinnamon bread, didn't mean that I had to wait for twenty minutes to get it. Yet I did! I could have 'cut my losses' after ten minutes and just walked across the road to the other bakery.

We might start every negotiation like an auction. We might set an arbitrary 'price' after which we just pull the plug. I might have said to myself, "If I'm not out of the bakery in ten minutes, I'll walk across the street or forego the cinnamon loaf altogether."

I used to have an old Saturn automobile. It needed little in the way of repairs over the early years of ownership, but in the last year I owned it, it just got more and more expensive to repair, find parts, get the environmental certificate, etc. I could have poured about $2,000 dollars into its restoration and rehabilitation, but I'd still only have an old car that might end up 'junk' at any time. There seemed to be no point in "throwing good money after bad." I had budgeted $700 for repairs and maintenance on this vehicle for this year and it was exceeded, not by a little but by a lot. I pulled the plug on the old darling.

f) Clustering Bias
Our brains are pattern-finding machines. How, in a crowded room with scores of people, can we easily and sometimes almost uncon-

sciously recognize the face of someone we know - even after not having seen them for years? Our brains work overtime trying to put a pattern onto everything. We find patterns in sound of the wind, howling around the house and think we hear voices. We find patterns in the stars and call them "constellations." We find patterns in completely random numbers, like a lotto draw, and think we can predict the next winning set.

We might think that we've seen two consecutive numbers in random, winning lotto draws, so we always make sure we have two consecrative digits in the numbers we select for any lottery in which we participate.

We might begin to believe that after a series of red numbers on a roulette wheel, another red will appear. Or we might believe the exact opposite. After a string of reds, we're 'due' for a black. In either case it's exactly a 50/50 chance that red or black will appear, but our brains want to put a predictive pattern to a limited set of observations.

We tend to put patterns where, more-often-than-not, there are none. Or we may recognize one pattern in a data set, but not recognize another.

The dangers of clustering bias, of course, is that we might begin to believe we can predict the next event from a limited series of observations just because we found what we think is a pattern.

How Can Clustering Bias Be Overcome?

We need to recognize that our brains want to put a pattern on everything. Is there really a "hunter" in the Orion constellation or a 'bear' in the Ursa Major constellation? Of course not and if you look hard enough, and apply your imagination, you'll find other patterns in those same constellations. One culture might call the "Big Dipper" constellation an inverted plough while another might recognize it as a smokers pipe.

We must exercise caution when it comes to assigning patterns to what are demonstrably random series. When we want to cross the road, we look left and right, gauge the speed and spacing of the cars, then make our move when we perceive that there will be an opening in the pattern of traffic. We're usually right. We've been doing it years. Still, we need to recognize that despite the 'fact' that we've seen the pattern and believe it's safe to cross at the prescribed time, we have to recognize that some driver may decide to pull out of a parking spot or driveway and enter the stream and invalidate our pattern, making crossing dangerous. A police vehicle, ambulance or fire truck may enter the stream and bring everything in our pattern crashing down, again, making it unsafe to cross. Even when we get it right and there's a safe space to cross, what if we trip over a shoe lace?

Unless it can be mathematically "proven" that a pattern exists, don't take your brain's word for it … especially when there is a limited data set from which to draw conclusions.

g) *Conservatism Bias*
Similar to Anchoring bias. In this case, new information is slow to displace older information.

A story is told.

Nan-in, a Japanese Zen master during the Meiji era (1868-1912), received a university professor who came to inquire about Zen. Nan-in served tea. He poured his visitor's cup full, and then kept on pouring. The professor watched the overflow until he no longer could restrain himself. "It is overfull. No more will go in!" "Like this cup," Nan-in replied, "you are full of your own opinions and speculations. How can I show you Zen unless you first empty your cup?"

There is a bias of holding onto *old* data because so much of our identity and value system is wound up in that older information. To accept new information is to re-think who we are and what we believe.

How Can Conservatism Bias Be Overcome?

We need to take the time to understand and interpret new information that comes to us. If it's too difficult to quickly understand or incorporate then we need to take a deep breath and learn about the new material at our own pace.

New Information Weighting Shortcut Rule; In short, when new information arrives, especially if it's difficult to understand, you must assume it should be more heavily weighted and valued than the old information which you already understand. Then, once you understand and assimilate the new material you can decide for yourself how the information should be weighted. Where and when you simply cannot understand the information, you should turn to a professional who has nothing to gain from either side.

h) Stereotyping Bias

This bias occurs when we think, for example, that all members of a political group will think and behave as a block. Even though any political group (or social group, or club, or religion or culture) is made up of individuals, we may *still* believe that members of that group will behave as a homogenous unit. We imagine we know the answers any individual of a group will provide on any given topic. What do we think or feel, when we hear political pundits tout the importance of, 'getting the Black vote,' or the 'Latino vote,' speaking of both groups as though they are a homogeneous amalgamation of like-thinkers. Even *Hari Seldon* knew the dangers of trying to predict the future too finely.

How Can Stereotyping Bias Be Overcome?

Like any bias, simply recognizing that it may exist within your own mind is an essential step. It is wise to constantly remind ourselves that there are independently acting individuals within any given group and, as individuals, their behaviour is not predictable.

i) Pro-Innovation Bias

In 1993 Apple introduced their Newton, personal digital assistant (PDA) that was, for its time, quite advanced. Hand writing recognition, peer-to-peer infrared data transmission, touch sensitive screen, built in apps, optional internet connectivity, etc. In theory, it could deliver powerful computing solutions in a package about, 18.42 cm H × 11.43 cm W × 1.91 cm D and weighed in at 0.41 kg. Small enough to easily slip into the pocket of a suit jacket or easily toted along in a purse or small briefcase. It was well received when first introduced, selling some 50,000 at roughly $900 each.

While the device proved useful, it turned out not as useful as Apple had hoped. - They had overestimated its utility, speed, handwriting recognition abilities, etc. One of the main drawbacks was that it was not equipped with desktop connectivity, meaning that data input into the device was difficult to get out and use on a desktop machine - a fact that made its utility less than stellar.

There is a tendency to overestimate the value of new products, new innovations, new devices or new methods, while underestimating their drawbacks.

How Can We Overcome Pro-Innovation Bias?

There is considerable wisdom in exercising patience around the adaptation of new technology. Stop jumping onto every new bandwagon that drives through town. Look carefully and with an open mind about what this new innovation will bring. How will this new innovative device or methodology be used? Can it be integrated into how I already work? Are you concerned that North Haverbrook has a monorail and your Springfield doesn't?

- Some companies put out a "free trial" version of new software that may last for 30 days and then stop working. These are great because you can try them and see if they fit with how you work
- Read reviews of new hardware to see how it's being received by the public at large and then, determine if it will easily integrate with how you work
- Don't buy the newest thing to hit the market – it's one thing to be at the 'leading edge,' but quite another to be at the, 'bleeding edge.' Let other people and other companies sort out the 'teething' problems that are sure to crop up.

j) Outcome Bias

Similar to, but not quite like early or anchoring bias and recency bias.

Judging a situation solely on the outcome, rather than the decision process that went into it. If you won money in Atlantic City, it's still not a good idea to gamble away your money. It's a certainty that you will, *eventually*, lose for the odds are statistically stacked in favour of the casino.

How Can We Address Outcome Bias?

Outcome bias is simply seeing and giving weight to any particular outcome. To overcome this bias, we would be wise to remember that that any outcome is not self-arising, but has arisen because of a series of other things that came before it. Examining those circumstances will help us see through this particular bias.

When, we look at the gambling example, already given, we see the pleasant outcome of being a winner. Remember, however, that losing ones money is far more likely. Add to that the examination of the odds of winning, prior to even playing, and it's clear that the statistics heavily favour the house and a loss is far more likely than a win. In short, the wisdom comes in focusing not on the outcome, but on the process and circumstances that lead to an outcome.

k) Zero Risk Bias

This is the tendency to prefer the complete elimination of a specific risk, even where addressing other risks may be more beneficial in the long run.

Take for example, the fact that from 2001 to 2014 — 3,412 Americans died due to terrorist activities on US soil. In that same time, 440,095 Americans died due to domestic gun violence in America.* Put another way, for every citizen who died due to terrorist activity, 129 died from domestic gun violence. The 'War on Terror' has taken

---

* American deaths in terrorism vs. gun violence in one graph. Eve Bower, October 3, 2016. Source Centres for Disease Control, US State Department.

priority and a major slice of the American military and homeland security budget, and while gun violence is frequently talked about, it's never effectively addressed. In this example, if the concern was American lives, it would make far more sense to address domestic gun violence. There seems to be a belief that the risk from jihadist and other forms of terrorism can be eliminated completely (or made negligible), while gun violence is too great an obstacle to tackle, even though it would save more American lives.

How Do We Overcome Zero Risk Bias?

Recognizing that this bias exists can help overcome its effect on our decision making and actions. When we recognize that our minds have selected a zero risk solution to a problem, that should immediately be a red flag that we should stop and think about our biases. The best option *may* be the zero risk choice, but take the time to recognize other options, cost them out and see where, if at all, they have a place in addressing the common good.

l) Blind Spot Bias

In the end, this bias is probably our biggest challenge. We need to be aware of all the biases that come to bear on our thinking and decision making. We must overcome the belief that we are 'fair' people, are not racist, homophobic, intolerant or ego-centric. Not seeking out, recognizing, examining and doing something about our own cognitive biases, is a bias in itself. It's a major blind spot. Somehow we believe we are able to detect bias in the thinking of others, yet refuse to see the bias in our own thinking.

Erin McCormick, an author and Ph.D. student in behavioural decision research in CMU's Dietrich College of Humanities and Social Sciences wrote, in her research;

"When physicians receive gifts from pharmaceutical companies, they may claim that the gifts do not affect their decisions about what medicine to prescribe because they have no memory of the gifts biasing their prescriptions. However, if you ask them whether a gift might unconsciously bias the decisions of other physicians, most will agree that other physicians are unconsciously biased by the gifts, while

continuing to believe that their own decisions are not. This disparity is the bias blind spot, and occurs for everyone, for many different types of judgments and decisions,"

Conclusions

Everyone from the Dalai Lama to Sarah Churchwell suffers from bias in decision making. It is inevitable for we have been born into and formed by the societies, religions or cultures with which we identify. We develop ideas, preferences, theories and ideals that we hold dear and want to protect them. We will never be completely free from decision making biases, but recognizing they exist and knowing how they might be overcome can go a long way towards helping us make better decisions - and better decisions help give rise to greater wisdom.

Key Points Summary – Bias

Negativity Bias	• We seem to be hard-wired to be more influence by negative stimulus (loss) than positive stimulus (gain)
Confirmation Bias	• The tendency to search for, interpret, recall and re-use information that favours our existing ideas or values. New information is not weighted as heavily
Early or Anchoring Bias	• We have a strong tendency to believe any early data that tends to confirm our hypotheses. We might 'anchor' our evaluation on early data
Recency Bias	• A tendency to put more weight on recent data at the expense of earlier data
Escalation of Commitment Bias	• Simply, the more we have invested in an outcome, the more we tend to stick to the premise, even where contrary data is in evidence
Clustering Bias	• Our tendency to see patterns where, more-often-than-not, there are none. We may recognize one pattern in a set, but not recognize another. Our brains tend to see *clusters* and patterns
Conservatism Bias	• A situation in which new data is slow to displace old data
Stereotyping Bias	• A belief that individuals within a given group will be like-thinking and like-acting
Pro Innovation Bias	• A belief that when new innovations come along, they will inevitably be better than that which it is replacing

Key Points Summary – Bias (Cont.)

Outcome Bias	• A tendency to judge a situation solely on the outcome, rather than the decision process that went into it
Zero Risk Bias	• The tendency to select an option which seemingly eliminates a threat, even where other options would more completely address the situation
Blind Spot Bias	• We need to overcome the belief that we are 'fair people, not racist, homophobic, intolerant or egocentric • Not seeking out, recognizing, examining and doing something about our own cognitive bias, is a bias in itself

9. Theory of Mind

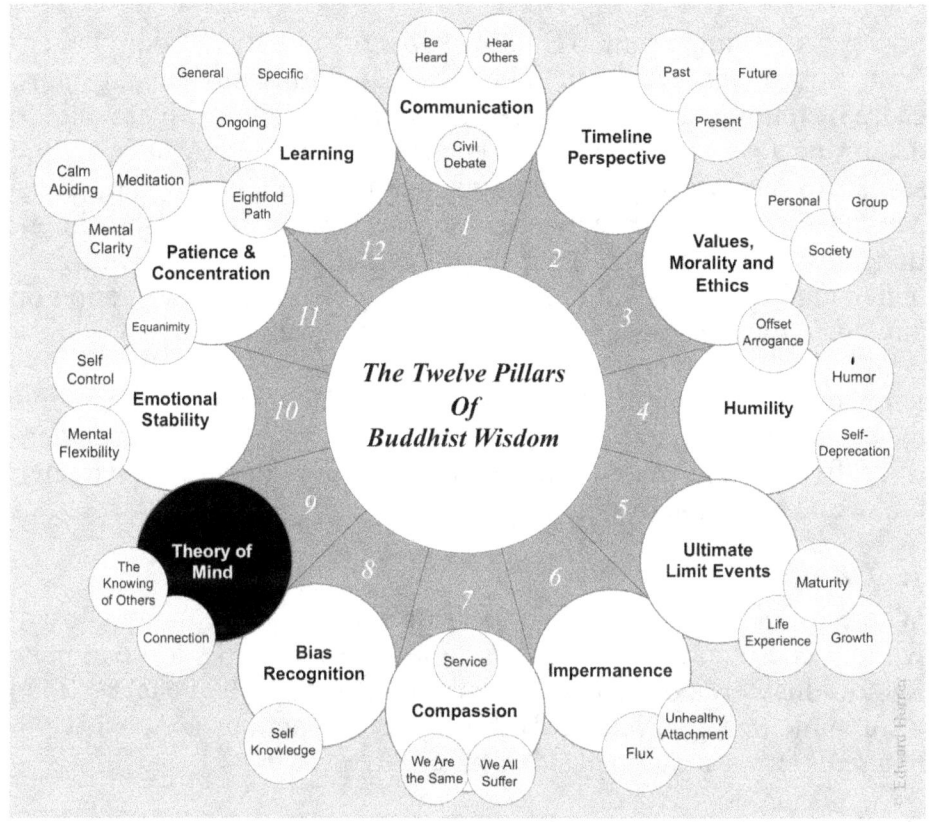

ATTRIBUTION THEORY LOOKS INTO HOW an observer is able to use gathered social cues to arrive at causal explanations for events or judgments about another persons behaviour. It's also known as Theory of Mind or ToM. While attribution theory is beyond the scope of this book, it is worth a few paragraphs.

There are two tracks running that we use to explain behaviour of others; internal and external. In the first, we might, for example, attribute *intentionally* bad behaviour to some internal flaw in a persons character. "They have a mean streak." In the later case we might attribute *accidental* bad behaviour to external causes, over which the observed individual appears to have no control or influence.

So how is this important to Buddhist wisdom or even wisdom in general? Simply that we come to believe that, within our social groups, cadre of fellow workers, congregation or social club, we are able to determine a persons intentions, because we believe they have a mind similar to ours with similar thoughts, similar beliefs and similar experiences. But of course, we can never really know a persons intentions, even when they tell us, for they, themselves, might not fully understand their motivations around any given thought or action on any given day. At best, we can only make a guess.

Drawing largely from JONES, E. E. (1976) How do people perceive the causes of behaviour? American Scientist, 64, 300–5. Jones identified five factors that we seem to use to determine the character, mood and intention of others;

1. Choice
Where we observe a behaviour or hear words that are freely chosen, without coercion or threat, we assume internal factors to be at play. Should the words or actions that are freely chosen be negative, then we assume negative intent. If the words and actions are positive in nature, then we assume positive intent.

2. Accidental vs Intentional Behaviour
Behaviour that we perceive to be intentional is usually attribute to internal factors, while accidental behaviours are usually attributed to outside forces, beyond the control of the individual. Accidentally knocking over a glass of wine, while rising from the table would be considered accidental behaviour and be considered as an outside force. On the other hand, telling the host that the meat is over or under cooked, in front of other guests, would be considered intentional and caused by a personality flaw, such as poor manners and/or rudeness.

3. Social Desirability
Behaviours or words that we would consider low in social desirability we tend to attribute to the person's personality. For example, fail-

ing to offer a senior citizen or an obviously pregnant woman a seat on the bus would be considered low social desirability and be judged a personality flaw - in some way delinquent, selfish or rude.

4. *Hedonistic Relevance*

Are the words or behaviours perceived to be of benefit to us or a harm to us? We are all ego-centric and tend to think the world revolves around us and that we are the cause of so much action in our little world. When someone exhibits anger or an element of aggression towards us, we tend to think it's something about *us* that has caused it. However, we are often only 'bit players' in other peoples dramas and their apparent focus on us is likely not personal.

If the behaviour or words, directed at us, are kindly and positive, we might perceive the intention to also be kindly and positive. Should the words directed at us be rude and offensive, we might consider the intention to be rude and offensive.

5. *Personalism*

When the words or actions of another appear to have a direct impact on us, we usually consider it "personal" and not just the by-product of an unfolding situation in which we are simply 'caught up.'

There's much more to this attribution theory business, but like I said, its beyond the scope of this book.

> When we interact with people, listen to their words and observe their actions, we try to put our observations into some kind of social context and then judge the behaviour using the five principles noted above. However we can't depend entirely upon those cues.

Is that fellow approaching us with a little knife, going to stab us or help us slice our apple? In this case, even if he looked friendly, we might err on the side of caution and take our apple elsewhere.

Mirror Neurons

Another theory that seems popular of late is that our brains possess 'mirror' neurons . These specialized neurons seem to have some importance around understanding the actions and emotional state of other people as well as our ability to learn through imitation. It's suggested that the brain has a 'simulation' function and these mirror neurons seem to allow us to run a simulation of the observed behaviours of others to empathize with their mood and estimate their intentions.

All this is very speculative and most of this research has been done with monkeys, but there certainly seems to be something in our brains that helps us instantly determine if a person is genuine or false and to what degree.

A Personal Anecdote

I once owned an espresso bar and there was this fellow who would wander around the neighbourhood, nattering away to himself, kicking at lamp posts and parking meters and generally sounding and acting incoherent. He would mutter about pies, pies, pies, all the time. "Nut job, and likely a little dangerous," is what most observers would think.

On the one or two occasions he came in, I ushered him out (kindly, but firmly) fearing for my physical safety and that of my patrons. He never expressed that he wanted anything other than to be bothersome. You could see the look of gratitude on the faces of my customers and almost hear the sighs of relief.

Then one day, a friend of his came into the shop and wanted to introduce him to me. I was hesitant and it must have shown. His friend told me that the fellow wandering around suffers from 'Tourettes Syndrome' a neurological condition that involves, among other things, nervous ticks, uncontrollable spasms, involuntary utterances and repetitive words - at least in this particular fellow. Being anxious only tended to make it worse for him. His name was Daniel.

He brought Daniel in and you could see on Daniels face, relief that I wasn't going to throw him out. His condition was not his fault and it turned out not to be dangerous to others. When allowed to sit down, order a coffee and relax, almost all his obvious outward signs of distress faded away. Then, when someone else came into the café you could see him get agitated again, but then calm down. When he and I spoke, he began a lot of his sentences by repeating 'pi, pi, pi' before getting to the topic.

Occasionally Daniel suffered minor seizures, in which he would just stop whatever he was doing and stare into space for a few minutes. I don't know if it was from the Tourettes Syndrome or some other, non-disclosed ailment, such as epilepsy. When this first happened, I called 911 and they arrived just after he recovered. Both he and they said it likely wasn't necessary to call them for this particular symptom, but if it lasted more than ten minutes, I might want to call.

Over the months that followed, Daniel and I became well acquainted and even friendly. While he never became what I'd call a 'regular' customer, he would make an occasional appearance at various times and for various durations. Other patrons became comfortable with his ticks and spasms and would occasionally exchange a few words with him.

The take away is, even with ToM and mirror neuron findings taken into account, our conclusions about other peoples intentions are not always accurate and need to be careful when trying to parse peoples words, looks or actions.

To Wrap up the Section
We need to be careful that we don't falsely attribute intent to the words or actions of people. We too easily fall into the trap of believing that any given member of a group will behave in concert with the group to which they belong - and that just isn't true. We can, with some degree of success, predict the behaviour of the group, but we can rarely predict the behaviour of any individual within the group.

When people 'choose' to misbehave we assume some social maladjustment on their part - some nefarious intention that may or may not be present. On the other hand, if a person misbehaves, but we judge that circumstances 'forced' them to behave in that way, then we are less likely to look upon them too unkindly. This is further complicated when we bring in the hedonistic aspect - is this misbehaving directed at me? If we judge the behaviour is personally directed, then we may think of the person in less than glowing terms, relative to them just behaving badly towards the world in general.

So what does all this mean when it comes to wisdom? Simply that we need to think deeply about the nature of words and behaviour of others. We can easily be misled as to what people think, say and do if we don't examine the circumstances.

9.1 Motivation, Skills and Resource Analysis in Wise Decision Making

Offering advice is a great thing. Many years ago, there was a television advertisement for UNICEF. It featured Canadian actor Peter Ustinov. Someone asks him for a donation of money and he replies something to the effect, "You ask me for money? Money is so, so sorted. Why should I give you money when I still have an inexhaustible supply of advice to offer?" To be clear, Sir Peter Ustinov was a kind and generous man and did a lot of fundraising for that particular cause but his point was that the most needed resource, at that time, wasn't advice, but money.

Motivation

The motivation of an individual plays a key role in how or even 'if' a person is willing to take advice and then act upon it.

Telling a tired fellow employee that they should get more rest might fall upon deaf ears if the person isn't motivated to do so. Being tired at work may be the price they are willing to pay to stay up and watch Steven Colbert on late night TV. Maybe they have to work two jobs to support their children. Essentially reciting the old adage, "Early to bed and early to rise, makes a man healthy , wealthy and wise," may have no effect at all.

Skills

Suggesting to a person that they run an anti-virus app on their laptop will fall upon deaf ears and cause their eyes to glaze over if that person simply doesn't have the skills to look up a good app on the web, identify their OS, down load the appropriate version, install it, open and run it. Their motivation may be high, but their skill level may not allow for the work to be done. With high motivation and low skills, a different approach to wise counsel might be necessary than for a person who possessed high motivation and high skills.

On the chart presented on the next page, we have two axis; the x=SKILL level (left is low skill level while right is high skill level) and the y=MOTIVATION (bottom is low motivation while top is

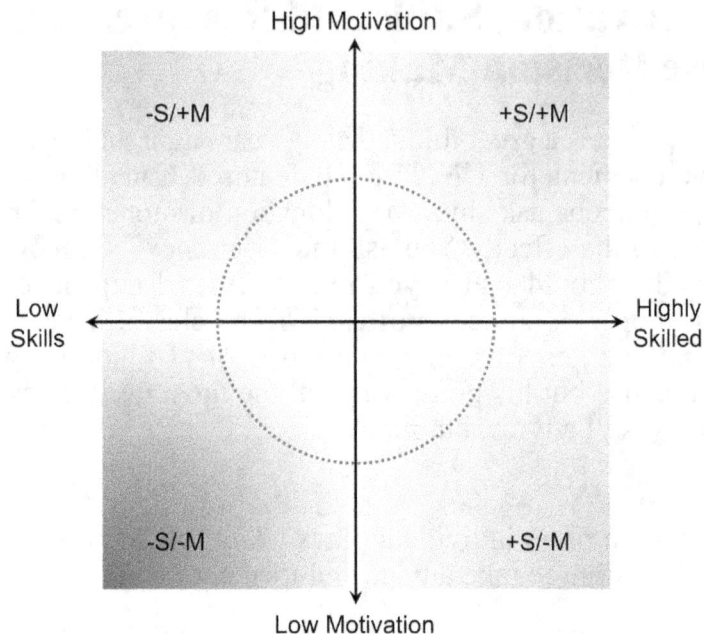

high motivation). The upper right quadrant represents an individual who is highly skilled AND highly motivated (+S/+M), while the lower left is an individual who is low in skills and low in motivation (-S/-M).

An individual who is highly skilled AND highly motivated (+S/+M) is more likely to listen to advice being offered, for their skills will allow them to act on the advice and their motivation to change their circumstances is high.

The individual who is low in skills AND least motivated (-S/-M) is less likely to listen to advice being offered as their skill set may not allow them to act on the advice and their motivation for change is low.

Resources
When a person complains about 'needing a vacation,' suggesting they try Havana, Cuba, might not be received if the person doesn't have any money to spend on a vacation.

Resources might include, but not be limited to; money, time, friends who can help, contacts within the community, knowledge (specialized or general), reading/writing/math skills, self-confidence, mental capacity, station in life, etc. After we consider the persons resources, then we are in a better position to offer advice. There's no point in suggesting a person actually take a vacation to Jamaica when they have not the money or the ability to take time off from work to do so. Offering other advice, such as taking a weekend off and staying at home with a good book, warm bath, glass of wine might be more sensible.

> A person who is well-resourced, highly motivated and highly skilled has more options available to them than an individual who is poorly resourced, unmotivated and lacking in skills. Bear that in mind when taking time to offer advice.

Before we offer advice, we need to do a bit of an inventory for ourselves as well;

- Examine our motivation for offering advice
- Examine our skills and ability with this particular situation
- Know our own resources.

That brings up the question of self analysis. Do *you* have the skills to offer advice? If a friend is having money problems, do you have the financial knowledge to help them? If not, do you know who does? What are your connections within the community if a person *really* needs help?

\Further, examine your own motivations for helping; are you being genuinely helpful in order to ease the suffering of another or are you being a busy-body and only helping because it makes you feel good or superior? as in, "I helped poor old Joe through his financial difficulties. Aren't I a great guy?" Are you being truly altruistic or are helping just so you can pat yourself on the back and think what a great person you are? Are you seeking applause or thanks for helping? If so, that might not be the right reason.

Key Points Summary - Theory of Mind

The Knowing of Others	• Because we are human and recognize our own thinking, we tend to believe that we can know what others are thinking • We tend to think we can predict the actions of an individual within a group, simply because that individual is part of the group
Choice	• When people behave or speak from their own choice, we tend to believe them more than if they speak or act under threat
Social Desirability	• Where people speak or act in a manner that is not socially acceptable, we tend to blame it on their personality and ascribe negative traits to them
Hedonistic Relevance	• We are all ego-centric and when people speak out or act up around us, we tend to think it's bout us. If it's negative, we tend to attribute negative attributes to the personality of the person acting out - even where it has nothing to do with us
Personalism	• f kind words are being spoken about us, then we tend to attribute positive personality traits to the individual doing the speaking
Mirror Neurons	• Early studies suggest that our brains have 'mirror neurons' that help us 'simulate' the thinking and emotional state of others
Advice Giving	• Before we offer advice, we need to take stock of the receivers skills, resources and motivation
Self-Knowing	• We need to self examine and determine out own motivations and resources before offering advice to others

10. *Emotional Stability And Wisdom*

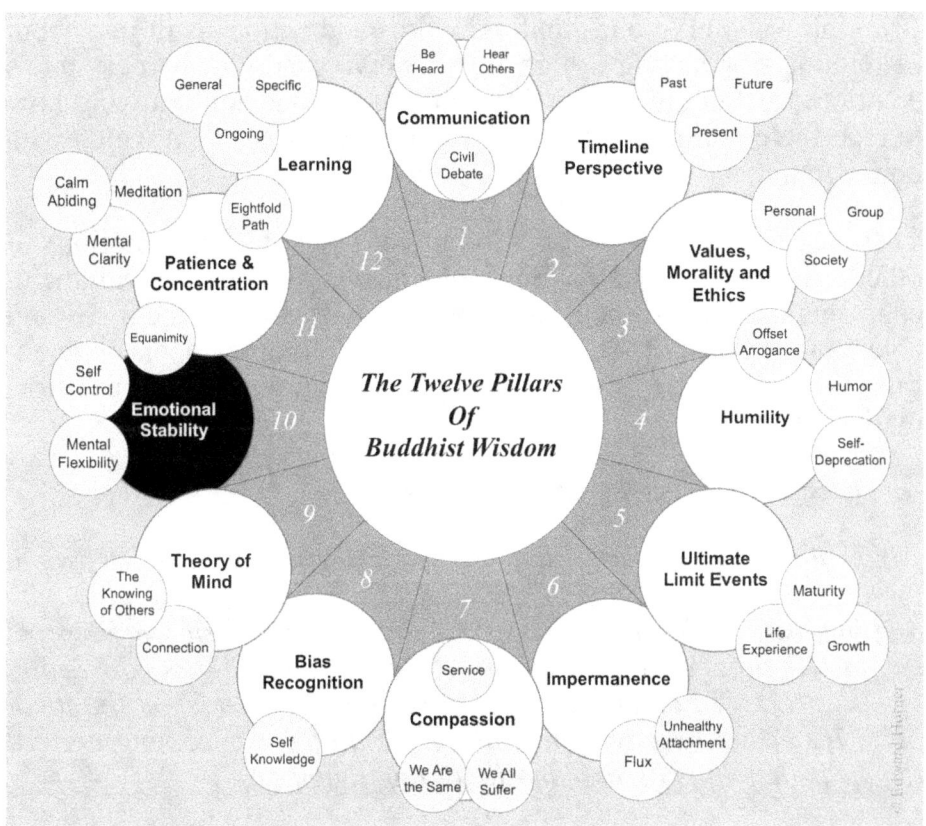

According to *Psychology Today*, emotional intelligence is, *"The ability to identify and manage your own emotions and the emotions of others. It is generally said to include three skills: emotional awareness; the ability to harness emotions and apply them to tasks like thinking and problem solving; and the ability to manage emotions, which includes regulating your own emotions and cheering up or calming down other people."*

Anyone who has ever worked for an employer who was emotionally unstable or unpredictable can attest to how difficult or even toxic that makes the work place. When a supervisor can fly off the handle for no known reason it makes speaking or interacting with them, in any way, a real challenge.

Bringing wisdom to our thinking, words and actions isn't just about being smart or having a high IQ. Knowing how to harness one's emotions, present to the world a stable personae and knowing how to read the emotions of others is yet another pillar upon which wisdom is built.

There are tremendous benefits to knowing how to read emotions of others. There's an advantage in being able to sympathize with them, calm them, energize them or, sometimes, exasperate them. Being able to identify, understand and work with complex social interactions is a major advantage in dealing with complicated and transformative issues.

As Dr. Susan Krauss Whitbourne writes;

"Transformative leaders can act as models who inspire other people by their vision of change. They have charisma, promote creativity and innovation, develop an environment in which their workers feel supported, and convey ambitious goals to their workers (Cavazotte et al., 2012). In other words, a transformative leader is the ideal boss. It's easy to see why part of the formula for becoming a great leader is that you possess emotional intelligence."

When we speak of wisdom and its role in public discourse, it's rarely about an individual, private citizen. Rather, it tends to be about public figures - those who open themselves up for criticism and put themselves in the limelight to be seen and to be critiqued, judged and held accountable. Rarely would a private citizen want their lives, past transgressions, decisions, policy choices or their intellect exposed to public scrutiny, but when one enters politics or entertainment or any position where they will be seen and heard by the public, that's exactly what they do. It's tough. Whatever errors in judgment, mis-quotes, trip ups, personality weakness or cognitive malfunctions occur will be immediately picked up and magnified by the media bullhorn - more so today than ever before.

Let's not forget that we have a bias towards retaining and even seeking out the negatives while tending to discount or undervalue the positives that we encounter. When a public figure does something 'wrong' or questionable, we jump all over them, seeking to heap blame upon blame. When that same individual does something 'right,' we tend to think, "Well, they're just doing their job. That's what we expect." As we discussed in Chapter 5, saying or doing something 'wrong' is to be avoided at all costs for the suffering at the hands of our fellow citizens is, seemingly, too great to bear.

When we think back to the *Eight Vicissitudes* or Eight *Worldly Concerns* discussed in Chapter 8, Bias in Wise Decision Making, it becomes clear that in trying to achieve the four things we are drawn to; fame, gain, pleasure and praise we open ourselves up to criticism including; shame, loss, pain and censure. It's a constant push/pull situation.

There is much wisdom in learning about ones strengths and weaknesses, because when we know of our shortcomings, we can better act to improve ourselves, prepare our defences or be proactive in some way that can minimize the impact of those weakness in our decision making, policy choices and public personae.

Effective Communication Skills

In some ways, this takes us right back to Chapter 1 - Communications. How we speak, the words we choose, the body language we present and the emotionality (or lack thereof) of the presentation all fuse to present a picture of the speaker. If the words are inappropriate, harsh, dismissive or rude, the speaker is perceived in one way. Should the words be kind, gentle, well spoken and sensible, they will be perceived in another.

One does not need to be a 'great orator' in order to be an effective communicator. When we think of great orators of the past eighty years we might conjure up names widely recognizable such as Winston Churchill, Franklin D. Roosevelt, John F. Kennedy, Ronald

Reagan, Mahatma Gandhi, Marie Colvin, Martin Luther King Jr. or Betty Friedan, yet, these men and women were not born with the inmate ability to stand and deliver speeches that proved to be moving, powerful, significant and transformational.

These men and women, along with their speech writers, had to sit down and work on what was to be said. They practiced and rehearsed every line. In some cases they recorded themselves so they could both see and hear what their message would look like. They were rarely confident in their abilities, although their resolve was unshakable. In the case of FDR, his wife, Eleanor, occasionally wondered whether her husband would be able to overcome his fear of public speaking and actually deliver the speeches he'd laboured so long over. She found the long pauses in some of his speeches almost unbearable and wondered if, indeed, he would go on.

As mentioned earlier, sometimes coming up with wise thoughts and words is a matter of sitting down and giving it deep and concentrated thought. It rarely comes naturally. Instead it's the result of effort and practice. It needs the ability to stay on message - and not go off script - to deliver a focused speech that is clear and concise.

In some speakers, we hear clear, unambiguous messages in their addresses. Churchill was not unclear in what he expected of the citizens of Britain when he delivered, "We Shall Fight on the Beaches." Martin Luther King Jr. was not unclear when he delivered, "I Have A Dream," in 1963. On the other hand we shake our heads when we hear rambling, off script, unfocused and confusing messages from other leaders.

Donald Trump, speaking in Sun City's Magnolia Hall, South Carolina, on July 21, 2016, is a notable example of extemporaneous public speaking, gone terribly wrong with the "My uncle used to tell me about nuclear before nuclear was nuclear," speech.

Another outstanding example of a speech gone wrong - even as heavily scripted as it was - is the Jimmy Carter, "What's Wrong With America" speech delivered back in 1979. He was trying to deliver an inspiring speech about the energy crisis dogging the country at that time, but didn't get around to the issue until nearly the end of the sermon at which point he offered exactly one short paragraph of ineffective, vague and not particularly useful solutions. Most of his time was spent telling the American public what was wrong with them.

When addressing the public, it's rarely a good idea to go off script, ad-lib, speak extemporaneously or make it up on the fly. It's much wiser to take the time to learn the speech, maybe help write it, fully understand it, fact check it, refer to notes on stage and not try to impress your audience with your off-the-cuff witticisms. Using a teleprompter might not be such a bad idea.

Still, if you know the material like the back of your hand and you're sure of your audience, an experienced speaker *may* be able to address a specific topic without notes.

Political Proficiency

Similar to organizational ability, one's political awareness and the ability to build a network of contacts both within and outside your sphere of influence and interest is critical. One needs to know who represents the 'enemy' and who represents the 'friend.' The wisdom lays in the ability to reach across party lines, bring in others with contradictory views and still be able to move an agenda forward to achieve the common good for the electorate or business organization.

Vision

This may be best described as an obsessive attention to achieving the identified common good through constant and unrelenting efforts of thought, speech and actions. An individual with vision represents and acts as the anchor for all policy and action decisions that could possibly be utilized to help achieve the articulated common good.

Where a vision is lacking, there will be internal inconsistently, that, when viewed from the outside, may suggest confusion, incoherence and lack of good judgement, which serves only to erode trust and allow the thin-end-of-the-wedge for attack on policy or actions from those opposed to the individual or their cause. Employees, staff or electorate will be less supportive of a leader with a lack of vision, for they will never know if the actions they take, on behalf of their leader, are 'right' or 'wrong.' They will not fully understand their role in the organization or how they will best achieve the common good.

Elon Musk, then CEO of SpaceX, Tesla Motors and other business ventures, is nothing, if not visionary. His vision is to literally drag the personal and cargo transportation industry out of the fossil fuel era into the electric era - singlehandedly if necessary. There is no ambiguity in what he wants to do. When he says, *"I really do encourage other manufacturers to bring electric cars to market. It's a good thing, and they need to bring it to market and keep iterating and improving and make better and better electric cars, and that's what going to result in humanity achieving a sustainable transport future. I wish it was growing faster than it is,"* there is little room for wondering what he means.*

The wisdom here, lies in the ability to not only to create and hold a vision of the common good, but to clearly and accurately articulate that vision to bring about meaningful change in support of the common good.

Cognitive Style

Cognitive style refers, not to an individuals decisions or actions, but to the mental process they go through in order to reach those decisions. We all vary in how we gather, correlate, process, store, retrieve and interpret information. *How* we solve problems is also a component of our cognitive style. When individuals exhibit a cognitive style similar to ours, we tend to agree, believe and trust them more.

Left Brain, Right Brain

It's widely agreed among psychologists, that there is something of a duality in our brains. The left half (or left hemisphere) of our brain is adept at handling facts, figures, statistics, process, sequence, logic

---

* Musk's response during a 2013 earnings conference call, when Morgan Stanley analyst, Adam Jonas, asked about the BMW i3.

and what not. The right hemisphere, being more adroit at handling spacial concepts, colour, images, sound and the interpretation of emotions, among other things. Left and right hemisphere work in concert to bring some sense to the incoming information from the world at large.

We occasionally hear the term, 'She's a right-brain thinker," or "He's coming at the problem from a left-brain perspective.' These terms suggest two different ways to approach or interpret a problem—the first from an analytical, data-driven methodology and the second using concepts, sound and emotions. Both can be equally valid and produce a wise way forward, but their styles are different and may seem foreign to one another.

Up And Down

Cognitive psychologists have also identified a second dimension to our thinking, that usually referred to as up and down or abstract vs concrete. In the abstract, we exhibit aptitude at handling speculative, hypothetical and abstract concepts. In the concrete, we are more adept at handling the here and now - the ideas that can be verified with our senses.

There are a few other personality indicator assessment tools out there which are widely used;

- **Myers-Briggs** (Myers-Briggs Type Indicators or MBTI) is a popular assessment tool, in which individuals 'score' themselves on various statements and in the end they fall into various personality types in which the individual prefers to operate, given their judgments and perceptions.

- **Predictive Index** (Pi), "A person's behavioural pattern provides a nuanced understanding of their drives and needs. But when you need to understand someone with a quick glance our reference profiles can distill countless behavioural patterns into a handful of recognizable profiles."

- **The Adaptiv Resilience Factor Inventory** uses the concept of emotional resiliency as a lens through which to view the individual. People's lives are never a straight line. Each life is bedevilled

with ups and downs. This tool attempts to assess how a person handles major setbacks and failures
- **Traitify** displays a set of photos or images to test-takers, and the candidate clicks "Me" or "Not Me." After a couple dozen images, you get an assessment. I took the 3 minute test and my assessment reads as follow;

Action-Taker/Naturalist

"You are an independent hard worker who is active and full of energy. You feel best when experiencing the natural world, and you try to be outdoors as much as possible. You have a fondness for animals and don't shy away from hard work. You prefer to take matters into your own hands and complete projects yourself. If you are going to spend time with others, you would prefer getting together to work on shared projects or hobbies, or to take part in an activity like hiking, camping, or gardening. You don't like to be idle and always want to have a project either for work or pleasure. Your friends and family know they can always count on you when they need anything. You recharge when alone, enjoying solitary time to get lost in your work and appreciate a job well done."

It's like I'm reading the first paragraph of my résumé. This is pretty much how I think of myself, most of the time. There are always occasions where I have to put on the hat of "accountant" and crunch numbers but it's not my favorite task. What this might mean is that I'm probably not the first choice for a team-based project that is supposed to overhaul the accounting system of a major corporation, even though I have a solid grasp of bookkeeping and managerial accounting (I went to college for it, after all). It's also very true that I don't like to be idle and always need a project on the go. It's odd that there's no mention of my fondness for fedoras.

From a wisdom point of view, knowing *how* we think around specific issues and understanding how *others* might think around those same issues, means that we might better understand them. Better understanding means we may be better able to find common ground and thinking in order to move more quickly and smoothly to decisions and actions that better obtain the articulated common good.

This is all brought up in discussion, not because it gives you an edge to "manipulate' someone, based upon their thinking preferences (this isn't a PSYOPS situation after all) but so we can quickly find common ground so that both parties can move forward towards the common good - whatever that may be.

Cognitive style is not a 'locked in' mindset. It can vary from situation to situation. Comfort, competency, urgency, timeliness, resources, etc. can all influence an individual's cognitive style. An individual who is not naturally a 'leader' may easily assume that role in the event of a natural disaster in which time is of the essence. Still there is a tendency towards a 'default' style upon which any individual typically relies.

10.1 Mental Re-Training

So, we've talked a little about what emotional intelligence or emotional stability might look like and perhaps how it might be recognized, but what can we do to become emotionally stable ourselves or at least encourage our emotional stability? Can we re-train ourselves so that we can get our emotions under control quicker and with less lasting effect? After all, being able to see and think clearly, being able to understand issues and communicate effectively are two building blocks that help us give rise to wisdom.

Speaking from my own experience, I can say that when negative feelings arise I try to do three things to help me regain my emotional balance;

1. Re-train my emotional reactions
2. Modify my thinking
3. Change my habits

Re-train Emotions
When it comes to emotions – especially the dark emotions such as grief, anxiety, fear or despair – that trigger major depressive episodes, we are not completely powerless, although sometimes it may seem like that. Like a dark storm approaching, we may be able

to see it coming, but think there is little we can do about it. We must recognize that dark emotions exist and they will have a tendency to seem much more powerful than positive emotions, but they can be controlled, at least to some degree.

If we were to identify a lasting sadness, we do things that help counteract the emotions. We take a walk in the countryside, go out with friends, take some exercise. We might talk about our negative feelings with someone we trust. We cannot simply wave a magic wand or pop and pill and expect these emotions go away, but we can minimize the length of time they dominate us and limit their impact on our psyche. Recognize them, name them and try to see how they impact us. Of course, where deep and lasting sadness arises, it may be a good idea to talk with a psychotherapist or other mental healthcare professional.

Reappraisal

When we begin to experience negative thoughts, as above, we need to recognize and name them without judgement. Once we do that, try to look at any positive benefits of the situation that have brought up the negative emotions. Is there some way we can identify any good from this or at least identify aspects that aren't completely devastating? Is there some way we can look at this as a difficult challenge to overcome rather than an emotionally devastating situation? Perhaps we could imagining what a trusted friend or advisor might say about this situation would help. Thinking back to how we handled a similar episode in the past might help overcome lasting negative emotions.

Stabilize the Whole Self

When we are trying to get our negative emotions under control, we shouldn't ignore other aspects of our lives. The other areas, some of which may even be a source of positivity, can be supportive in our attempt to recover from the negativity. Going out with friends, eating well, taking exercise, doing things that help you de-stress will go a long way to improve your mood.

View Setbacks as Opportunities

Setbacks are part of everyone's life. This probably won't make us feel any better when all we can see and hear is failure and stress over a particular situation, but remember that we've overcome other negative situations before. We might look at how we solved them or what activities we participated in that brought us out of a negative mood. There is considerable truth in the adage that adversity builds strength - but you may need help along the way.

10.2 Modify Thinking

Compartmentalize Your Thinking

More easily said than done, for our lives have become so interconnected between, sports, work, home, travel, etc. that it's not easy to separate one out from the others. Still, if work is causing the negative mood, we might try to compartmentalize that section of our life so it doesn't seep into and contaminate *everything* we do. Try to leave the worries of work, *at work*. We might think about the enjoyment we receive from our favorite sports team, or our home life or hobbies. Try not to let the concerns of our job drain enjoyment from other areas of our life. Identify where the stress or negativity is coming from so it can be addressed and not taint everything.

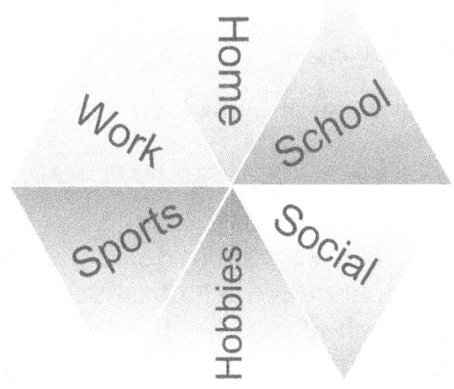

Remembering Differently

If you just got fired from work, that memory will linger for a long time and threaten your general well-being in many ways. Try to remember the circumstances of that day differently. Obviously you're not going to forget that you were fired, but you might think about other aspects of that day; how you were dressed, what the weather was like, how you got to work, who you met afterwards, etc. Try to remember the situation differently, focusing on any positives.

Our brains can, with attention and diligence, learn to think differently and bad experiences (those which may give rise to negative emotions and unhealthy stress) can, essentially, be 'overwritten' with positive thinking.

According to WebMD.com stress and worry will have adverse affects upon pre-existing conditions, including, but not limited to;

- Heart disease
- Asthma
- Obesity
- Diabetes
- Headaches
- Depression and anxiety
- Gastrointestinal problems and
- Alzheimer's disease

Getting stress and worry under control will have obvious health benefits.

Think Neutrally

It's very hard to think positively after you've just experienced a negative situation that has put you into a negative mood. That much of a mental leap is a bit much for most of us. Instead, try moving from a negative emotion to a more neutral one. If you're experiencing negative emotions around your poor performance at a pubic speaking engagement, then you might try thinking, "With more and perhaps smaller gigs, I'm only going to get better at this." Going from negative to neutral is a more natural step than going from negative to positive.

If we have a heated discussion with a friend, we may be in a negative mood for a) having said things we might now regret b) having put them in a bad mood and c) acting unskilfully in the first place. We may quickly remind ourselves that we've been here before and will be here again. We're all adults and will get over it. An apology from one side or the other does wonders. Remembering and taking action will move us from the negative emotions, to neutral feeling to finally end up in a positive mood again. It may take a few hours, days or weeks, but we get there, if we apply ourselves to the task.

Be Mindful

In the case of negative emotions, being mindful is recognizing that often the negativity comes from memories of the past and worries about the future. Both of these are largely beyond our control. The past is irretrievable and the future is only hypothesis. When we can take a moment, centre ourselves and focus on the here and now, we can regain some balance. When we get a little further on in this book, specifically the chapter on meditation, we'll go into this much further. For now, coming back to the present might simply mean sitting down, closing our eyes, being aware of our breathing and concentrating on that - nothing else.

Focusing on the body, through our breathing, can bring us back to the present, but an effort must be made to get there. Sitting outside, perhaps on a bench in the sun, we might think, "The sun feels nice. The breeze is relaxing. I hear the birds and distant traffic. I can feel the bench beneath me. I can feel the ground under my feet." When negative thoughts arise, don't fuel them. Just identify them, name them and gently bring yourself back to the sun, breeze, birds, bench and ground - bring yourself back to the present.

10.3 Modify Habits

Build Connections

Keeping the friends we have and expanding our social network can often help when we experience emotional setbacks. Having friends to talk with will almost always help. But there may come a time when even your friends can't help and that's where professional therapy comes in. A registered psychotherapist or sociologist can help guide you back from debilitating, negative experiences, help find a positive way forward, provide coping strategies and sustain that progress over time.

Associate with Stable People

We all know we are affected by the individuals we associate with. When we hang out with unstable, emotionally negative individuals (who are not seeking help) they tend to bring us down. When we associate with positive, emotionally stable people, we tend to become more positive ourselves. When you identify with people who are negative, mistrustful, toxic and ridden with anxiety, we might begin to believe and feel that this is a normal state of affairs, but it is not.

Set Healthy Boundaries

We need to set boundaries that help us maintain good mental health. Sometimes we simply need to say, 'no' to a request if we think it will be too stressful. At the outset, this isn't always easy. If shopping with your partner is stressing you out, how do you gently say, 'no' in a way that won't offend. Your partner may have thought that you actually liked shopping with them. It may even be true that at one time you did, but not now, and you need to make that clear.

You may have had enough of American politics for now. Perhaps it's stressing you out. You might say to your friends, "Do you think we might avoid that topic for a week or so?" This isn't to say you'd never speak of politics again, but you may just need a rest, for now.

Recognize Co-Dependency

According to Mental Health America; *"Co-dependency is a learned behaviour that can be passed down from one generation to another. It is an emotional and behavioural condition that affects an individual's ability to have a healthy, mutually satisfying relationship. It is also known as 'relationship addiction' because people with codependency often form or maintain relationships that are one-sided, emotionally destructive and/or abusive. The disorder was first identified about ten years ago as the result of years of studying interpersonal relationships in families of alcoholics. Co-dependent behaviour is learned by watching and imitating other family members who display this type of behaviour."**

Becoming too emotionally reliant on others is a symptom of co-dependency. You may begin to feel that your peace is dependent upon their happiness. You may begin to share activities that make *them* happy, but may not bring you peace or joy. Sometimes in relationships, we feel the need to take care of others more than we need to take care of ourselves. But when we begin to recognize we are our own person, we can begin to separate ourselves from emotional dependency upon others.

Co-dependency usually is the result of early childhood development, within a family unit that displays co-dependent behaviour. Treatment typically involves exploration of the patients childhood and the links to their current behaviours. Treatment generally also involves helping the individual to get in touch with repressed feelings that may have been buried since childhood, thus allowing the patient to experience a full range of emotions once again. Of course, this discussion is really well beyond the scope of this book, but being able to recognize a co-dependent relationship can be helpful, as then professional help can be sought to break negative patterns.

Wait it Out
Trite, but true. Everything passes with time. Once again, change and impermanence is the central theme of all our lives. As we age, there is a tendency to be more calm. What troubles us today, may not trouble us tomorrow, or next week or next year. As we age, fewer things send us into an emotional free fall or if they do, the episodes tend to be less severe and of shorter duration.

How all This Helps
Remember, the key point of this chapter is that we learn to build emotional resilience and stability so that when it comes to approach-

---

* Mental Health America. https://www.mhanational.org/issues/co-dependency

ing decisions or actions that are going to require our best thinking, we are calm, as objective as we can be and as free from debilitating emotions as possible.

None of this is to suggest that we try develop stoic personalities, free from emotion, but only that we recognize when we are being driven by negative emotions. This is especially important at a time when good decision making is needed. When we learn to recognize how our emotions may be driving our decision making, we will be in a better position to make wise choices.

Conclusions

Don't try to control everything. Much of our everyday life is beyond our control and when we recognize that, come to grips with it and act accordingly, our emotions become more stable.

Don't believe everything your mind tells you. 5 + 5 = 11. If you read that and thought, "5 + 5 = 11" you knew it was wrong, even though your mind *thought* it. Your mind doesn't always tell you reasonable things. Just because you *think* something, doesn't make it true.

Try not to judge yourself for how you feel. Sometimes our emotions get the better of us and we should try to avoid judging ourselves for having negative feelings. Give yourself a bit of compassion. You wouldn't chastise a friend if *they* had a bit of cry over a beer, so why do that to yourself.

Don't try to find meaning in everything. Not everything is about us. While our brains run themselves ragged trying to find meaning in every little scrap of information or every occurrence, that doesn't mean that everything has meaning. Sometimes stuff happens for no meaningful reason. We all *want* things to have meaning, but things just aren't that accommodating.

Try to make decisions based on your values, not your emotions. Sometimes our feelings get in the way of our values and that conflict may lead to bad decisions. "It feels good lo lay in bed, because I'm not motivated," may be in direct conflict with getting out of bed and doing something which you value, like going for a walk, meeting friends, grocery shopping, etc. We make decisions both on our emotions *and* our values, so we need to recognize that and take it into account around wise decision making.

Key Points Summary - Emotional Stability

Re-Train Negative Emotions	<ul><li>Reappraisal - is there some way we can re-assess the situation or recognize any positive aspect</li><li>Stabilize the whole self - When we experience negative emotions, don't forget the other, more positive areas of our life</li><li>Setbacks as opportunities - think of any positive things that can be learned from major setbacks</li></ul>
Modify Thinking	<ul><li>Where possible, compartmentalize your thinking - negative aspects of life at work can bleed into home life</li><li>Remember differently - When negative situations arise, you may be able to remember other aspects of that day that we more positive and focus on those</li><li>Think neutrally - going from negative feeling to neutral feelings is more natural than going from negative directly to positive</li><li>Be mindful - recognize that often the negativity comes from memories of the past and worries about the future. Leave the past where it is and concentrate on improving things for the future</li></ul>
Modify Habits	<ul><li>Build connections with others - get out with friends, join clubs, take a course, walk in nature</li><li>Hang out with stable people - limit contact with those who bring you down</li><li>Set healthy boundaries - learn to say, 'no'</li><li>Recognize co-dependency - avoid developing relationships that are one sided, emotionally destructive and or abusive</li><li>Wait it out. We would do well to remember that all things pass with time.en and understood, compassion can well up more easily</li></ul>

11. Meditation, Concentration and Patience

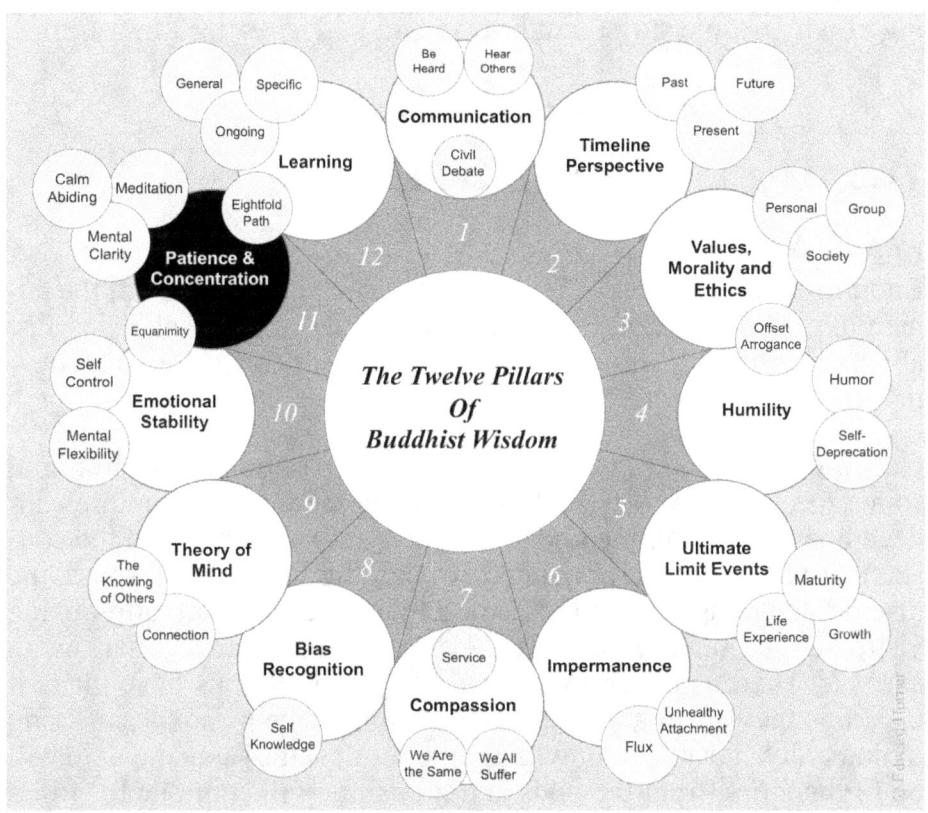

11.1 The Four Noble Truths

IT'S ALMOST IMPOSSIBLE to think, write or talk about Buddhism and its relationship with wisdom, without referencing the The Four Noble Truths and coming to some understanding of their role in the life of a practicing Buddhist. Unless we understand how we suffer, what the causes are and how suffering can end, we can't really get to how we can encourage the development of wisdom and so we need to spend a few pages on the Four Noble Truths.

When Siddhartha Gautama (the man who ultimately became The Buddha - the Enlightened One) finally decided to sit down under a bodhi tree in the town of Bodh Gaya, in what is now the Indian state of Bihar, he was intent on not only coming to a complete understanding of why people suffer, but how to end it. He realized four truths.

11.2 The First Noble Truth

People Suffer
Buddhism doesn't treat suffering as some tangential branch of the human experience, but rather as a central tenet of its teachings. Just about everything begins with suffering and seeking a way of relieving it.

One might imagine Siddhartha standing on a hill one moonlit night, sometime around 528BCE. Looking up at the stars, he implores, indeed begs, any or all the gods of India to intervene and end the constant suffering of human beings. To end the wars, the sickness, the disease, the hunger, the injuries or any manner of deprivation being visited upon human kind. He cups his ear and waits. There is no answer. There is never an answer. Any and all gods have made it clear that they are either unable or unwilling to help end the suffering of humanity. Unable or unwilling, the result is the same; no help will be forthcoming from the gods and humanity will continue to suffer. This was the obvious first truth.

The Suffering of Existence
In this first truth, People Suffer, we might start with the simple recognition that just being alive, just being human is a guarantee that we are going to experience pain and suffering. We experience suffering in childbirth, sickness, disease, injury, old age and death.

Simply being human means that pain, suffering and death await each and every one of us. There is no escaping it. No deity is going to bail us out. No diet or exercise regime is going to save us from our ultimate end or help much in the suffering department. Tummy tucks, facelifts, hair pieces and laser vision correction will only give the illusion of assistance or, at best, exchange one suffering for another.

"All our days pass away under your wrath;
We finish our years with a moan.
Our days may come to seventy years,
or eighty, if our strength endures;
yet the best of them are but trouble and sorrow,
for they quickly pass, and we fly away."

~ Psalms 90:9-14 NIV

I go to my doctor about three times a year. He takes my blood pressure, listens to my chest with a stethoscope, occasionally takes some blood and asks me, "So, how are you feeling, generally?" I might reply, "I have sore knees when I first get out of bed," or "If I stand up too quickly I get a little light-headed." He typically offers some suggestions, but also includes the adjunct, "Of course that's normal for a man of your age." I take no particular solace in that, in-so-far as dying will be "normal" for a man of my age, at some point.

"If I'd known I was going to live so long,
I'd have taken better care of myself.

~ Adolph Zukor as he approached his 100th birthday

All Pervasive Suffering

The second way we suffer is on the personal level. This is beyond the suffering of being human and having a vulnerable body. This is not merely an intellectualizing of the outside world's suffering, but our own, personal and deeply felt mental suffering.

We might not have lost our house or loved ones in a tornado, but none-the-less, we suffer almost daily. We suffer the wait for the streetcar that should have been here five minutes ago. We suffer the indignity of having to wait for a slow internet connection at The Remarkable Bean. We suffer having missed the last blueberry scone at Starbucks that we had craved and must now settle for the cranberry-lemon. We suffer a loss at having an "economy" car waiting for us at the car rental place, when we had specifically ordered a "luxury" sedan. We suffer when we hear that a friend is earning more money than us for doing the same job at a different company. We suffer when we learn that the University of Toronto hasn't accepted us for admission and now we have to attend our second, third or fourth choice.

This suffering is caused by things or situations not meeting our expectations. We became attached to one idea or one expectation and when that idea doesn't pan out, we get disappointed and suffer.

Now clearly the vast majority of us don't suffer every day all day long. In fact, we get a few good days in there, where everything looks pleasant and we have a bit of fun and we forget about wants and cravings. It's a good thing we do, otherwise we'd all end up jumping off a bridge in despair. Still, eventually we will begin to think that even these good days aren't good enough and we will begin to crave and suffer all over again.

From our own experience and observations we know life is like this. This is all pervasive suffering. This is dukkha, a Pali word suggesting a feeling that life is somehow not fully satisfying. We might characterize it using words such as, disappointment, sadness, displeasure or disillusionment. When we recognize dukkha, accept it, and live our lives understanding it, then we can begin to examine why and how this is so, and work to suffer less.

Pain vs. Suffering
This might be a good time to bring in the idea of pain, that physical manifestation of the body that tells us something is wrong, something is amiss. When we talk about pain we almost always seem to bring in suffering as if to have pain is to suffer or to suffer is to experience pain, but this isn't quite as it seems.

Pain, simply put, is the body's way of telling us that something is wrong. The pain of a sprained ankle is clear evidence that the ankle has been damaged and needs attention and should not be walked on. The pain of an aching back is clear evidence that something is pulled, overused, damaged in some way and needs rest or attention. Pain is not really an optional manifestation of human existence. It comes when it comes for whatever reason or reasons. The difference between pain and suffering is that suffering is optional and we address this in the next Noble Truth.

The Suffering of Change or Loss

A third way we suffer is through attachment. We get ideas into our head about how things ought to be and when we realized that they are not, we suffer. When we sprain an ankle, we experience the unpleasantness of pain. That pain, unless we take some pain killing drugs, is not optional. It comes because the body is telling us that something is wrong. The suffering comes in when we begin to deliberate over what a sprained ankle might mean.

Let's say that we sprained our ankle training for a marathon. We'd been training a lot. We were putting in 50 miles a week and getting ready to peak our performance next week during the big event.

Sure, we didn't have any real plans on winning the event, but we had our goal set of lowering our personal best time. We had enlisted the help of our spouses, employer (taking time off to train maybe) a trainer and a unique diet that would all converge next month at the marathon. Then comes that fateful evening when we're out for a training run and we step off the curb not quite right. Down we go! The pain, while uncomfortable and even tolerable, is nothing compared to the thought that all our time and effort has been wasted in training for the marathon. It's instantly clear that we are not going to be able to run the race. Not only that, but we likely won't be able to take that canoe trip we had all planned. Crap! We likely won't even be able to play softball every Friday night at the local park.

Disappointment, heaped upon disappointment. This is suffering caused by change. Things are going to change and we don't like it one bit. We agonize over our misfortune and wonder, "Why has this happened to me? What have I done that this should be so?" We suffer along, trying to figure out why something has occurred.

We start with denial that anything has really changed, but that quickly drops away when the ankle begins to swell to the size of a grapefruit. We then imagine there must be some way to make this work - some bargain to be struck somehow that will allow us to run the race, but that quickly fades when we realized the recovery time for this type of injury is well over a month. We then try to blame someone else for our misfortune. "Damn that curb designer! If only the curb had sloped rather than dropped, I'd not be in this predicament now. Maybe I can sue the City."

We run through all this mental anguish every time we do things like this. We are not quick to accept things as they are. We have delusions that we are in control, when really we aren't, but we are not able to see that and that is where the suffering comes from - thinking that things should be one way, but turn out another. There is no wisdom in ignoring that we are not in control of everything at all times and things will often change.

The Suffering of Conditioning

Another way we suffer is found in our conditioning. In a way, and apart from the suffering of being human, we are programmed to suffer. We are a product of our form; our seeing, our hearing, our smelling, tasting and, physical sensation. These "sense doors" are the only way we interact with the world and they are limited in what they bring to us.

Imagine if you had the eyes of an eagle or the strength of a lion or the scent facilities of a blood hound. Your world would be very different. You could see and smell things that normal humans could not. You could leap higher, run faster and lift heavier objects than any normal person. You'd interact differently with the world because you'd experience the world differently.

In Buddhism, we say we are the product of our Five Skandhas discussed in Chapter 4.1 - Wisdom and The Three Mental Defilements. Our lives are tied up in the psycho-physical aggregates, the Five

Skandhas or Five Aggregates of experience. All our future experiences are bound up in our present and past experiences because they are pre-conditioned by our skandhas.

An apple smells like an apple, not because it actually is an apple, but because we are preconditioned by our nose sense organ to identify it as being such. If an apple were to smell like a veggie dog on the BBQ, we'd be understandably confused.

A brief reminder that the Five Skandhas are;

Form; The body and all the sense organs (ears, eyes, tongue, etc)

Sensation; Feeling an object or situation as being good, bad or neutral

Perception (cognition); Being able to determine the existence of a tree or the sound of a bell, for example

Mental Formations; Thoughts, opinions, mental habits, preferences, aversions, etc.

Consciousness; That part of us which discerns or supports all experience.

These are the five filters through we interact and experience the world around us. Everything is affected by their presence. Understanding this, it is no surprise that we have come to see the world as we do. It's the blending and mixing proportions of the five skandhas that allow people to interpret the world differently from each other. Some people may place great weight on form sensation while others may placer greater weight on mental formations, thus having a different take on the world.

Some people will place great value on what they hear, despite what they may see or smell. Others may place great value on what they see, despite what is heard, etc. then using their mental formations and life experiences, preferences and aversions will draw conclusions on this recent experience - good, bad or indifferent. Different conclusions will be drawn by different people because we employ the five skandhas differently.

When people have a different view from our own, it is largely because of the five skandhas and the unique life experiences which they possess. There is great wisdom in understanding this. When we recognize that we too are affected by our five skandhas, we can better understand the world around us and how or why people may have different views of the same circumstances.

11.3 The Second Noble Truth

Suffering Has Causes

Just as pain in the body has physical causes, so suffering has mental causes. First and foremost of these is the illusion of permanence and that was discussed in some detail back in Chapter 6 .

The Delusion of Independence

Another way we suffer is that we fail to understand that everything - absolutely everything - is dependent upon other things that came before. We have this fascinating illusion that we are "financially independent," "independent business owners," "independent contractors," or "free lance writers," etc. Nothing could be further from the truth.

We too often fail to recognize that there is no such thing as independent arising. Nothing comes from nothing. Everything manifests only because other things have come before, Lawrence Krauss notwithstanding.

Take, for example the notion of "financial independence." Without a global financial system to support our Canadian dollar, we only have paper promises that can be destroyed by water or fire. We are absolutely and utterly dependent upon someone else accepting our money. How, "independent" do you feel when the debit card machine isn't working at the store? Without a bank to store your money, where would you put it, the stock market? Then you are at the mercy of the stock traders and their good will – and their goodwill extends exactly as far as your margin account allows. Would it be safer in a money market fund? Maybe, but they are invested in the stock market and dependent upon the vagaries of that machine as well – and we know the investment houses have your best interests at heart. I mean you just have to look at the loving kindness they displayed around packaging bad mortgages with other bad debt and selling them as "investment quality," instruments. Only through the interventions of your elected officials did this Zhentarim of jackals not drag the world financial system back to the middle ages.

So, to say or believe in your financial independence is, really, a bit too much to accept. And, in the end, if you truly believe you are the Warren Buffett of your neighbourhood and control your own financial destiny, you are still utterly and totally dependent on hundreds of thousands of people who are charged with enforcing the banking laws, trading practices, internet security, bank vault designers, accountants, lawyers, judges, etc, to protect your money. Your "independence," is really *interdependence*. Without the legions of 'others' we are quite frankly, screwed. Again, the idea of "independence" is sheer fantasy.

Karma

The idea of karma is a concept well established and imbedded in all Buddhist traditions. It's the idea that as we go through life, our thoughts, words and actions have consequences. In non-Buddhist terms we might just say, "What goes around, comes around." Those consequences, those "comeuppances," may not be apparent or even manifest in any obvious way, but they occur none-the-less. Unless the consequences are obvious and immediate, we tend to forget about karma - we might have forgotten that something we said or did five years ago, is coming home to roost today. Other times, the consequences are more obvious and immediate.

Let me give an example from my personal life. Some years ago, I failed to renew the little sticker on my license plate by the due date. I had just opened an espresso bar in Toronto, and was having a tough time making ends meet. I was hoping to put off the renewal until the end of the month, just a couple of weeks away. Well, I got caught and was issued a ticket. My fault, I totally get it. So, about a month later, I received a reminder in the mail about the fine, which I failed to read fully, for included in the reminder (it turned out) was a little bit about paying by a certain date otherwise my license could be suspended. Well, of course I didn't pay – like I said, I didn't read it fully. To be clear, I had renewed the sticker by this point, but I had not paid the fine. So about two months after that, I open my mail and was quite surprised to see my drivers license has been suspended! My shock, was quickly followed by laughter with the instant recognition of the shifting world of dependent arising and karma. The cause was eventually followed by the effect. My actions, or in this case inaction, had resulted in the suspension of my license. I paid the fine, then the re-instatement fee to get my driver's license back and everything has been right since.

That, of course is an obvious example of karma hard at work. The difficulty for most people is that there often isn't a direct and obvious link between words or actions and a karmic effect. Without that obvious link, we tend to either forget about karma or dismiss it as irrelevant in our daily lives.

Giving a homeless person a couple of dollars to help buy his or her next meal is an action that has karmic effect. It might not be obvious at the time of giving, but it will, somewhere down the line, have an effect. Many years might pass until the effect comes home to roost - and that's even if you're aware of it.

Those unfamiliar with Buddhism may think of karma as "good karma" or "bad karma." When something happens to us that is bad (we might have our car stolen) people occasionally say, "Oh, bad karma," but karma is neither good nor bad. Just because something 'bad' happens to us, doesn't mean it was necessarily karmic in nature.

Like the ocean, karma just exists. We tend to personify things around us, giving them human qualities that they, in and of themselves, don't really possess. The ocean isn't "good" or "bad." The ocean is just the ocean. Any characteristics we give to it, are our own projections, based on the fact that we are human. In the same way, karma is not good or bad, it just is. Karma is what Buddhists understand as a condition they create and carry around with them all their life.

As we accumulate karma we are giving rise to conditions that will be in effect when things happen to us. Have you ever notice that when bad things happen to some people, they come out of it smelling like roses? Might it be because they've accumulated a lifetime of 'good' karma? Maybe, but maybe not.

This isn't to say that all things that happen to us are karmic in nature. Things happen for lots of reasons; natural phenomenon, genes and chromosomes, random chaos and of course, karma.

Rebirth

One can't really talk about karma, without bringing up the Buddhist idea of rebirth. It's rather amazing, really, that we managed to get this far without broaching the topic at all. Volumes have been written on the topic by Buddhist scholars, venerable Rinpoches, Monks, Gegans, Lamas and lay practitioners aplenty, so we won't dwell on the idea here, but some discussion needs to take place, for, after all, a lot of wisdom in Buddhism is aimed at providing the practitioner with a 'good' rebirth, a rebirth at a 'higher level,' with the ultimate goal of escaping rebirth altogether and disappearing from this Earthly realm to enter a place of no–birth/no–death - Nirvana.

In simple terms, we humans are born into a difficult world. We've already seen that just being human we inherit a life that sort of sucks. A life that's filled with suffering of all kinds is the legacy left to us by those who gave birth to us. Our parents had lust, they had sex and we were born. It may sound trite, but I believe we are here because we were born and we haven't died yet – not much more to it than that. Our existence on this planet is a result of dependent arising. Circumstances came together and we arrived nine months later.

The question remains, "Is this our first go 'round on this planet?" Most Buddhists come to conclude that it is not our first trip here, but rather, we have been reborn time and time again. The same conditions repeatedly arise that continue to create the conditions of our rebirth–death–rebirth cycle. We are born, suffer, age and die, time and time again. The same conditions arise and the result is the same – a lot like Bill Murray in Harold Ramis and Danny Rubin's film, *Groundhog Day*.

It sounds a bit hackneyed, but I believe we are here because we were born and we haven't died yet – not much more to it than that.

The good thing is we don't seem to remember any past lives. Nothing of what we think of as "us" seems to survive a rebirth. Let's hope it doesn't because then we'd be wracked with anxiety around all the stupid, bad or even evil things we might have done in earlier lives.

In one of my earlier books —*My Buddhist Journal*, 2016—I questioned the very premise of rebirth;

"Have I lived in other lifetimes? A good question for someone who has no illusions about an afterlife and some real issues around rebirth. How would I know if I had been around the block before? The Buddhist texts I've read offer only the most elusive suggestions as to how you might know, but nothing you could test. Yet, rebirth seems to be a continual narrative in Buddhism and a few other eastern religions. This rebirth business is, in fact, the one area of Buddhism that I have great doubts about.

Everything else about Buddhism asks that you, "Don't just take our word for it, go and test it yourself." Rebirth does not offer this adjunct. I once asked one of the instructors at my meditation centre about this business and how to test it. His response was that we have dreams that tell us of our past lives and that we, "know" what lives we've lived once we awaken. That is the closest I've come to an answer and I'm totally unsatisfied."

It really comes down to three possibilities;

1. The Buddha promoted the idea of rebirth, rebirth is a thing, so he was right
2. The Buddha promoted the idea of rebirth, rebirth isn't a thing, so he was wrong
3. The Buddha promoted the idea of rebirth, we have no way of testing, so we don't know if Buddha was right or wrong.

I tend to think in the realm of the third possibility - I don't know if The Buddha was right or wrong, but does it matter? Everything else I 'know' about Buddhism has been tested, tried and true. The four noble Truths, The Eightfold Path, the Five Precepts the Eight Worldly Concerns, etc. have, proven, upon examination, observation and direct first-hand experience, to be valid and found fit-for-purpose – which is to create better understanding of the human condition and help relieve suffering.

It seems clear that what The Buddha taught were ways of thinking, speaking and acting that would, when diligently applied and with good intent, at the very least, help us reduce our suffering in this lifetime. When we apply these prescriptions to our life, we see transformative results - we suffer less and those around us suffer less.

It seems reasonable to imagine that if there is rebirth, and our experience of the dharma has lessened our suffering in this lifetime, then having good karma might help us in our next go 'round - if there's another go 'round to be had. There seems to be no downside. Obviously this isn't any form of 'proof' but if the benefits of preparing for a rebirth have no downside, why wouldn't we so prepare? There seems to be some wisdom in accumulating 'good' karma in this lifetime if only to help us relieve our suffering (and that of others) within this lifetime. Then, if rebirth *is* a thing, we may have set ourselves up for a 'good' rebirth or maybe even reaching Nirvana and the possibility of not returning to this crumby life on Earth ever again.

Samsara

The world we have come to know and love or know and despise, or know and be indifferent about, is not perfect, regardless of your circumstances. We've identified it's imperfections and called it *dukkha*, a feeling of dissatisfaction and disillusionment. It's a world in which dependent arising has created conditions that have caused us to be born, feel pain, suffer, age and finally die. The same conditions exist after our death and the result is the same - we are born again, feel pain again, suffer some more, age once more and kick off in the end. But the conditions still haven't changed! We have to go through that again and again and again for countless re-births, because neither us or the conditions which gave rise to us, have changed. It's an endless cycle and that cycle is called *samsara*.

Samsara is a Sanskrit word and it is variously translated as 'wandering' or 'world," and implies a cyclic or circuitous existence. Like karma, it's a well established and understood concept in all Buddhist traditions. It is a world in which we go 'round and 'round, being born, ageing, dying and being reborn again. Eons of cyclical human suffering and pain – a *Kafkaesque* world from which any reasonable person would want to escape, but, being born human, into a world that hasn't changed, being heavily influenced by our five skandhas and having delusions about how the world works, it seems impossible that we will be able to change anything!

We need a major intervention

Nirvana

It seems that any religion that has a major deity, hopes for it's disciples to 'escape' into their god's realm, whatever that may be or look like. When we perform meritorious tasks, lead a "good" or "holy" life, helping others, kneeling in just the right way when worshipping the select god, reading or memorizing certain books or passages, then we will be rewarded with a "get out of samsara" card. We are allowed, or become able, to leave this cyclical life of suffering behind us.

Most religions seem to make it fairly simple. When we die we are usually "judged" by the deity or his/her surrogate and, if we are found to be in good standing, get to go to heaven. If we are found wanting in virtue, we either go to Hell (fire, brimstone, everlasting torment or some variation) or must return to Earth and go 'round again with the expectation of improvement, to get better, perform more meritorious tasks and deeds until our next judgement and are found, hopefully, to be up to snuff.

You'll recall our earlier allusion to Siddhartha, standing atop a hill on moonlit night, asking the gods to intervene in human suffering, but, receiving only silence in response. The man, quite reasonably, concluded the gods seemed either unable or unwilling to help. Siddhartha further concluded that we are left to find our own way out of samsara and our own way to relieve suffering.

As Siddhartha sought an answer to permanently end the suffering of humans, he asked for help from religious persons, land owners, men of royal descent, philosophers, doctors, wise men, men of business, yogis and aesthetics. He tried many suggestions, but found them all wanting in results. In the end, after years of trial and error, he came upon the realization that if we could have life, without birth, then there would be no further suffering. If we could, somehow, change the conditions that give rise to our re-birth into samsara, then re-birth could be prevented. There had to be a way to prevent re-birth into samsara.

Jumping ahead a bit, this brings up the question of what would take the place of samsara? Siddhartha, began to envision what a life without re-birth would look like. This world, this state of existence, he called Nirvana - a situation into which one "disappears" from the universe. It may be characterized as the extinction of all earthly desires and delusions. It would require a lot of change. It meant that one would have to extinguish the Three Poisons of the mind that would be a barrier to such a place; passion, aversion and ignorance. Once these fires are extinguished, then we can gain release from the cycle of samsara and rebirth and enter a place of no-time and no-death, without suffering or the causes of suffering – existence without birth. All very heady stuff. We will come back to this a little further along.

11.4 The Third Noble Truth

Suffering Can Cease
This third noble truth follows directly from the first two; IF people suffer, THEN suffering has causes. IF suffering has causes, THEN they can be addressed. Sounds simple enough, but there's a lot of ground between mental anguish and permanent relief.

It seems clear enough that if we were to address and remediate the causes of suffering, then suffering would cease - or at the very least be reduced. After The Buddha's enlightenment and his realization of these truths, he spent the rest of his life, some 45 years, telling people about his observations and his ideas to relive suffering.

Knowing that you suffer and that suffering has causes isn't really an answer though. What was needed was a path that one could follow, some method that a person, with an open mind and the right motivation, could actually follow and get results. It was one thing for Siddhartha to observe the universal truth of suffering but another to provide guidance to end that suffering. This is where the Eightfold Path comes in.

11.5 The Fourth Noble Truths

The Eightfold Path Is The Way To Cease Suffering

What Siddhartha taught, talked about, discussed, demonstrated and modelled for the rest of his life, (after he awoke and actually became The Buddha or "the Enlightened one") was his solution to the permanent relief of human suffering.

Immediately after his enlightenment, he didn't want to talk much about it, since what he had to say was, at the very least, radical and at worst heresy. It devalued the influence of the Indian gods in vogue at that time and was not looked upon fondly by the vast majority of religious orders that made their living from pilgrims and by performing various rites for their followers. Discontent and discord would follow The Buddha for the remainder of his life. Indeed, not only discord, but outright hatred and loathing.

As a bit of an aside, there were three assassination attempts on his life, but worse, they were all attempted by his *cousin*, Devadatta. His cousin was jealous of the influence and perceived power that The Buddha had gained. He marvelled that people would listen to the man's words and follow his teachings and wanted that for himself for he thought he was just as wise and just as enlightened. In the first attempt on The Buddha's life, Devadatta asked followers of Buddha to give him (Devadatta) the chance to run the sangha, but no one would then follow him, so he sent a group of paid archers to kill his cousin, The Buddha, as he sat in meditation. As the archers neared The Buddha, they became envious of his serenity and peaceful *sangfroid*. They lay down their weapons and joined the sangha. This infuriated Devadatta and some time later he, himself, caused a large rock to fall onto the path of The Buddha. The rock split in two during the descent down the hill and one half grazed one foot of The Buddha, causing a minor injury. Finally, Devadatta had caused a drunken elephant to go on a rampage and charge at The Buddha and his followers, but this too failed. When outright violence didn't work, Devadatta began to lure away the followers of The Buddha. Some came, but soon returned to Siddhartha after seeing little wisdom from Devadatta.

What The Buddha had to say about how humans could gain relief from suffering was as different from everyday human experience as light is from dark. He could not find the words to properly express himself, in a manner that would be understood and accepted by others. How do you describe music to a deaf person, or colours to one who is blind? The language just doesn't exist to describe the experience. It seemed too difficult. For this reason, he continued to sit beneath the tree for many more days.

In the end, according to one story, it was Braham, King of the Gods, who appears and ultimately persuades Siddhartha to spread his knowledge by saying that some people only have a little dirt in their eyes and might be awakened if only they could hear his story.

The Buddha relents and gives his first talk to some ascetics - earlier acquaintances he met on his journey - his Setting the Wheel of Dharma in Motion talk, or the *Dhammacakkappavattana Sutta*. In this first talk, he gives his observations about the Four Noble Truths and outlines his path to permanent relief of human suffering, the so called Eightfold Path.and how it leads to Nirvana.

11.6 The Eightfold Path

This path, simply put, might best be considered as a set of instructions or guidelines, that, when followed patiently, conscientiously and with good intent, will deliver a human being from samsara.

Even though all the components of the Eightfold Path start with the word "right" it should be noted that the word isn't being used to suggest right or wrong. In this context, "right" only means that we are attempting to support our efforts for personal development so that we may suffer less, not harm others and take ourselves nearer to wisdom. Further, while the Eightfold path is generally laid out in a manner similar to that below, the path isn't a series of steps to be mastered one at a time. They are best practiced together, for each supports the others in our quest for less suffering.

In brief, the Eightfold Path can be divided into three sections. Interestingly, and most importantly for this book, the first two steps are about the CULTIVATION OF WISDOM, while the remaining six are about ethics and mental development. Yet, putting wisdom in with the first two steps of the Eightfold Path is a little curious, because wisdom is the ultimate goal of the Eightfold path - something to be attained after diligent application, understanding and practice of all elements of the Eightfold Path. In a way, The Eightfold Path is a bit like climbing a mountain. While you may begin with your view set upon the summit, you still have to climb over the foothills, jump the crevasses, find the route and make the effort to ascend.

WISDOM

1 Right View
(Pali, Samma Ditthi)

Since wisdom is the antidote to ignorance and ignorance of how the world operates (or how we operate within the world) is what keeps us from ending our suffering, it follows that any view that supports us in the development of wisdom must first be developed in order to end suffering. This is called Right View.

It's been noted that the Eightfold Path isn't so much a path as a set of disciplines to be practiced in concert, each supporting the other. So how does one begin? It should be understood that without a view of the world that accepts we are the architects of our own suffering, there can be no real beginning. Unless we recognize that when we participate in meritorious acts (generosity, donations, kindness towards others, giving alms, etc.) there is benefit not only to others, but to ourselves as well, there can be no first steps. If we don't realize that words and actions that harm others will have karmic consequences for us in the future, there can be no initial setting out on the Eightfold Path.

Right view, then, assumes that you have given thought to, understand and have had direct experience of the suffering to which the Four Noble Truths refer. You may not know exactly what the four truths mean, or exactly how they work, but you've at least developed a view that agrees with the conclusion that; all humans suffer, suffering has causes and once the causes are eliminated, we can end suffering. You will have had direct, personal experience with the Four Noble Truths and know suffering for what it is. Without that fundamental understanding and acceptance, there can be no right view, and without right view, there will be little benefit gained from following the Eightfold Path.

2 Right Intention
(Pali, Samma Sankappa)

Sometimes called Right Thought. This, along with right view is supportive of our quest for wisdom.

I have occasionally heard it expressed that our thoughts don't matter, only our words and deeds make a difference. But that just isn't so. Everything we become and everything we do, begins with our thoughts. Just because our thoughts can't be heard by others or 'policed' by some outside body, doesn't mean they don't have an effect on us and those with whom we interact. Someone acting poorly is doing so because poor thoughts and poor intention arose in their mind first. As a cart might follow a draft animal, so do our words and deeds follow our thoughts. When we think in negative terms, then we speak in negative terms and manifest negative actions. When we have good thoughts, then we - and those around us - are the beneficiaries of good speech and good deeds. Peace and happiness are the result of peaceful and positive thinking.

Right Intention has three components;

1. RENUNCIATION to counter the desire to seek sensual pleasures or worldly possessions. This isn't to suggest that we give everything away and denounce material goods or sensual pleasure, but rather that we recognize our unhealthy attachment to these things. Giving away our goods, while maintaining an emotional attachment to them is not beneficial

2. The intention of GOODWILL to counteract any inclination towards ill will. This is to suggest that we cultivate a "loving-kindness" towards all humanity (not just the people we like) to overcome anger, hatred and aversion. It is an effort to minimize the differences between, "you" and "I," or "us" and "them"

3. The intention of HARMLESSNESS to offset any intention to harm. This is the simple effort to not harm or do violence to anyone or anything. It is enhanced with an effort to arouse compassion for others.

Four practices that might help us with our Right Intention;

1. Ask yourself, "Are you sure?" Write the question on a piece of paper and tape it to the bathroom mirror. Wrong perceptions often lead to wrong intentions

2. Ask yourself, "What am I doing?" This helps bring you back to the present moment where Right Thinking can once again arise

3. Be aware of your 'auto pilot' moments. When you recognize you're doing something or thinking something wholly through

habit, say, "Hello habit energy, old friend." This can also help bring you back to the present moment

4. Cultivate bodhicitta. This is the raising of compassion for all sentient beings and the wish to end their suffering, preferably by dropping one's attachment to, "self," and devoting one's practice to helping others gain freedom from suffering. See entry on Tonglen in Chapter 7.0.

The Gates of Paradise
A Tale of Anger

A warrior travels many days to sit at the feet of Zen master, Hakuin Edaku.

The warrior asks Hakuin, "Is there a heaven and hell?"

Hakuin reflects and eventually asks the warrior, "Who are you?"

The warrior replies, "I am samurai! Proud member of the military class, serving a powerful daimyō. I am skilled and menacing."

Hakuin replies, with disgust, "Indeed? You seem but a simple, greedy mercenary. What master would have you? You have the face of a beggar!"

At this, the samurai stands and begins to draw his sword.

"So, you have a sword. I doubt your skill to wield it. It's probably too dull to chop cheese," taunted Hakuin.

The samurai draws his sword in anger and raises it to strike at Hakuin.

"There! Right there opens the gates of hell," responds Hakuin.

Hearing this, the warrior recognizes the wisdom of the master and returns his sword to its sheath and deeply bows.

"And there, open the gates of paradise."

ETHICS

3 Right Speech
(Pali – samma vaca)

As we discussed early on in this book, our age of mass-media, social media and almost instant communication around the globe, we might sometimes forget that our words have meaning. The words we use and how we use them help convey our intent. Our words express our thinking process; clear, muddled or somewhere in between. The words we use have weight and when they are heard or read, people make judgements about us

When US president Abraham Lincoln (R) wrote to Messrs. H.L PIEROE, &c in 1895 and said, "This is a world of compensations, and he who would be no slave must consent to have no slave. Those who deny Freedom to others deserve it not for themselves, and under a just God cannot long retain it." We knew what he meant. He was not muddled. He was not unclear. He was speaking against owning slaves and denying freedom to others. His words had weight and continue to have weight today. His meaning was concise and we knew his intent.

In the Theravada Buddhist tradition, it's simple enough and the advice is unambiguous;

1. Abstain from telling lies or using words that deceive
2. Avoid divisive language
3. Do not participate in idle gossip
4. Renounce uncivil, discourteous or insulting language

In addition to the above advice, we might also add;

- Do not boast
- Do not speak of your spiritual achievements
- Do not speak of you achievements in general, where it would cause another to feel demeaned or dismissed
- Do not repeat hearsay.

Right speech is more than simply using the "right" words, it's also about being skillful in how you use them. Avoiding hurting others and speaking negatively behind people's back. It's about trying to bring light and civility to discourse, even when there is disagreement ... *especially* when there is disagreement.

It's so easy to tear people down with words and actions. It requires little in the way of skill or effort. Unkind words, unkind looks and unkind actions can leave irreparable harm. It creates an environment of distrust. It's often done without intent and that of course is at least as bad as when it's being done intentionally. It means the person is being unkind without even giving it any thought! Creating an environment of distrust, in which people don't want to speak openly, is not a wise action, for it stifles creativity, communication and engagement - those very things that are so important in any community.

This isn't confined to local community of course, but extends to the subway car, busses, local coffee shops, trains, planes and out on the street. We hear people being uncivil and divisive all the time. It's become all too common.

The wisdom is in recognizing when we are engaging in this type of behaviour and knowing how to cease. When we continue in this conduct, our ego gets boosted and it wants more. It positively thrives on our being dismissive, discourteous, mean, insulting and backhanded with others.

The ego likes to keep busy with this type of activity. It's always active, reacting with zeal to aversion, attachment, greed and hatred. The more appreciable our level of aversion and desire, the more alive we feel and the more tangible the ego seems. Who hasn't enjoyed a good rant against a local or national politician? The greater the rant, the more alive the ego feels – the more alive *we* feel.

Yet, we don't seem to recognize that when we talk poorly about people behind their back, we make ourselves look mean and small in the eyes of our audience and we demonstrate a lack of civility, discretion and we appear egotistical and insensitive.

- Wisdom is speaking of people in a positive, supportive manner
- Wisdom is speaking in a way that put people in their best light
- Wisdom is displayed when we hear divisive or insulting talk, and speak up to put an end to it, or, at the very least, do not participate ourselves.

Poorly chosen words can easily hurt others, misrepresent them and even reflect poorly on us.

But is there a time for harsh talk? Of course. When people misbehave, there is wisdom in correcting them. They should hear in words that are not uncertain, that their behaviour is poor, disruptive, unwanted, harmful, undesirable, illegal or inappropriate to those around them.

The words chosen should not be about the *individual* offending, but about the behaviours that should be corrected - it should not be a personal attack. The words should be delivered in a kindly manner and not in such a way that would imply insult. You do not want to do harm to the offender, but rather, in correcting, you offer them an opportunity to alter their behaviour and their karma to better effect their life. Should the individual improve their behaviour and they become kinder because of your words, then they will have a beneficial effect on those they come in contact with.

When correcting people, do so with kindness backing your intent, not malice. Do not correct someone simply for the sake of correcting them. Use compassion as a guide when corrective words are required. Be light, but be clear. Use words wisely.

4 Right Actions
(Pali, samma sammanta)

Abstain From Taking Life

The first thing to recognize here is that we should abstain from killing each other – for any reason. We are all desirous of life and wish to continue as long as we can. Our lives are short enough without others cutting it shorter still. It is wise to follow such a rule, for we would not want someone to cut short *our* life.

Don't kill other sentient creatures. If we agree that all sentient creatures can feel pain, then inflicting pain upon such creatures runs contrary to moral behaviour. Killing such creatures would, similarly, be contrary to moral behaviour.

Abstain from Sexual Misconduct

For the purposes of this discussion, from a Buddhist perspective, it's fairly simply and straightforward and has been discussed, at some length earlier in this book, back in Chapter 3.1;

- Abstain from sexual encounters those who are under age
- Abstain from sexual encounters with engaged or married people
- Abstain from non-consensual sex

If it's not clear, this still leaves a lot of room for personal preferences, proclivities, sexual orientation, kinks and fetishes. So long as we're talking about consenting adults, Buddhism has very little to say about who you do. There is no concern about same sex coupling or multiple partners, pre-marital sex, BDSM or whatever you're into.

For monastic purposes, at least in Buddhism, sexual contact is widely discouraged. Sexual and sensual pleasures are viewed as a distraction for those who are seriously on the spiritual path. The passion to which it can give rise is one of The Three Fires of the human mind that must be dealt with before approaching Nirvana, that of passion. For the average Buddhist on the street or the so-called "householder" this prohibition is not applicable.

Abstain From Theft
Abstain from taking that which is not freely given. When we take things which do not belong to us, we are injuring others and causing them suffering. Not only that, but we are negatively affecting our karma. Then there's the legal difficulty one might find oneself in, possibly facing a conviction that would haunt you for the rest of your life, and possibly even ending up in jail or prison.

5 Right Livelihood
(Pali, samma ajiva)

In the Vanijja Sutta we read The Buddha as having said;

"A lay follower should not engage in five types of business. Which five? Business in weapons, business in human beings, business in meat, business in intoxicants, and business in poison."

It seems reasonably clear that dealing in such goods would cause harm and suffering to humans and other sentient creatures. After we discount those ways to earn a living, we are still left with an almost limitless number of jobs or business that won't harm others.

When we combine the Five Precepts and suggestions that were attributed to Buddha himself we get a pretty clear picture of what a "right livelihood" looks like. You could be, among hundreds of other things; a writer, poet, artist, ad writer, film director, doctor, dentist, veterinarian, furniture maker, carpet cleaner, automobile mechanic, arborist, farmer, taxi driver, gas station owner/operator, truck driver, window washer, house builder, steel worker, lawn care guy, pool guy, clothing designer, pharmacist, TV repair person, HVAC installer or designer, lift operator, crane operator, wind turbine technician, installer of photo voltaic cells, plumber, electrician, gardener, tow truck driver, police officer, streetcar or bus driver, airline pilot … oh the list goes on and on. All you need to avoid is killing, lying, stealing, sleeping with the wrong people, dealing with intoxicants and poisons.

Can you be a lawyer or politician? So long as you keep in mind the Five Precepts, practice skillful speech and do not harm others, it would seem possible. Can you be a soldier? That's a bit more difficult as you may well be expected to kill an enemy, but maybe if you were conscripted you could work in an administrative capacity to fulfil your duty to your country. Can you be a butcher? That's difficult as well, for you are enabling the slaughter or maybe even slaughtering animals yourself - sentient creatures. Right livelihood would mean that you couldn't work as a butcher - at least not without some of moral gymnastics.

MENTAL DEVELOPMENT

6 Right Effort
(Pali, sammā-kammanta)

This is the desire and intention to better develop wholesome personal characteristics. It consists of four elements;

　　1.　Do not allow unwholesome emotions, such as greed, anger and ignorance, to arise

　　2.　Where unwholesome mental states have arisen, there is an effort to extinguish them

　　3.　Make the effort to cultivate and give rise to generosity, loving kindness, and wisdom - the opposites of greed, anger and ignorance

　　4.　Where wholesome mental states have arisen, effort is exerted to maintain them.

These efforts should not be a burden to you, rather they should bring some joy. Your practice should not drain you, but rather provide spiritual nourishment.

A Tale of Generosity
The Buddha lets it be known that on a particular day, he would be personally accepting contributions for the poor. On the appointed day, The Buddha sat beneath a tree, ready to accept offered donations.

The first to arrive was a wealthy, local land-owner and business man, along with his lawyer, scribe, personal assistant, body guard and entourage. He offered The Buddha money, the deed to a small piece of land and various grain products from his farms, all while being certain he was being seen by others. The Buddha was pleased to accept these gifts and did so with one hand, thanking the land-owner.

Next to arrive was a minor member of a royal dynasty. She too arrived with a complete entourage and a scribe to record and report on the event. Her offered included jewels, rare art works, and the labour of 100 men. All this The Buddha gratefully accepted with one hand, thanking her for her efforts.

So it went throughout the day, rich men and women would arrive, intermingled with kings and other members of royal families, offer The Buddha precious items or services and The Buddha would gratefully accept them with one hand, all on behalf of the poor, destitute, homeless and less fortunate.

Late in the afternoon, a poor woman arrived, dressed in dusty clothes that were near the end of their usefulness. In her hand was half a pomegranate. She explained to The Buddha that she had, only hours ago, heard that he was accepting donations for the poor. She had nothing to offer, but her half eaten pomegranate and so she walked five miles to give it to The Buddha. Hearing this, The Buddha extended both hands and accepted her donation.

Seeing The Buddha had used two hands to accept her gift, but used only one to accept theirs, the royals and wealthy persons of business asked The Buddha why this was so. He explained that while he was grateful for their donations, they gave but the smallest fraction of their wealth and did so more for recognition and glory, not charity. The poor woman who had nothing, gave everything and did so happily, so I needed both hands to accept her donation.

A Plan for Giving

There are basically two ways to be generous; we give through sense of duty or we give through an upwelling of generosity.

The first is good. Being taught to give isn't a bad thing. Giving because you have a reasonable expectation that you or someone else expects you to give isn't a bad thing. Hopefully it will be skillful and the recipient will see some benefit. This is often how corporate giving is done.

The corporation sees some value in giving and so makes a calculated donation that will maximize their benefit, while at the same time, the receiver gets some benefit as well. This is very common and seems well accepted as part of doing business – abuses not withstanding.

The other mode of generosity is simply an upwelling of desire to do so. I think this is the one that is suspect. This seems so unlikely to happen in our culture that when it does happen, it appears unseemly. There seems to be something about generosity that is too often called into question by others.

- What are they trying to get, by giving as they do?
- What is their hidden agenda?
- What strings will be attached to this gift?

Purity of giving is questioned in our society. There seems to be no sense that generosity can just arise – without all the other stuff.

Still, Al Gore in his book The Assault on Reason, makes it pretty clear that giving by corporations to political parties comes with plenty of strings attached.

We must remember, that, in the end, we all give away everything.

Generosity is the Antidote to Selfishness

When we willfully give money or donate time or some other resource to those in need, it's natural that we feel empathy and compassion for those to whom we are giving. It also works the other way around; when we feel compassion for someone we naturally want to help.

Of course, we can't help everyone, so, what do we do? One method of giving, without getting yourself into financial trouble, is to set aside a specific amount to give every week. Then, when you've given it away, it's done - at least until the following week. It might be $5, $10, $20 or $50. It might be more. Only you can decide what you can afford to give, but when it's gone, it's gone. If you still want to help, then you might donate your time at a food share facility, an outreach program, answering phones at a help centre, etc. If you're at all like me, you probably have more spare time than spare money.

You might have a specific cause that you wish to donate to. It might be an illness, for which there is no cure, or an environmental project or a homeless youth program, etc. For these, you might want the convenience of giving a certain amount each month on your credit card. Again, the amount you decide upon must be an amount which you can afford. You should not suffer financially because of your generosity. There will always be people or organizations which are worthy of our money, but we will never have enough to help everywhere.

I know of one Buddhist monk who leaves his change in vending machines for others to find. He receives a small, monthly stipend from his monastery and donations from public speaking to help with his living expenses and his donations come from those sources. It's not a lot, but it's what he can afford.

This anonymous form of giving relieves the giver of making judgements about the uses the receiver is going to put that money towards. Would you give money to someone who you believed (rightly or wrongly) was going to spend it on something you find wrong, illegal, immoral, un-sustaining, etc? Probably not. Yet, when you give you should not attach strings.

When we give we may have to remind ourselves that it isn't really about us - I mean it is about us, in so far as we want to feel good and do meritorious acts that have the potential to help us develop good karma - but we shouldn't expect applause, adulation or even thanks. If we give money to a street person and they respond with a 'God bless you friend,' we don't need to feel offended if we are an atheist. If we give and receive *no* thanks, it's OK, gratitude may be nice, but giving isn't about that - it's about helping.

Finally, one must be mindful that what is given is not harmful to the recipient. It might not be wise to give a bottle of wine to someone known to be addicted to alcohol. This would only further their suffering in the long run. Is there something else that could be given, in place of alcohol?

Decide what you can afford and who should receive your money and execute your act of generosity with good intention and no expectation of return or applause. Avoid giving that which may cause harm.

#7 *Right Mindfulness*
(Pali, sammā-sati)

The Pali word *sati* can, depending on context, means, retention, recollection or alertness. When we say we are mindful, we are saying we are present, in the moment, aware of our surroundings and aware of our state of mind. We are not thinking about what to have for dinner. We are not worrying about our taxes. We are not daydreaming or remembering our vacation experiences. We are here and now with full attention on the present. We are cultivating or refining the quality and power of our mind to become aware of what is happening now, without judgement and without our usual perturbations.

Of course awareness of the now is not exclusive to Buddhism, for many spiritual practices incorporate awareness, but for Buddhists, awareness is a specialty, an essential part of the practice.

The importance of mindfulness is that it's a direct link to what's happening, without our usual mental filters. The reason that's important is that if we are to achieve enlightenment and attain Nirvana (and the ultimate end to suffering) it is done through direct experience of the conditions that give it rise and that means being in the present moment to receive the experience.

When we talk about mindfulness and bringing energy to bear on our mind, creating some element of discipline, we are not talking about beating the mind into submission. We are not talking about systematically depriving your life of interest, variety or excitement. We're not talking about robbing ourselves of hope and a future. In one very real sense, it's like walking on a hiking trail in the middle of a hot, humid and sunny day, feeling the effects of the weather, then coming across a cooling waterfall, under which you can wade and cool yourself. Mindfulness is a lot like that. It brings us to the point where we see the emotional state of our mind and give us a chance to cool off - take a time out, as it were - taking a moment to find your centre, feeling a bit of calm and peace.

Being able to centre the mind, and be aware of its state is important when it comes to wisdom. When the mind can be settled, when emotions can be recognized and set aside, even for a moment, then we can see more clearly the nature of the problems before us. This calming down and knowing the mind gives us pause where we can see our problem more clearly and be able to better synthesize some wise thinking, words and actions.

When we begin to recognize that we tend to repeat the same patterns over and over then we can raise awareness to recognize when those mental states begin and we can nip them in the bud to help avoid unhealthy patterns.

Participate in Altruistic Activities
Mindfulness is often found in strong connection to community. When we participate in local charities, we develop a sense of compassion for those around us. We see that their pain is not that different from our pain. We become more aware of our environment

Develop a Meditative Practice
We discuss the practice of meditation in Chapter 11.7, but for now, suffice it to say that when we are able to sit with our thoughts, look at them, examine them and set them down again without getting confused, upset, angry or jealous then we are practicing mindfulness.

Keep a Journal
Looking back over the day and recording those things that have upset us, calmed us, angered us, made us jealous, hateful, demeaned us or any other mental state allows us to identify what situations trigger us. Knowing where and how we are tossed about by our environment, it becomes easier to see where we can right ourselves.

Engage in Physical Exercise
A lot of mindfulness can be found in the present moment and physical activity can often bring us into our bodies and so bring us into the here and now. When we are exercising, we rarely think about the future or worry about the past. It's all we can do to keep ourselves working in the moment and so the past and present fall away.

Take a Mini-Break in Nature
If circumstances allow, take a walk in nature. Sit by a stream or on a hill or some sort of outlook. Visually take in the scenery, listen to the sound of the wind or water or nearby birds. Feel the wind and sun on your skin. You will almost certainly notice that the mind becomes calmer. Enjoy that feeling for as long as it is present.

When we are aware of our mental state and what circumstances negatively affect us, then we can apply our efforts to minimize those circumstances and better allow our mind to function in a clear and disciplined manner.

#8 Right Concentration
(Pali, Samadhi)

Right concentration means that there is an effort to delve into the four deeper levels of concentration known as 'jhanas.' However, from a practical everyday point of view, we're not going too far down this rather esoteric road. Instead we concentrate on the first level of concentration for it casts the widest net and provides a firm stepping stone should you decide to go deeper into the practices of meditation.

Discussing the circumstances that give rise to wisdom without discussing right concentration is almost impossible, for it's the ability to direct the mind to *focus* that is key to deep, meaningful thought. Possessing a thorough understanding and some practical experience in the practice of meditation is essential if we are to have any hope of controlling our mind and directing it to our will.

We will discuss meditation and how to meditate in the next chapter, but for now, know that the act of meditation has been clinically proven to provide many mental and even physical benefits to the practitioner.

In writing for Healthline, July 5, 2017, Dr. Matthew Thorpe, MD, PhD notes 12 benefits of regular meditation, including; reduced stress and anxiety, improved emotional health, greater self-awareness, improved attention span, reduced memory loss in persons ageing, improved sleep, etc.

While meditation is central to a Buddhist practice, there is no need to be a Buddhist to practice meditation. It's a mind training technique to help improve deep concentration and can be incorporated into almost any lifestyle, religion or culture.

While numerous benefits can accrue to the practitioner, meditation is really about focusing attention and preparing the mind to give rise to wisdom.

"There is no concentration without wisdom, no wisdom without concentration. One who has both concentration and wisdom is close to peace and emancipation."

~ Bhante Henepola Gunaratana

11.7 Meditation, Concentration and Patience

Not to put too fine a point on it, but a lot of wisdom simply requires sitting down and thinking about something and coming to a well thought out conclusion. As we discussed in the introduction of this book, we have become lethargic thinkers. Learning to deeply and effectively reason, requires a bit of re-training. This is even more true when we consider the vast quantities of information that are available to us today, in comparison to the data desert in which The Buddha lived.

Thinking is rarely done in any meaningful way while watching TV or surfing the internet. Deep thinking is rarely done while driving to or from work and profound thinking is rarely done at work - even if you're getting paid to do it, as there's just too many phone calls, emails, letters to be opened and people poking their head into your office or cubicle for a 'moment of your time.'

Indeed, thinking requires attention, intent, concentration and effort. It is not for the feint of heart, for thinking, as we've already noted, can sometimes bring up conclusions that we don't like and we are either forced to accept the conclusion or rally against it and against our own mind often becoming conflicted or split.

In all Buddhist traditions, meditation is usually a daily practice. Meditation is simply sitting down, turning off the TV, radio, computer, Play Station and stereo, and allowing the mind to wander a bit, watch where it goes and then gently bring it back to the present.

Cautionary Note

Before we get too far into this, it must be pointed out that meditation can, occasionally, bring up some uncomfortable emotions. It can bring up memories of things we might have been repressing or blocking. It's for these reasons that you might join a meditation or Buddhist centre before you begin the practice - if only to get a bit of training or advice. In a safe, supervised environment, any negative experiences can be dealt with by those who are, at least nominally, trained to help. Where deeper issues arise, beyond the meditation centre, then professional mental health practitioners might be able to help.

In the Theravada tradition of Buddhism, there are two primary forms of meditation, vipassana and samatha.

Vipassana Meditation

Vipassana or "insight" meditation provides techniques to "purify" the mind and ready it for deep-seeing of the nature of ourselves so we can unravel the causes of our suffering and general disillusionment of our lives. It's mind training that helps to take away the stories we've added to our observations and allow us to see and know, clearly, what is unfolding before us. It helps us cut through conventional perception to perceive mind and matter as they really are: impermanent, unsatisfactory, and impersonal. With training, we learn to detach ourselves from our ideas and opinions so desire and delusion are gradually diluted - and don't forget, delusion is one of the major factors betraying our wisdom.

Samatha Meditation

For the purposes of this book, samatha meditation is the key to preparing the mind to allow for the raising of wisdom.

Also known as calmness meditation or focused meditation. The purpose of samatha meditation is to bring the mind to a single-pointed state of concentration on an object of meditation - often the breath. Focusing on the breath we can practice fixing the mind in place to enter a deep, trancelike stillness. By quieting the mind, by suppressing negative emotions, you prepare the field for "insight" or Vipassana meditation.

Vipassana and Samatha meditation are two sides of the same coin. Each enhances the practice of the other.

It's not obvious to most people, but we spend most of our mental energy thinking about the past and looking ahead to the future. We rarely sit, focus and allow the mind to see what's happening right now, right here. When we do allow the mind to rest, it naturally wants to go to the past or future, for there is little for it to do in the present. Our brain is a machine that's beautifully designed to forecast, calculate, draw conclusions, commiserate about the past - do just about anything really, except stay in the present.

Usually, throughout the day we have the feeling that we need to respond or react to almost everything that arises. The telephone rings, we answer. An email comes in, we read it. Someone pokes their head into our cubical, we engage. Someone honks their horn, we give them the finger - or want to. In fact, it's more than a feeling, but an imperative of most of our work. We push away and pull towards things all day long and it's this feeling that we are trying to get under control during sitting meditation.

The practice asks only that we be there without "doing."

This book isn't about meditation, it's about raising wisdom, so getting too "instructional" is beyond the scope of this book. Indeed, there are many, many well-written books about meditation by real masters and learned persons. Still, when we talk about wisdom in Buddhism, we can't skip over meditation, so a few pages are required.

Meditation, unlike religion, does not require 'faith' to work. There is no mystery. You don't time-travel, or astral-travel or levitate. You don't reach altered states of reality or genetically mutate like William Hurt in the 1980 film *Altered States*, although you can achieve a peaceful disposition.

What you need to know is that meditation disciplines the mind, through the application of clinically proven, tested and well documented means. The mind will become clearer, calmer and more concise. It will be less cluttered with hatred, delusion and desire. When bereft of these mental afflictions, the mind will be a better tool for deep thinking and raising wisdom. In one recent study from UCLA, they found evidence suggesting meditation has a positive effect on certain mental facilities that are contributors to higher levels of introspection.

"Since cortical gyrification relates to behavioural traits in humans (Awate et al., 2010), the observed alterations in long-term practitioners might reflect specific traits associated with meditation (e.g., higher levels of introspection, awareness, response control, compassion, etc.). However, this hypothesis remains to be tested with actual behavioural data and/or performance measures in follow-up studies."

So, while this book does not profess to instructional techniques of meditation, it's tough to speak of calming the mind without some methodology from which one can springboard.

The Environment

I usually meditate for 15 to 20 minutes twice a day – once in the morning, just after waking and once in the evening, usually about 30 minutes before going to bed. I have and continue to meditate at any time of day that may prove convenient, although I try to stick to a bit of a schedule.

When I sit to meditate, I seek a quiet, sheltered place in my home, usually the bedroom or living room and occasionally the small sunroom, if it's not too bright or hot. I turn off my phone, television, radio and any other distractions, although occasionally I may play a CD that features Buddhist monks, chanting quietly. While on the road, staying in hotels or camping, the same environment can usually be found, with only minor modifications.

I'm fortunate enough to live very near Riverdale Park East, just along Broadview Ave. in Toronto. There is a hill there, with a view of downtown Toronto. Between the hill and the city is the Don Valley Parkway, just hidden a bit from view. In the summer and on nice days in the spring or fall, I'll walk over to the park and sit in meditation about 1/3 of the way down the hill. The view is lovely and the noise of the city, while present, is not too distracting.

The Seating

I usually sit on a firm, but comfortable cushion, on a carpeted floor. Beneath the cushion, I usually place a folded blanket, so that the bones of my ankles don't get sore, pressing into the carpet. Occasionally, especially after a day long hike, where my knees might be a little tender, I'll sit on a straight backed chair of the sort you might find at a kitchen table.

I have been known to sit quietly by a stream, in the woods, upon a small inflatable cushion. I even sat upon a rock and enjoyed the quiet sounds of a "nature reserve'" nestled in the Oakridges Moraine. Taking ten minutes out of a day hike to sit quietly and listen to nature is a form of meditation that I find particularly enjoyable.

When sitting on a cushion, my legs are crossed, in the manner known as 'half-lotus', back straight, hands either in my lap or resting, palms down on my thighs. When I think about my back posture, I imagine all my vertebrae are joined by a string and the string is tied off above me. When I relax, I imagine the string lengthening and aligning all my vertebra in a straight column. I try to arrange the cushion to impart some forward pelvic tilt, as this seems to help align my vertebrae and improve my posture.

My head position is somewhat straight ahead, but with a slight downward tilt. The tip of my nose sits just ahead of the position of my belly button. When my eyes are open, I usually look at a spot on the floor about six feet in front of me. I don't stare at it, but just gaze at the spot, softly and comfortably. I often close my eyes, but sometimes not. In the morning, when my energy level might be good, I usually close my eyes to bring some calmness. In the evenings, when I may be tired, I tend to open my eyes to bring a higher level of energy. Also, when tired, I may imagine a bright light in my mind and that helps to bring a bit more energy and wakefulness.

Another technique I use to raise my energy is simple exercise. I don't mean running down to the gym and doing a thirty minute circuit. I'm referring to a quiet, meditative, reflective set of movements that awaken the body and energize the mind. I first found The Ten Mindful Movements on a Youtube video featuring Zen Master Thich Nhat Hanh at Plum Village, France. I have found these exercises to be perfect for raising energy and preparing myself for meditation, if I'm feeling a little tired. I might not always do the full set of ten, but I'll do what I think feels necessary to bring a bit of energy to my mind.

When I first began my meditation practice, I set a little plastic statue of The Buddha upon the floor, about four feet in front of me. I was helpful to have an 'object of meditation' upon which my eyes and mind could focus. I know some people have a painting or picture of The Buddha hanging on the wall, upon which they might focus. To be clear, these are not objects of worship, prayer or adoration. They are simply items upon which one applies their concentration. You could use anything really, a flower, an empty glass, a bowl - just about anything that you'd consider to be 'neutral' for you.

When using a chair for meditation seating, I sit on the front 2/3 of the seat, not utilizing the back support. I have my feet flat on the floor, back straight, hands resting either palms down on my thighs about mid way or gently clasped in my lap.

I imagine I can sense the ground beneath me and feel its pull. I relax and let me body weight drop through the cushion or chair and let the ground support me.

My breath process is typically inhalation through the nose and exhalation through the mouth. If I have a cold with related stuffy nose, then obviously I just breath through my mouth. My jaw is relaxed, and my top and bottom teeth are not pressing against each other. My lips are usually slightly parted. My tongue usually rests lightly against the back of my upper teeth and occasional against the roof of my mouth. My shoulders usually start lifted towards my ears, but with conscious awareness, they eventually fall to relax.

Time Keeping

After years of meditation practice, I've learned to fall into deep concentration much faster than I did when first beginning. Occasionally I lose track of time, which usually is no big deal. I've taken to using a meditation timer app on my iPhone that I can set for various intervals. For example, I can set it for 15 minutes with a 3 minute 'settling down' time and a 2 minute 'cooling down' period. At the end of the 3 minutes, a gong sounds to inform me that the 15 minutes is beginning. At the end of the 15 minutes, a gong chimes 3 times to signal the 'cooling down' portion of the session. You can set any of the intervals to your desired preferences. While a valuable tool, it's not strictly necessary for meditation practice. A simple alarm clock or any timer would do, if you feel the need to have one.

When you first begin the meditation practice, keep the time short, say 5 minutes. At the end of that short time, you walk away feeling like you could do it for ten, but build up your time slowly, over weeks or months. It's better to walk away feeling you could add a few minutes than to walk away feeling you should subtract a few.

Mental Attention

I then bring my attention to my breathing. I count my breaths, 1, 2, 3, ... I try to get to 10 without thinking of anything other than the breath. It rarely works, so I start over again. I try that for a few moments, then I focus on my body.

I'll bring awareness to the top of my head and then my forehead, eyelids, nose, etc. I'll work my down through my body, bringing awareness to ears, chin, neck, shoulders and so on, down to the soles of my feet. This usually help calm the mind as it brings the focus from the past and future, directly to the present and what's happening in the body.

The point of the breath-counting and 'body-scan' is that the mind will be occupied with what the body is feeling at this moment, and will not be focused on the past or future. In the moment is when the mind is the most quiet.

The outside world does not disappear for me. I am aware of it, but not focused on it. When I'm in the park, I can view the skyscrapers of Toronto in the distance or the parkland in the foreground. I can hear the streetcars making their way along Broadview Ave. behind me. I can hear and sometimes see the traffic on the parkway. The sound of birds, chattering squirrels, voices of children on the sports field all press in, but are not taken in. They are heard, but not responded to. Occasionally an ambulance will sound its siren as it races along to the hospital, but it does not require attention or response. After all, Toronto is a Big City and expecting silence *anywhere* is a bit of a stretch.

Meditation is deceptively simple. I'm reminded of a New Yorker cartoon some years ago; Two monks are sitting side by side, apparently in deep meditation. The younger of the two, casts a side-long glance at the elder, to which the elder replies, "Nothing happens next. This is it."

When I have an itch, I don't quickly jump to scratch it. Instead, I think to my self, "I feel an itch, so I will gently move my arm and allow my hand to scratch it." I try to avoid immediate attention to the itch, but neither do I ignore it. When a fly lands on my face or head, I do the same thing. I don't jump to immediately attend to the fly, but neither do I ignore it.

The same can be said for discomfort in posture. Should my knees begin to hurt excessively, I will think to myself that my knees hurt and will knowingly, slowly and with intent, alter my seating position to reduce the pain. Again, I don't flinch at the first twinge, but allow the discomfort to become part of the here and now meditative practice. It becomes part of the narrative. The pain or discomfort is in the present. It doesn't belong in the past and it doesn't live in the future. It will get attended to, but not after it has served its purpose as an object of meditation. Have you ever stubbed your toe? The pain flashes into your brain and dislodges everything else. There are no longer thoughts about yesterday or tomorrow or what to have for dinner or the difficulties you're having at work. All that is present is that throbbing, painful toe. Pain can *really* focus our attention, to say the least.

No matter what I do, I find my mind wanders around quite a bit. This is perfectly natural. When people first sit to meditate, they will sometimes describe their mental wandering as "monkey mind," which is to say, the mind jumps all over the place, seemingly untameable. However, with practice and time, the mind will be more controlled and focused attention can then be attained with greater ease and in less time.

It's Always the First Time

Even though I've been meditating for years, it often feels like the first time when I sit down. From a philosophical point of view, everything - no matter how often repeated - happens for the first time. Each time being slightly different from any earlier time. I jokingly think to myself, 'With practice, the first time gets easier.'

Don't Chase Thoughts

When thoughts come to you, give them attention, but don't feed them or chase them. Let them come, be recognized and then set them aside and return to your breath. If you chase the *thought-rabbits*, you'll only end up barrelling down rabbit holes and getting lost. Better just to see the thought-rabbit, acknowledge it's there, then let it go and return to focus on the breath.

There will be frustration at first. Now that I think about it, frustration occasionally comes even after years of practice. Attention to the here-and-now is difficult and not readily accomplished. It comes with practice. Don't think that you are a failure at meditation if it does not come easily. Everyone feels some frustration with this training. It's a bit like golf, even after years of playing, you're going to get those drives that end up in the woods. It isn't natural to be accomplished right off the bat, but as the weeks pass, the practice becomes easier and the results become apparent. Remember, as well, that The Buddha, after leaving the safety and security of his family palace, wandered for years, seeking meditation masters and learning how to meditate before he found the practice to be second nature - and in his case that's *all* he did - he wasn't raising kids, working full time or paying off a mortgage.

In Buddhism we use the term *calm abiding* to express the state or feeling to which we aspire in this meditation technique. A mental state in which we find peace and stability where we can rest in a state of non-distraction, aware of, but not reactive to, outside stimulus. A state of deep concentration.

The more often you develop this condition of calm abiding, the easier it becomes, but it will take time. It does not just arise without effort or practice.

For the individual who might want to go further with meditation and learn more about the eight levels of deep concentration, I suggest a book by Snyder and Rasmussen titled *Practicing the Jhānas: Traditional Concentration Meditation* as presented by the Venerable Pa Auk Sayadaw.

This Isn't Torture

Granted, sometimes it feels that way. I get that. At first it was a bit of torture for me. It's not natural to sit that way, for any amount of time. My knees hurt and my back muscles tired and cramped. The bones in my ankles hurt. I had to scratch any itch. It doesn't seem natural to not think about the future or the past and just focus on the body in the here-and-now. It's not natural to set aside any thoughts that come racing into your mind. Why am I doing this again!?

Where's it Going?

The point of all this is that when we free our mind from wandering and chasing any random thoughts that come into our head, we allow the mind greater potential for concentration. Greater potential to concentrate without disruption or interruption. The focused, concentrated undistracted mind is key to wisdom.

The benefits of meditation, valuable while seated upon the cushion, are most apparent in your everyday life. When you can sit and ponder a question, deeply, explore possibilities, turn over options, apply experience, education, knowledge, compassion and observations you have a greater chance of coming up with a 'wise' conclusion or answer than if you were not able to think, uninterrupted and without distractions. This is a key ability in our quest for wisdom and that which gives rise to wisdom.

Without the ability to focus our thoughts, control them and apply them, we dramatically hamper any attempts at wisdom.

The Role Of Patience In Wisdom

Often we need to balance our short-term satisfaction of desires against long term benefits. Almost anyone would recognize the need of 'saving for a rainy day,' but saving requires a long-term mindset and we too often operate within a narrow time band of minutes, hours and maybe days.

We rarely think long term, for we don't want to put off immediate gratification of desires. Smokers, the vast number of whom are reasonable, rational people, realize there are long-term health effects from consuming tobacco, but few are able or willing to quit, since meeting the short-term impulse to smoke is just so ... gratifying. This, of course, is not to diminish the addictive nature of the tobacco, but the act of quitting is a long-term mindset, while the act of smoking is short-term. We almost always opt for the short-term solution.

We are often reminded that;

"Patience is a virtue"

"All things come to those who wait"

"Patience is bitter, but it's fruits are sweet"

"Patience and diligence, like faith, remove mountains"

"Our patience will achieve more than our force ..."

Why is this so? What's this obsession with patience? In *Nicomachean Ethics VII,* Aristotle uses the term, 'akrasia,' essentially lack of mastery or lack of personal discipline, to describe an individual acting contrary to reason. When people make choices that satisfy their immediate desires, over long term happiness, Aristotle believed that exhibited a weakness, an incontinence or an impetuosity that is fuelled by emotions. Patience, like so much of Buddhism, is a personality trait that can be improved through practice and mental discipline.

In Homer's epic poem, *The Odyssey*, our hero, Odysseus, is on a long quest, trying to get home to Ithaca, after the Trojan war. At one point he must sail past a rocky shoal. Upon these rocks live the Sirens. He has been forewarned that he must not listen to their call, nor their promises of knowledge and wisdom or else he would be wrecked on the shores, eventually eaten and his bones would join the bones of other mariners to bleach in the sun.

"Approach! Thy soul shall into raptures rise!

Approach! And learn new wisdom from the wise!

We know whate'er the kings of mighty name achieved at Ilion in the field of fame; Whate'er beneath the sun's bright journey lies.

Oh stay, and learn new wisdom from the wise!"

Of course Odysseus is torn between the short-term satisfaction of hearing the knowledge they supposedly possess and the long term benefits of returning home to his wife and his rightful place as King of Ithaca. But he knows himself well and fears that he will be too greatly tempted by the Sirens, so (acting on the advice from the goddess Circe) orders his men to tie him to the mast and tells them to stuff their ears with bees wax so that only he could hear their call. Thus situated, they manage to sail by the Sirens and so home.

The practice of patience allows us freedom from life's changes, delays and detours. It helps us be calm and still in the face of disappointment. But patience, like wisdom, isn't something we are born with, rather it's an acquired skill that comes only with awareness and practice.

Slow Down

I have a tendency to be impatient when standing in line at the grocery store to pay. "Why are those people ahead of me chatting with the cashier?" "Why does that guy have 10 items in the 8 item express line?" "Why can't those people just use the self-checkout aisle?" "Why, why, why!!!???"

It's at times like these that I really have to slow down, take a deep breath, remind myself that they are just like me and equally anxious to get to wherever they're going. This lineup is just as much a burden for them as me. I monitor my breath and heart rate. I bring myself down before I get too wound up. I try to remember that getting impatient isn't going to hurry the line along. Sometimes, when I go to the grocery store on a Saturday afternoon, I slow myself down even before I get out of the car. I prepare myself for the crowd and/or lineup. I take a philosophical view and treat the shopping experience merely as an exercise in patience. In all honesty, it still tries my patience.

Meditate on Patience

Occasionally, consider patience during meditation sessions. Think about what it looks like, how it might manifest and how you can help it arise. Think about some consequences that you may have suffered when you were less than patient. Think about people you know who have shown patience with you or others. How could you emulate them? Try to imagine how you physically react as you become impatient.

Delay Indulgence

In this material goods obsessed world of ours, it's tough to even *think* about delaying gratification. I have a bit of a collectors streak in me when it comes to books. If given a chance I'd have a personal library that would stress my bank account and occupy an entire room in our house. I have neither the luxury of money *or* space. It may seem obvious, but it took me some time to realize that *owning* the book was not the same as *reading* the book. I really wanted to read, and not necessarily own the books I enjoyed. I re-discovered the joys of the public library. Going to the library has become an exercise in delayed indulgence, for they rarely have any of the Buddhism books I want to read and so I have to wait until they come in from another branch.

Knowing in advance that I may have to wait for something is good practice in patience.

Think Before You Speak

If we want to avoid inflicting pain or discomfort on others, we need to practice patience around speaking. If someone offends us, it's almost natural to want to strike out and respond to their remarks with cutting remarks of our own. From a Buddhist perspective, we don't

Key Points Summary – Meditation

Meditation Does Not Require 'Faith'	• Sitting, quietly with your thoughts, seeking a calm, does not require 'faith' or 'belief' in order to work
Environment	• Select a quiet comfortable spot as free from distractions as possible • Same time of day is generally preferred
Seating	• Comfortable position on a soft cushion, legs crossed, hands in lap, back straight • Eyes open or closed, depending on your energy
Time Keeping	• For beginners, sit for only a few minutes, but as you become more familiar with the practice, you may extend your time. It's better to come away from a session desiring more, not less
Mental Attention	• Focus your mind on your breath • Mentally scan your body from head to toe, noting and being aware of it's condition • Breath and body scan bring you into the present
Don't Chase Thoughts	• When thoughts and emotions arise, simply recognize them, name them and gently let them go. When they arise again, repeat the process
Back to the Room	• As yo unwind down your session, gently bring yourself, mentally, back to the room
Every Time is the First Time	• Not every session will go well. Expect set backs and treat each session as a new version of a 'first time.'
Join a Sangha	• Practice with others of like mind can be beneficial

want to cause harm to others, so we need to take a breath, calm ourselves and think about what we're going to say, before saying it.

Key Points Summary – Patience

Patience Is a Virtue	• A mind that is free to explore a wide range of possibilities and calmly deliberate is a mind more likely to offer wise words and take wise actions • Making haste, except in emergency situations, rarely results in the best choice • The human mind needs to pick over the facts and the emotions of important topics
Delay Indulgence	• This isn't about 'going without' or developing a mindset of scarcity. It's about the practice of patience. It's about recognizing that that we won't die if we don't get immediate satisfaction. It's about curbing attachment to sensual pleasure and desire. It's about not grasping at every straw. It's about taming the ego
Slow Down	• Many of us live in a fast-paced urban environment where everyone is 'hurry up.' We can, from time to time, slow down, monitor our breathing and mental state. We can look around us and appreciate the birds, flowers, trees, even the architecture and the streets that we inhabit. It's about bringing awareness to our lives • When it comes to decision making, determine if the decision needs to be made in a hurry, or if there is benefit in waiting a bit, taking some 'soak time' and gathering more info and testing how we feel about our choices
Meditate on Patience	• Thinking about how impatience harms you and others is good practice before you allow impatience to manifest when out in public
Think Before Speaking	• From a Buddhist perspective, this allows us time to practice speech that does not harm, demean, devalue, discredit dismiss or injure others

Patience, then, as it relates to wisdom in Buddhism is that understanding and practice that allows us to slow down and think before we react with words or actions that may prove to be unwise in the long run. Being patient is the recognition that hurrying to a decision is usually not

12. Learning

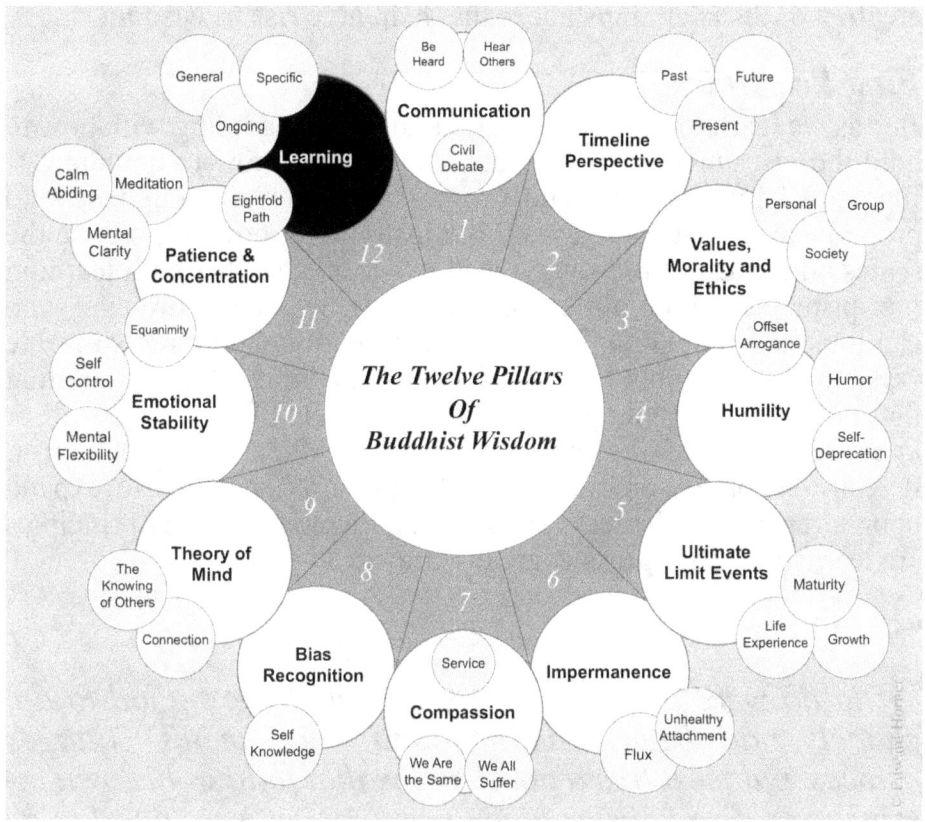

ONE WHO IS CURIOUS about the workings of the world and the universe, humanity, society, politics, science, literature, trades and professions is a person who sees and can hold many views and understand their heterogeneous nature. Who would make a virtue of ignorance?

Learning serves wisdom, in that knowing the ways of the world, in general, allows us to see that one point of view is rarely *the* point of view. But, of course, this can be learned through simple life experiences and does not require any formal or systematic education to be learned.

As we will see, learning, for the sake of learning and expanding one's mind through credit or non-credit courses is a direct aid to the creation of those circumstances that help give rise to wisdom.

First Principles

Just as we learn to play a musical instrument, beginning with how to hold the instrument, how to store it in its case, how to maintain its function, know its parts and progressively move through how to properly place one's fingers on the instrument, how to practice the scales and learn simple songs, read music, etc. so it is with learning first principles about almost anything. Rare is the individual who can look at a flute, pick it up and beginning playing a recognizable version of Telemann's 12 Fantasies for Flute Solo. Only by learning first principles can you progress to high levels of expertise, skill or knowledge. While one *could* learn to play a flute by trial and error, it really becomes somewhat self defeating as one tries to expand upon a repertoire. Unless fundamental, elemental or first principles are learned first, progress is greatly impeded.

"If to do were as easy as to know what were good to do, chapels had been churches and poor men's cottages princes' palaces. It is a good divine that follows his own instructions. I can easier teach twenty what were good to be done than be one of the twenty to follow mine own teaching. The brain may devise laws for the blood, but a hot temper leaps o'er a cold decree. Such a hare is madness the youth—to skip o'er the meshes of good counsel the cripple.

~ Portia, William Shakespeare – Merchant of Venice

I remember reading a quote attributed to Abraham Lincoln that went something like, "Give me an hour to chop down a tree and I'll spend the first 45 minutes sharpening the axe."

That's exactly what it's like when trying to learn something. Start honing your skills by learning (or reacquainting yourself) with fundamental principles. Learn to ask 'why,' 'what' and 'how."

The problem of course, is what we've already looked at in this book ... we are impatient. We have monkey mind that can't sit still for ten minutes. We are always trying to jump ahead and don't want to wait for the tree to grow before we can enjoy the shade of its leaves. Patience, as we've already noted, is a virtue.

Learning something is not always easy for everyone all the time. It requires that we learn those boring first principles – those principles that we think we already know from elementary school or college, but have likely already forgotten or remembered incorrectly. But, as we are human, we want to rush past all that to get to the higher principles. The trouble is, that without a solid base of knowledge about a given topic, it's often either very hard or impossible to grasp the higher concepts. But we don't have to learn everything from the ground up.

It reminds me of a cartoon recently in the New Yorker. A young woman is practicing the piano under the watchful eye of her accomplished instructor. "Can't we just skip all this practicing and get right to the part where I'm awesome?"

Comparison Thinking
To both contrast and compliment first principles thinking we have comparison thinking.

In a lot of ways, learning things is about drawing the lines from one relationship to another. Will eating this berry be OK or will it poison me? If you see other people eating the berry with no ill effects then you might reasonably conclude that eating it yourself will be OK. You compare their behaviours and results to expected results for you.

Still, you can't know for certain. Perhaps those others have built up an immunity to the poisonous effect (if it exists) or perhaps their constitutions are very different from yours. Perhaps they've eaten other things earlier in the day that may have offset any ill affects. You just don't have all the information, but you can make reasonable guesses, based upon what you *do* know and what you've experienced in the past. Rarely can all things be known or even knowable. We work with what we have and learn from past experience - in short - we compare and contrast *this* vs. *that*.

Comparison thinking encourages analogies, which have their uses. We love analogies, not because they prove anything, but because they make us feel at home. If I were trying to explain how a keyboard on my MacBook Pro functioned (how I'd use it) then I might use the analogy of a typewriter from the 1940s. In so many ways, the two are different, but in one important way they are the same ... the keyboard is laid out exactly the same today as it was then. A typist from 1940 would understand what a Mac keyboard is and how it might work. Clearly the keyboard has far more functionality today than it did in the 40s, but the analogy is solid enough for comparison, although it does fall short.

Comparing different things becomes a problem. Analogies may become false. We can't really compare a plum to an apple. True they both grow on trees and are both fruits, but that's about where the comparison ends. They have very different taste, texture and visual appeal. They are transported and stored very differently and have very different uses (although some shared uses, such as pies). You may have an allergy to one, but not the other.

Further, comparing one thing to another doesn't really advance the cause. Little learning is achieved from, "A deer is a bit like a moose." It both is and isn't. The differences are critical to the understanding of both a deer and a moose. Comparing them isn't really learning.

So, while comparison thinking has its place, the greatest bang for the buck is in the first principles thinking.

The more experiences we have the greater our ability to link relationships. Learning fundamentals about electrical engineering, personal transportation infrastructure, energy production and basic physics might put us in a good spot to learn – more easily – how to build an electric car. Elon Musk created Tesla (the all electric car company) and he was not an expert in automobiles. Obviously Elon had a lot of help, but his fundamental grasp and working knowledge of a few disciplines allows him to see linkages between such varied disciplines as rocket science, electricity storage, transportation and photovoltaic cells in order to build out a vertically integrated business that draws from many disciplines.

Learning across many fields has advantages in that knowledge can be transferred between disciplines.

In Elon Musk's Reddit AMA interview, Elon wrote, in response to the question, "Do you have any advice on learning?"

"It is important to view knowledge as sort of a semantic tree — make sure you understand the fundamental principles, i.e. the trunk and big branches, before you get into the leaves/details or there is nothing for them to hang onto." Furthermore, "If we put in the time and learn core concepts across fields and always relate those concepts back to our life and the world, transferring between areas becomes much easier and faster. As we build up a reservoir of 'first principles' and associate those principles with different fields, we suddenly gain the superpower of being able to go into a new field we've never learned before, and quickly make unique contributions."

History

Being a student of history might make you a master of hindsight, but it might not, by itself, contribute to wisdom. Knowing what has happened needs to be augmented with what is happening today, in the here and now. More, as we learned in Chapter 2, (Timeline Perspective) context and period *need* to be addressed. We can't just rely on platitudes such as, "If history tells us anything," or "History repeats itself," and "What we did in the past was …" These bromides have some merit but they are too vague to be of real benefit. We need specifics.

"The farther backward you can look, the farther forward you can see."

- Winston Churchill

Churchill wasn't completely wrong. Human nature doesn't really change. So long as power is being held out, someone will grab it and do almost anything to keep it. As I've come to learn in my life, people don't really change, circumstances do.

Life Satisfaction

Our western world is an ever-changing and ever-faster changing environment. New opportunities come along almost every day. Being able to keep up with current events, new technologies, transportation innovations, etc. is gratifying, if only because we won't feel, 'left out of it,' at work when others are having a conversation. Knowing the score of last night's baseball game and who-scored-when is 'nice to know' and good for smalltalk but hardly conducive to career development or advancement. Better to keep up on emerging trends in your industry and what research is being done and by whom. One might imagine, being able to tell you boss (say, Elon Musk) that you've just read up on a non-silicon based photovoltaic that might be used by his company is likely going to impress him more than who scored first in last nights baseball game.

Learning and then being able to discuss or demonstrate new knowledge is good for ones self-esteem. No one wants to be at the bar with co-workers when the conversation turns to how Artificial General Intelligence is going to revolutionize your jobs, and not know the first thing about what everyone is talking about. What can you offer to the conversation beyond, "Well. Didn't you see Terminator?" Rather, having some intelligent, thoughtful and accurate information or opinion feels far better and may also advance the conversation.

We all have innate abilities. We might be good at drawing birds, but never gave any consideration to being an illustrator for bird books because we were never 'professional' enough. Participating in an illustration or graphic design course might help us explore our abilities, learn where we have interests and how we might expand upon them.

A lifetime of learning will be of benefit to others, which will be of benefit to you. Older persons who have been interacting with the world for decades may be able to offer some useful insight gained from that experience to help make things better for their community.

Job/Career Prospects

Learning new things is a sure way of opening yourself up for new opportunities. If I was a Kentucky coal miner, knowing that the price of coal has been falling for decades as the domestic market got smaller and smaller as new sources of cleaner, cost-competitive, energy become available, I might recognize that I'd soon be out of a job. What will I do? What skills/knowledge do I possess that would allow me to find another job or career? Learning new things, intentionally and as a matter of daily practice allows for personal growth and greater opportunities.

While many factors contribute to income and wealth inequality, the role of education is a key piece of the puzzle.

Economic Benefit

There is a strong correlation between education and income. Having a good income allows for greater opportunities for yourself, your family and your community. Having financial resources available provides one with options.

Correlation is not causation. Looking at the chart below, it would seem a higher level of education will bring greater levels of income, although it's not a certainty. There are at least a few other factors with significant impact on income.

Assortive Mating. This simply means that we select mates that we are comfortable with and/or see some advantage beyond physical attraction. People with higher levels of education will tend to seek out and partner up with others who have a similar level of education. This may double the income of the household.

Education (2013)	Percentage of Families	Median Income	Median Wealth	Wealth-to Income Ratio	Millionaires (Family Income)
No High School Diploma	12%	$22,320	$37,766	1.43	1 in 110
High School Diploma	50%	$41,190	$95,072	2.15	1 in 18
Two or Four Year Degree	25%	$76,293	$273,488	3.45	1 in 4.6
Advanced Degree	15%	$116,265	$689,100	5.58	1 in 2.6

Chart derived from, Economic Research Federal Reserve Bank of St. Louis, Jan. 2017. Education, Income and Wealth. Scott A. Wolla, Ph.D., Senior Economic Education Specialist and Jessica Sullivan, Economic Education Intern

Inheritance. People with higher levels of education are more apt to be from families which have accumulated wealth and so will be more likely to receive an inheritance, increasing the household income. Combine this with the principles of Assortive Mating and household income can rise dramatically.

Financial Literacy. Separate from higher levels of education is one's knowledge of finance. Having a good understanding of the financial tools available to the average household can really help with wealth accumulation.

Longer Life. People with higher level of education tend to have better health, can work longer and so accumulate greater lifetime earnings. They will also live longer to reap the benefits of CPP and Old Age Security and other benefit programs.

Now clearly, having a higher income does not, by itself, make you wise. However, a higher level of education, reading, attending seminars, etc. *does* contribute to wisdom. A good education brings a lot of this learning into one place, making it easier to give rise to the conditions that contribute to wisdom. Still, one wonders that some of the most educated people we know are a complete disaster when it comes to offering wise words or taking wise actions.

Should you be so lucky to have a good education on your side, you don't need to be a snot about it. Examine whether or not you have social obligations (real or self-imposed) around wealth and privilege. Are you being generous to those around you and are you behaving in an honourable manner, including your words and actions? Do you believe in the French phrase *Noblesse oblige*, or Nobility obliges?

Social Awareness

When you step out of your comfort zone and make the effort to learn new things, attend night school classes, go to a local TEDx talk, a conversation salon, makers workshop, art course or just about anything, you meet new people. These people may have very different views from your own. They will have different talents, skills and abilities. Having a place to practice and knowing how to interact with varying cultures or parts of society is a great skill to have.

Portability/Transportability

The desktop computer has become a 'universal tool' in that it can be used for writing, graphics, gaming, spreadsheets, advertising, social media, watching/making movies, banking, paying bills, buying goods and services, etc. The list is almost without limit. Similarly, some knowledge is 'universal,' as it can be used across a broad range experiences.

Reading, for example, is a universal skill. It translates into all manner of situations; science, religion, society, schooling, work, recreation, transportation, business, teaching, research, etc. Whatever you do, you're all but certain to need to know how to read.

Basic arithmetic is a universal skill. Like reading, it can also be utilized in almost every aspect of life. Will the five litres of gasoline remaining in your gas tank allow you to drive the necessary 80km for a refill at your usual gas station or will you have to look for a closer alternative? $80 \div 5 = 16$ If your vehicle travels more than 16kL (kilometres per litre) then you're good. If you got 15kL then you better have a plan B. Fundamental stuff for sure, but applied almost every day.

Another universal skill might be a good working knowledge of how to use Microsoft Office Suite. This is a set of computer applications that is shared by millions of offices and industries around the world. Knowing the fundamentals of how to use Word or Excel is a skill that transcends many industries.

Longevity in Ageing

There is considerable evidence that keeping the mind hard at work, learning new things and practicing skills, helps the brain age well.

According to Nancy Merz Nordstrom, author of *Learning Later, Giving Greater*;

"Lifelong learning enables us to put our lives in perspective ... It increases our understanding of the whys and the whats of previous successes and failures, and it helps us understand ourselves better. We more fully develop the wisdom that can come with later life."

The New Millennial Learners or NMLs

Not everyone learns using the same methods. Some people are very good 'book learners' which is to say, they can take the concepts presented in a book and apply them immediately. Others like to 'talk it though' with others, to better understand presented ides. Some people like to 'see' the principles in action, while still others prefer to have a hands-on approach, actually taking the ideas and building models, charts or simulations, etc. This isn't to suggest that people can't learn using different methods, only that they have a default in which they are most comfortable. Some people might use many methods to learn difficult concepts.

People born after 1982 have grown up with digital communication devices and social media at their fingertips. They do not generally appreciate a 'stand and deliver' methodology of learning. They expect their teachers to deliver higher level concepts, while they, themselves, do the 'grunt' work of learning basic concepts at home, either from textbooks or from online material. Millennial learners also expect 'high yield' discussions among small groups and their teacher. This is commonly known as Small Group Learning or SGL. Further, they exhibit a learning preference that includes team-based learning projects that brings to the forefront the skills and strengths of individuals within the group. Finally, for the purposes of this section, there is a definite preference for 'hands-on' learning where models, simulations and active participation are utilized by the teacher. This isn't to suggest that lectures be completely dismissed as a teaching methodology, only that it become part of a larger toolbox for the teachers.

Dr. Christy Price, from Dalton State College, has written extensively on the Millennial Learners and has summarized her findings as;

- Relevance - NMLs prefer a link between material and current events and culture
- Rationale - NMLs tend to be more engaged where they understand the rationale of the particular topics under discussion
- Relaxed - NMLs tend to learn better in a less formal atmosphere
- Rapport - NMLs prefer a strong connection with their teachers
- Research-based methods - NMLs prefer a variety of learning methods.

Essentially, Price suggests, "The needs of millennials may not actually be generational at all. Today's students may simply be showing us the benefits of paying more attention to what's working and the importance of gathering student feedback on teaching methods."

12.1 Seven Steps to Reinforce Wisdom

Know Yourself First - Meditation

As discussed in the previous chapter, meditation, is the simple act of sitting quietly and allowing the mind to relax and experience the here and now. It is a practice that promotes practical wisdom by having the mind disengage from our usual patterns of aversions and attractions to various people, objects and circumstances.

In order to best help others, and ourselves, through wise decision making, we need to intimately know who we are. We need to understand our motivations, sticking points, skills, attitudes and knowledge. Meditation and deeply looking at our own mind is a proven way to gain such insights. When we fully understand ourselves, then we have a much stronger platform upon which wisdom may arise. We also need the ability to concentrate and bring our mind to a single pointed focus on any given subject, without disruption or interruption. Meditation, particularly samatha meditation, helps support this ability.

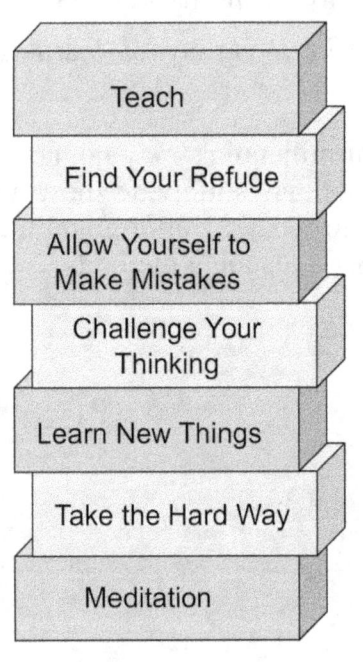

Do Some Things the Hard Way

We are simple creatures really. We like to do things in a simple way, the easy way. We tend to drive, ride or walk to work along the same route every day. Without awareness, we take the easiest route offered or known. We will pick up the same newspapers, read the same columns day in, day out, skip Beetle Baily and go directly to Bizarro. Step out of that mindset and try walking to work along another route. Turn off the GPS and let your brain do some navigating. Grab a different newspaper. Try memorizing five phone numbers, rather than relying on the address book in your smartphone. When the brain flexes its mental muscles, new connections form and old ones are strengthened. The brain, it turns out, is very plastic and adaptable to new situations, if only we give it a chance.

Learn New Things – Seek Novelty
Most legendary geniuses excelled at more than one thing. This isn't an entreatment to run amok, seeking new and novel experiences for their sake alone. What is being asked is that we open ourselves to novelty and new ideas as they present themselves and not just automatically close them out. Learn about black holes, string theory, magnetically levitating high speed rail travel, furniture making, pottery or any number of experiences that will widen our horizons and cause our brains to work a bit. Use some creative non-conformity and take a few pages from the life lessons of Picasso, Joyce, Freud, Stravinsky or Schoenberg … don't feel bad if you have to look up a couple of those names.

Challenge the Way You Think
Do not accept everything on face value. Learn to ask questions and actually listen to the answers. Examine the premise of the argument and draw your own conclusions based on your experience, understanding and observations. Test your brain with quizzes, puzzles, riddles and word games. Read widely. Attend movies that might not initially attract you. If you usually go to rock concerts, try going to the symphony or opera and let you mind experience something different. If you're an opera fan, try taking in a bluegrass music festival. If you're a Superman fan, trying reading The Flash or Batman. Expanding your experience base will not harm you and will bring benefits.

Allow Yourself to Make Mistakes
Notwithstanding our discussion about being wrong back in Chapter 5, making mistakes is allowable. Making mistakes is good. Errors are how we learn as individuals and how we move ahead as a species. We humans are the product of millions of years of errors, failed experiments in genetics and natural selection. For good or ill, we are the best that nature has yet to offer. When new products come to the market, they are almost always the result of multiple failures in design or manufacture. The iPhone owes much of its success to Apple's failed Newton. Dramatically improved automobile safety is

the result of decades of failed experiments in design of seat belts, air bags, crumple zones, antilock braking, collision avoidance sensors, etc. Do not be embarrassed by failure. Learn from mistakes.

Find Your Refuge

Having a place to go to, either physically or mentally, (preferably both) is an important aspect when attempting to create the circumstances that allow for wisdom to arise.

There is a cat in our neighbourhood whose name is Tokyo. He does not belong to us, but comes to our home every morning. He belongs to one of the neighbours. Years ago, when Tokyo was just a young cat he lived with other cats in their home. He was never "king of the castle," and always took a back seat to the other cats. When they eventually died, he had his chance to be well loved and cared for, but the neighbour, missing the other cats, bought in two new kittens, again, relegating Tokyo to a second class status. Eventually, he decided to move out and move in with us! Our neighbours know where he is and when he's out, they play with him, but his new home, his refuge, has become our house. After an evening out fighting with other cats, avoiding racoons and other denizens of the night, he meows at the door and we let him in, feed him, give him his belly rubs and then he falls asleep, usually for the rest of the day.

Teach

When you stand up and present something and then take questions, you're really opening up to some vulnerability. You may not have an answer or only have a vague answer, based upon your gut and not a well researched and thought out answer. You may feel a little uneasy about all that ... good! This uneasiness may be just the feeling you need to inspire you to gain further knowledge, incorporate new ideas and ways of doing things to better equip yourself for teaching others. Remember the Eight Worldly Concerns.

Another important thing about teaching of course, is the you impart knowledge to others, helping them become wiser, more intelligent, more widely read, better able to assimilate information and become actual thinkers. When others become better thinkers, they begin to assemble the building blocks of wisdom and can help themselves and others to ease suffering and live more meaningful lives.

Shortly after Siddhartha Gautama achieved his enlightenment and became known as "The Buddha" he began teaching and spreading his knowledge. He spent the next forty years of his life teaching. So, to follow in the footsteps of The Buddha, at least in this regard, is a noble way to spend your time.

You might not be a teacher, presenter or professor, but you might be able to speak at a club, organization, place of business or even just amongst your interested friends. You may decide to write a book.

Final Thoughts

You've stuck with it this far, so no doubt you're looking for the brief answer to the question, "What is wisdom in Buddhism." Having read through the book, you've likely discovered that there is rarely a brief answer to any important question. There is no silver arrow. Still, I have promised you an answer, and an answer you shall have - brevity not-withstanding.

First, in it's most narrow definition, wisdom from the Buddhist perspective, is thinking, speaking and taking actions in a manner that will lessen our suffering and move us forward on the Eightfold Path towards Nirvana. The Buddha really only taught two things after his enlightenment, i) the nature of suffering and ii) how to lessen suffering. Of course it seems he had a lot to say about other things, but almost everything related to the lessening of our suffering and the suffering of other sentient creatures. I expect that's not really the answer you're looking for - most of us don't really have any aspirations to become 'enlightened' this go 'round or achieve Nirvana any time soon.

So, more widely, and perhaps more *practically*, wisdom is the ability to draw useable, valuable, implementable conclusions and associated recommendations and actions that help you, your social group and humanity as a whole, suffer less, but that wisdom will rarely arise unless we can;

- Effectively communicate our thoughts and accurately hear and understand the ideas of others (Chap. 1)

- Understand, as far as we can, the full timeline of a problem, its past, present and possible future. Reference the past, analyze the present and make thoughtful forecasts that include; possible, unlikely and probable scenarios (Chap. 2)

- Reference and use a set of values and morals that are widely agreed upon and will give benefit to the whole, but not without considering the individual (Chap. 3)

- Be humble and self-deprecating about our abilities and use humour to build bridges between people and social groups (Chap. 4)

- Utilize the lessons we've learned from our life to benefit others. Recognize, understand and act in a manner that shows you don't see the world in black or white, but rather, in shades of grey. (Chap. 5)

- See and understand the impermanent nature of our lives and everything around us (Chap. 6)

- Know the situation and/or suffering being experienced by others and give rise to feelings of compassion (Chap. 7)

- Investigate our personal biases and know how they affect our view of the world (Chap. 8)

- Understand how the minds of others might work so we can better relate to them (Chap. 9)

- See our emotional nature and reference it to help relieve personal suffering and the suffering of others (Chap. 10)

- Harness our minds to improve our concentration so that deep thought can be given to problems. Do not speak or act rashly. Be patient and take your time when responding. Practice meditation and deep reflection (Chap. 11)

- Enjoy an ongoing education, both specific and general, that can be referenced and harnessed in a way that will help reduce suffering in ourselves and others (Chap. 12)

- See that our words and actions are not always about deciding what is best for an individual, although the needs of the individual need to be addressed and considered

- Draw conclusions and take actions for the benefit of many with support of the many. – the common good.

When we apply that *super suite* of mental faculties; concentration, intellect, foresight, humility, humour, learnedness, emotional stability, patience, a calm mind and historical awareness, and combine it with a broad experience base, then wise decisions and conclusions can manifest. Balance the benefits to the common good with due consideration to self-interest and the individual.

Remind yourself daily that death sits upon your shoulder and, if you listen, you will hear in no uncertain terms, that the days remaining to us are few. Open your mind and strive for wisdom.

Wisdom from The Buddha

At one time, The Buddha and a small group of bhikshus, wandering in the countryside, came upon the town of Kālāma. When they stopped, people of the town came to see them and speak with The Buddha and hear his teachings. Below is a distillation of one portion of those teachings, drawn largely from the late Ven. Soma Thera translation of the Kālāma Sutta from Pali to English

- *Do not believe, speak or act from revelation alone*
- *Do not believe, speak or act simply from tradition*
- *Do not believe, speak or act from rumour or hearsay*
- *Do not believe, speak or act solely from authority of sacred texts*
- *Do not believe, speak or act from logic alone*
- *Do not believe, speak or act only from a view that seems rational*
- *Do not believe, speak or act from appearance alone*
- *Do not believe, speak or act from a view simply because you agree with it*
- *Do not believe, speak or act on the grounds that the person is competent*
- *Do not believe, speak or act just because I have told you.*

Kālāmas, when you yourselves know: These things are unwholesome, these things are blameworthy; these things are censured by the wise; and when undertaken and observed, these things lead to harm and ill, abandon them ...

Kālāmas, when you know for yourselves: These are wholesome; these things are not blameworthy; these things are praised by the wise; undertaken and observed, these things lead to benefit and happiness, having undertaken them, abide in them."

Glossary

APADĀNA TEXTS

This is a collection of stories, presented as being told in the words of The Buddha. The work is completely in verse and tells tales of some 587 Buddhist monks and nuns. The tales relate meritorious deeds, acts of piety and charitable service, not only in this life, but often in previous lives.

ATTACHMENT

When we hold onto people, things or ideas too tightly, it can too often lead to great suffering when these things are taken away or disproven. We fall into despair, bad behaviour or gloomy moods. We may have a favorite coffee mug and if it breaks we will feel bad. Sometimes we will be angry with others or ourselves for the mug breaking. We need to remember it's only a mug and that all mugs will eventually break or fall into dust.

AWAKENING/ENLIGHTENMENT

For the purposes of this book, awakening and enlightenment may be considered to be the same thing. Awakening is the realization and understanding (from direct personal experience) that everyone suffers, everything is impermanent and we are all interconnected as human beings. This knowledge, and following the Eightfold Path, leads to a cessation of dukkha, our release from samsara and, upon our death, a state known as Nirvana.

BODHICITTA

This is the raising of compassion for all sentient beings and the wish to end their suffering, preferably by dropping one's attachment to, "Self," and devoting one's practice to helping others free themselves from said suffering.

Bodhisattva

A being who is able to achieve Nirvana but delays doing so in order to stay in the mortal realm and help all sentient beings gain relief from suffering.

Buddha (The)

Literally "The Enlightened One." The man who was born Siddhartha Gautama (c. 563 BCE/480 BCE – c. 483 BCE/400 BCE) - spent the first half of his life searching for and finding, the key to the end of suffering for all human beings. He then spent the rest of his life teaching people how to end or at the very least, reduce, their suffering. The Buddha was not a god or deity of any sort, yet he has been elevated to such by some cultures. He is generally believed to have died at the age of 80.

Buddhahood

In the Mahayana tradition, Buddhahood is the highest goal - one gains Nirvana, then returns to the world of samsara to help other sentient beings seek their ultimate relief from suffering.

Buddhist

One who is a follower of Buddha. Today, a Buddhist is really one who studies and follows the teachings of The Buddha, through one of the many Buddhist traditions or schools. One of the key aspects of any Buddhist practice is that of meditation.

Calm Abiding

A mental state or feeling to which we aspire in samatha meditation in which we find peace and stability where we can rest in a condition of non-distraction, aware of, but not reactive to outside stimulus. A state of deep concentration. (Also see Samadhi.)

Compassion

As wisdom covers the intellectual side of us, so compassion covers the emotional side of our being. "Co" means together while "passion" refers to a strong emotion. Hence the coming together of strong emotions.

When we see another person in pain or suffering, we may feel their pain or suffering as our own and want to help them. This is compassion - the spontaneous uprising of a need to help, based on a shared emotional bond.

D*alai* L*ama*

A title bestowed upon the leader of Tibetan Buddhism. The current (14th) Dalai Lama is Tenzin Gyatso, shortened from Jetsun Jamphel Ngawang Lobsang Yeshe Tenzin Gyatso; born Lhamo Dhondup.

D*elusion*

Insisting that we see the world working as we think it works, rather than how it actually works. Even when presented with evidence to the contrary we may continue to see the world only as we imagine it. Delusion about how the world operates creates much suffering us. Until we can let go of our stories and see the world in a clear manner we have no hope of ending our suffering.

D*ependent* A*rising*
(Dependent Origination)

The recognition that nothing comes from nothing and that all things, relationships and circumstances are the result of past events having combined to set the scene for what exists today.

D*evas*

In Buddhism Devas are non-human creatures with godlike longevity and powers. They are happier than humans and live in 'other worlds.' While they are respected and admired, the same level of veneration is not accorded them as to Buddhas. For the most part, Buddhists do not attribute any importance to such creatures.

D*harma*

The essential teachings of The Buddha as told through the oral and written traditions and practiced by the many schools of Buddhism. The dharma is also one of the "three jewels" of Buddhism a refuge, as it were; as in, we seek refuge in The Buddha, the dharma and the sangha.

Dukkha
The feeling or conditions that makes us feel a lack of satisfaction with life. Not necessarily "suffering," per se, although that may be part of it, but more a feeling that life is ultimately, unsatisfactory, perhaps characterized by such feelings as; failure, disillusion, anxiety, dissatisfaction, dismay or weariness, etc.

Eightfold Path (The)
The prescription given by The Buddha to help humans seek relief from suffering. The path is generally divided into eight attitudes and actions, which are categorized under Wisdom, Ethics and Mental Development

Wisdom

1. Right view
2. Right thinking

Ethics

3. Right action
4. Right livelihood
5. Right speech

Mental Development

6. Right concentration (meditation)
7. Right mindfulness
8. Right effort

Eight Vicissitudes (The)
(See Also the Eight Worldly Concerns)

We all seek, one way or another, fame, gain, pleasure and praise. We tend to avoid shame, loss, pain and censure. In fact, we go to great lengths to avoid those situations that will cause uncomfortable feelings.

Five Aggregates (The)
(See Also the Five Skandhas)

The five elements that constitute the sentient being;

1. Form. The body and all the sense organs (ears, eyes, tongue, etc)

2. Sensation. Feeling an object or situation as being good, bad or neutral

3. Perception (cognition). Being able to determine the existence of a tree or the sound of a bell, for example

4. Mental formations. Thoughts, opinions, mental habits, preferences, aversions, etc.

5. Consciousness. That part of us which discerns or supports all experience. In the Khajjaniya Sutta (SN 22.79) the Buddha distinguishes consciousness in the following manner:

"And why do you call it 'consciousness'? Because it cognizes, thus it is called consciousness. What does it cognize? It cognizes what is sour, bitter, pungent, sweet, alkaline, non-alkaline, salty, & unsalty. Because it cognizes, it is called consciousness."

Five Precepts (The)
These are core principles of training in the Buddhist tradition. Unlike the Ten Commandments, the precepts are to be undertaken, not as a matter of law or dictate, but a matter of conscious - undertaken freely. The precepts should not be a burden to your practice.

The Five Precepts are;

1. Do not kill
2. Do not take what is not freely offered
3. Do not lie
4. Do not engage in inappropriate sexual relations
5. Do not take intoxicants

Five Skandhas (The)
(*See The Five Aggregates*)

Four Noble Truths (The)
A fundamental Buddhist understanding that, through direct, personal experience and observation, all of humanity experiences life in a similar manner. When the man known as Siddhartha, was enlightened and became The Buddha (The Enlightened one) he saw clearly that there were four truths that all humans lived with;

1. Humans suffer
2. Suffering has causes
3. Suffering could end
4. The end of suffering may be found on the Eightfold Path

Impermanence
The Buddhist teaching is that all things are impermanent. Everything we know, everything we built or did in our lives will, eventually, fall to pieces and be lost. In human terms, nothing is forever.

Independence
The belief that things can arise without any external cause. Buddhist teachings hold that everything has a cause and everything is dependent upon other things having first arisen.

The opposite of independence is interdependence. This is the idea that things cannot exist without other things first existing. We cannot have an apple pie, until we have apples, sugar, flower, an oven, fuel, etc. As Carl Sagan notes, "The nitrogen in our DNA, the calcium in our teeth, the iron in our blood, the carbon in our apple pies were made in the interiors of collapsing stars. We are made of star stuff."

Karma

The Buddhist teaching that as we go through life we can think, speak and behave in certain ways. If we were to act in ways that hurt others or cause others to suffer, then it might be that hurt and suffering may gravitate to us. If we were to act in a skillful manner to help others relieve their suffering and to assist them through life, then similar things may drift towards us.

This cause and effect may not happen immediately - it may not even happen in this lifetime, or the next, but it is said to accumulate and will eventually manifest itself.

Having "good" karma at the end of this life may help set one up for a better life in the next rebirth. It should be noted that trying to develop good karma for the sake of one self is far less effective than trying to help others and not worrying about accumulating karma.

In non-Buddhist terms we might just say, "What goes around comes around."

Mahāyāna Buddhism

According to the teachings of Mahāyāna traditions, "Mahāyāna" also refers to the path of the Bodhisattva seeking complete enlightenment for the benefit of all sentient beings. A bodhisattva who has accomplished this goal is called a samyaksaṃbuddha, or "fully enlightened Buddha". A samyaksaṃbuddha can establish the Dharma and lead disciples to enlightenment. Mahayana Buddhists teach that enlightenment can be attained in a single lifetime, and this can be accomplished even by a layperson.

The Mahāyāna tradition is the largest major tradition of Buddhism existing today, with 53.2% of practitioners, compared to 35.8% for Theravada and 5.7% for Vajrayana in 2010.

Meditation - Meditating

For the purposes of this book, meditation is the precise process of resting the mind on the here and now, in order to obtain a conscious state in which we are aware, but not focused on the outside world. Bringing our attention to a single point of focus, the breath for example, allows meditation to deepen.

A simple definition of meditation is sitting quietly, with focused attention for religious, spiritual or relaxation purposes.

Merit

That which accumulates to a Buddhist through kindly acts, good deeds, considerate words and positive thoughts for others. Merit takes one through this life and helps with a good rebirth in subsequent incarnations. In some Buddhist philosophy, meritorious deeds or actions can be done by one person and shared with another. This especially so when a person is near death. Those around the dying person my make donations or perform meritorious deeds and share it with the soon to be departing in the hope that they will have a good rebirth.

Mindfulness

Mindfulness is a translation of the Pali word sati and is a major part of all Buddhist traditions.

The practice of bringing one's awareness to the internal and external environment occurring in the moment. Watching oneself for a tightening in the stomach and clenching of the jaw, for example, is bringing mindfulness to rising anger or anxiety. Knowing how you're responding to a given situation is the first defence against a poor choice of words or action.

In the West, there are many MBCTs or Mindfulness Based Cognitive Therapies that are used to treat; depressions, anxiety, drug abuse, poor self-esteem, etc. MBSR or Mindfulness Based Stress Reduction is used widely in hospitals, prisons, schools with good results.

MORALITY

Any social group will have a shared sense of what is 'right' and 'wrong,' with the intention of promoting that which is deemed 'good' for the society as a whole, with a balanced of what is acceptable to any given individual. Not all social groups share the same moral code, indeed, even within a given social group, individuals may not have the same morals. These individuals, if their behaviour is deemed unacceptable to the group, may be considered outliers and held accountable in some way, to some extent that the group deems acceptable.

NIRVANA

A Sanskrit word commonly used to describe the ultimate goal of following the Eightfold Path. Other words that are used include the Pali *"nibbana"* or *"nibbāna."* These words have various meanings, including; "blowing out" and "quenching."

In most Buddhist traditions, in order to achieve the goal of Nirvana one must practice the doctrine to ultimately extinguish The Three Fires or Three Poisons of the mind; passion, aversion and ignorance. Once these fires are extinguished, then we can gain release from the cycle of samsara and rebirth and enter a place of no-time and no-death, without suffering or the causes of suffering.

In the Theravada tradition, Nirvana is the highest goal - existence without rebirth. In the Mahayana tradition, Buddhahood is the highest goal - one gains Nirvana, then returns to the world of samsara to help other sentient beings seek their ultimate relief from suffering.

REBIRTH

Buddhists often believe we are re-born time and again. The karma we accumulated in our previous life or lives will determine how we are reborn into the next lifetime. If nothing changes, we will be reborn into this life countless times until, or if, we better our karma and can be reborn into Nirvana, which ends the cycle of rebirth. (See Samsara, below)

Samatha Meditation
(Sam-ah-TA)

Also known as calmness meditation or focused meditation. The purpose of samatha meditation is to bring the mind to a single-pointed state of concentration on an object-of-meditation - often the breath. Focusing on the breath we can practice fixing the mind in place to enter a deep, trancelike stillness. By quieting the mind, by suppressing negative emotions, you prepare the field for "insight" or Vipassana meditation.

Vipassana and Samatha meditation are two sides of the same coin. Each enhances the practice of the other.

Samadhi
A state of mind, primarily during meditation, in which the mind becomes still but does not merge with the object of attention, and so is able to gain insight into the ebb and flow of the present experience. Also see Calm Abiding.

Samsara
The idea of samsara is closely associated with the belief that the person continues to be born and reborn in various realms as a human, animal, or other being, depending on the nature of their karma. It's cyclic and repetitive and is dependent upon human beings grasping and fixating on a self and pursuit of sensory experiences.

This cycle of samsara is dukkha, a feeling that nothing is fully satisfactory and that life is, at best, a disappointment.

Sangha
A Buddhist community or association to which one belongs so that one might receive guidance or advice regarding the dharma and Buddhism. Various schools of Buddhism have varying forms of sangha. One does not need to belong to a sangha to practice Buddhism or to meditate.

SIDDHARTHA GAUTAMA
(See The Buddha)

SINGLE POINTED CONCENTRATION
Turning our attention repeatedly to a fixed, unchanging object sharpens and strengthens our ability to pay close attention to life. Single Pointed Concentration is the trained ability of the mind to set itself upon a topic or object without being easily distracted. The practice is to see while being awake to the fact that seeing is taking place.

SUFFERING
Simply put, suffering is the desire to have things other than the way they are. A broken foot may contain pain, but the suffering comes when you realize you won't be able to play baseball this summer, or go surfing, like you had planned. Suffering is what comes after the pain and is, in my way of thinking, an optional, mental construction. Things, not being what we want them to be is a major source of suffering for all sentient beings. It's this suffering that The Buddha sought to end for humanity.

SUPER SUITE
When it comes to wisdom there are twelve sets of skills in order to complete the 'super suite,' and those pillars are what is discussed in this book. The more familiar one is with these pillars and the more frequently they are applied to thinking, the greater the ability to give rise to wisdom. Working to obtain the super suite is a long and arduous task, and , sadly, no one is born possessing the suite. It's a hard won battle to obtain and put to use.

SUTTA OR SUTRA
Most of the exhortations and lectures given by The Buddha were witnessed or memorized by his cousin and close friend and attendant, Ananda. Shortly after The Buddha's death, about 400 BCE, monks and followers gathered and wrote down what each of them had heard from The Buddha. So, most of the recorded sermons start with the Pali phrase *Evam me sutam* or "As I have heard."

These teachings or suttas were passed down within the monastic community largely through storytelling. Some time around 100 BCE the first, substantial accounting of the stories and sermons were written down by Sri Lankan Sinhala scribe-monks.

Clearly, we can never know if the Pali Canon contains the actual words uttered by the historical Buddha. Still, the wisdom within these Canonical texts served for over two millennia as a vital guide for millions of Buddhists around the world.

THERAVADA BUDDHISM

One of the oldest traditions or schools of Buddhism. Literally, Doctrine of The Elders. The language of Theravada is Pali (a dialect of Magadhi, the language likely spoken in central India during Buddhas time).

VAJRAYĀNA BUDDHISM

A school of Buddhism. Vajrayāna is usually translated as Diamond Vehicle or Thunderbolt Vehicle, perhaps referring to the Vajra, a mythical weapon which is also used as a ritual implement. According to Vajrayāna scriptures, the term Vajrayāna refers to one of three vehicles or routes to enlightenment, the other two being the Srāvakayāna (also known as the Hīnayāna) and Mahāyāna.

VIPASSANA MEDITATION

In Theravada Buddhism two primary types of meditation are often practiced; Vipassana and Samatha.

Vipassana or "insight" meditation provides techniques to "purify" the mind and ready it for deep-seeing of the nature of ourselves so we can unravel the causes of our suffering and general disillusionment of our lives. It's mind training that helps to take away the stories we've added to our observations and allow us to see and know, clearly, what is unfolding before us. It helps us cut through conventional perception to perceive mind and matter as they really are: impermanent, unsatisfactory, and impersonal. With training, we learn to detach ourselves from our ideas and opinions so desire and delusion are gradually diluted.

Vipassana is a compound Pali word. "Passana" to see or perceive. "Vi" may have several meanings, including "through." Vipassana insight literally cuts through the curtain of delusion in the mind. The idea of "seeing separately" the difference between the "truth" and our delusions is relevant.

Vipassana and Samatha meditations are two sides of the same coin. Each enhances the practice of the other.

Self-Assessment Tools

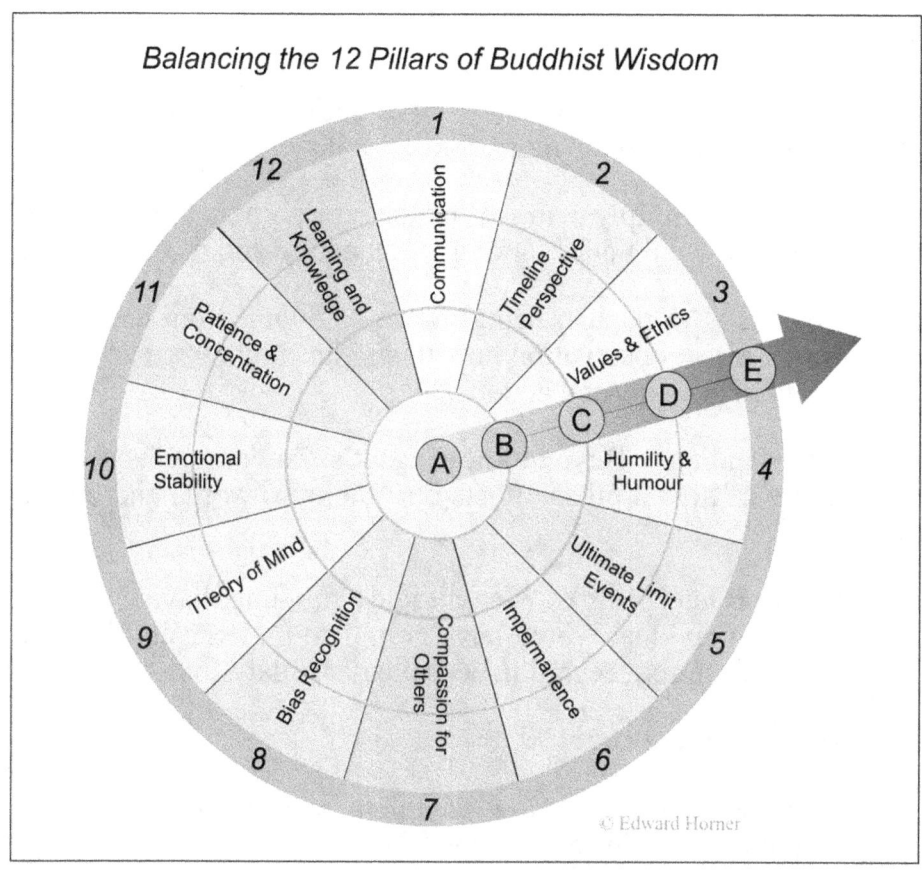

Conversation and Communication	Compassion for Others
Timeline Perspective	Recognize Bias
Values, Morality and Ethics	Theory of Mind
Humility and Humour	Emotional Stability
Ultimate Limit Events	Concentration and Meditation
Impermanence	Learning and Knowledge

In the graphic above, we see the 12 Pillars of Buddhist wisdom, 1 through 12. By now you are familiar with them.

There are five rings;

A. Ignorance (Innermost Circle) – Total lack of awareness at all of the pillar - not even on the radar. Skill not developed.

B. Awareness – Simply being aware that any particular pillar exists, but not have any real understanding of its nature and its effect on us.

C. Knowing – More than being aware, knowing from experience and through direct observation how this pillar might have an impact on our thinking, words and actions.

D. Understanding – Beyond knowing, it's the comprehensive understanding of how a pillar effects our thinking, words and our actions.

E. Mastery (Outer Ring) – Beyond understanding, having reached this ring, an individual would have complete mastery and intimate knowledge of the self, regarding a particular pillar.

How to use this chart

Referencing chart A1 below, we might be asked for our input on a new computer system for our workplace.

1. <u>Conversation and Communication</u>. I may have to interact with others, hear their opinions and have mine heard. If I cannot listen, without getting upset, I may not have fully mastered the skills of conversation, therefore, I can't really put myself on the outer ring of the diagram above, but I'd have to put myself somewhere.

2. <u>Timeline Perspective</u>. I may have to consider a full timeline, including what we had in the past, the reasons we have it, how it was integrated into the current system and whether or not it will be usable in any future system. If I consider all aspects of the past, present and future needs of the company, then I might have full mastery of that aspect of wisdom - at least for this topic.

3. Values Morality and Ethics. Do I understand the common good that is trying to be addressed? Do my values and ethical behaviour have any negative effect on the decisions I may be proposing? Does a friend of mine own the software company that I'm recommending and will this have any bearing on my recommendation? If I have examined my motives, checked my personal interests, looked at my values and not found any problems, then I may have fulfilled my obligations and can say I have entered the ring of Mastery, on this topic.

4. Humility and Humour. Can we laugh at our own shortcomings? Do we use humour to unite people and show where we have commonalities? Do we avoid using humour to distance, divide and dismiss other people and their ideas?

5. Life Experience and ULEs. Do I have sufficient life experience to offer recommendations? You may be fresh out of college with a computer engineering degree, but still may not yet have real world experience in working with other people. Again, you have to place yourself somewhere along that A,B,C,D,E spectrum.

6. Impermanence. Do I recognize that all the past computer systems have been replaced, for one reason or another, and that my recommendation will also, ultimately have to be replaced? Do I fully understand that all things change and that to get too attached to a recommendation is going to result in a feeling of rejection? Once more, you have to place yourself somewhere along that A,B,C,D,E continuum.

7. Compassion. Do I have compassion for others as I discuss and offer input on the replacements? Do I recognize that they have the same emotions and concerns as I do? Do I appreciate the fact that their ideas, while different from mine, are worthy of consideration?

8. Recognize Bias. Have I given due consideration to the pre-existing biases I might possess? Am I aware that my thinking is largely governed by these biases? Depending on how I have examined these biases, once again, I have to set myself somewhere along the E to A spectrum. Once a Mac user, always a Mac user.

9. <u>Theory of Mind</u>. When we are able to 'read' people, pick up on their nuanced body language, words and facial expressions, then we are better able to address how we speak to them. Do they respond better to facts and figures or are they more of a 'feeling' person? We are not trying to 'manipulate' people, but when we better understand their personality then we might be better able to express ourselves and better understand their point of view. Some people are very good at identifying people in this way. Where do you place your ability to assess people on the A to E band?

10. <u>Emotional Stability</u>. Have we looked into our own mind and seen where it becomes agitated and what types of situations cause it? When we recognize where and when we become emotional then we can use that knowledge to maintain greater emotional stability when discussing emotionally charged topics. Where on the A to E spectrum will you place yourself when discussing the new computer system for your workplace?

11. <u>Concentration</u>. When we come to a meeting to discuss important topics, we need to be focused and ready. Having a mind that easily drifts aways from the work at hand is not given to formulating wise plans of action. Clearly, our ability to concentrate can be affected by lots of things; a good night's sleep, proper diet, home life, physical condition, etc, but on any given day and for any given discussion, we need to place ourselves somewhere along that A to E spectrum. Concentration is helped with a consistently applied program of meditation.

12. <u>Learning and Knowledge</u>. Having general knowledge about related topics, combined with specific knowledge in an area of interest is usually the best way to approach problems. We need to place ourselves somewhere on the spectrum from complete ignorance of a topic, to being an expert - A to E.

Wisdom is a balance of the 12 pillars, along with various levels of achievement. The more pillars that have achieved the Mastery ring, the greater the possibility of making wise choices around a particular circumstance. However, one does not need to have achieved the 5th ring in all aspects in order to make a wise decision. One or more pillars may have little bearing on a decision. The trick is recognizing which pillars are critical, which are 'nice-to-haves' and which (if any) are redundant.

Of course, the opposite is also true. The more pillars that reside in the inner circle of ignorance, the less likely we are to dispense wise words and perform wise actions. Rarely can we lay claim to wisdom when our mind excludes the ideas of others or findings that we disagree with. Rarely does wisdom flow from the mouth of a bigot, racist, religious zealot or ultra anyone. What passes for 'wisdom' in those circumstances is merely the best way forward to advance a narrow agenda for a particular group or individual.

Self-Assessment Tools - Continued

A1	New Computer for Office	Low A	B	C	D	High E
1	Conversation and Comm.		X			
2	Timeline Perspective			X		
3	Values, Morality and Ethics				X	
4	Humility and Humour		X			
5	Ultimate Life Experiences		X			
6	Impermanence	X				
7	Compassion			X		
8	Bias Recognition		X			
9	Theory of Mind			X		
10	Emotional Stability			X		
11	Concentration/Meditation		X			
12	Learning					X

Referencing the chart on the previous page, (A1) a young employee, recently arrived to a company, has been asked for input on a new computer system for the workplace. Her life experience will be low while perhaps her learned knowledge of computer system might be very high. Being young, her emotional stability might not be well developed, etc. Her input might be very valuable based on her learning, but she might have difficulty accepting rejection or making her opinion heard clearly and precisely. She may not use humour constructively and she may have a limited grasp of the timeline. It would be well for her to identify her strengths and how they might be brought to bear on the problem, while also looking at her weakness and how they might be improved.

		Low				High
A2	Worker Rights Policy	A	B	C	D	E
1	Conversation and Comm.					
2	Timeline Perspective					
3	Values, Morality and Ethics					
4	Humility and Humour					
5	Ultimate Life Experiences					
6	Impermanence					
7	Compassion					
8	Bias Recognition					
9	Theory of Mind					
10	Emotional Stability					
11	Concentration/Meditation					
12	Learning					

On the above chart (A2) We see an older individual who has been asked to work on a team to develop a policy around worker rights. Perhaps she has been a policy wonk for years so her ability to hold a conversation and easily communicate her ideas may be high. Her values, morality and ethics might fit perfectly with the job and so be identified as 'high,' as might her knowledge of this particular aspect of government policy. If this individual was asked to contribute to a committee tasked with developing policy around a spaced-based weapons program, the chart would likely look very different.

A3	Abbey Relocation	Low A	B	C	D	High E
1	Conversation and Comm.	■	■	■		
2	Timeline Perspective	■	■	■	■	■
3	Values, Morality and Ethics	■	■	■	■	■
4	Humility and Humour	■	■	■	■	
5	Ultimate Life Experiences	■	■	■		■
6	Impermanence	■	■	■	■	■
7	Compassion	■	■	■	■	■
8	Bias Recognition	■	■	■	■	
9	Theory of Mind	■	■	■	■	
10	Emotional Stability	■	■	■		■
11	Concentration/Meditation	■	■	■	■	■
12	Learning	■				

In chart A3 (above) an elderly Buddhist nun has been asked to join a committee to determine where their new abbey might be built. While she may possess a firm grasp of the timeline, values, morality and ethics of the situation, there may be little available to her from a learning perspective (real estate). Having been a monastic for a long time, she might not have a great deal of worldly experience or know how to interact with the world at large so her life experience might be minimal. Identifying her strengths and weakness, when it comes to real estate, might create a chart that looks like A3. The committee might not turn to her for location advice, but she may be able to offer guidance around ethical considerations and historical perspective, etc.

Clearly all three charts (A1, A2 and A3) are different from each other and all represent a range of development around a particular situation at a particular point in time. They will, of course, change. If the older employee was asked for input on a new computer system, things would probably look very different on her chart. It's situational and it changes all the time.

Still, one could argue that if you continually use humour to make fun of people, then that characteristic might not change too much from situation to situation, but it may over time as you mature and gain more life experience.

In all cases, the further towards the right hand side of the chart, the greater the mastery of that particular aspect of the individual, in that particular situation at one particular point in time.

Blank Charts For Self-Assessment

		Low				High
		A	B	C	D	E
1	Conversation and Comm.					
2	Timeline Perspective					
3	Values, Morality and Ethics					
4	Humility and Humour					
5	Ultimate Life Experiences					
6	Impermanence					
7	Compassion					
8	Bias Recognition					
9	Theory of Mind					
10	Emotional Stability					
11	Concentration/Meditation					
12	Learning					

		Low				High
		A	B	C	D	E
1	Conversation and Comm.					
2	Timeline Perspective					
3	Values, Morality and Ethics					
4	Humility and Humour					
5	Ultimate Life Experiences					
6	Impermanence					
7	Compassion					
8	Bias Recognition					
9	Theory of Mind					
10	Emotional Stability					
11	Concentration/Meditation					
12	Learning					

		Low				High
		A	B	C	D	E
1	Conversation and Comm.					
2	Timeline Perspective					
3	Values, Morality and Ethics					
4	Humility and Humour					
5	Ultimate Life Experiences					
6	Impermanence					
7	Compassion					
8	Bias Recognition					
9	Theory of Mind					
10	Emotional Stability					
11	Concentration/Meditation					
12	Learning					

		Low				High
		A	B	C	D	E
1	Conversation and Comm.					
2	Timeline Perspective					
3	Values, Morality and Ethics					
4	Humility and Humour					
5	Ultimate Life Experiences					
6	Impermanence					
7	Compassion					
8	Bias Recognition					
9	Theory of Mind					
10	Emotional Stability					
11	Concentration/Meditation					
12	Learning					

Bibliography

Social Intelligence; The New Science of Success – Dr. Karl Albrecht
    Jossey-Bass Publications – Copyright 2006
        978-0787979386

Crises of the Republic; Lying in Politics – Hannah Arendt
    Harcourt Brace and Company – Copyright 1972
        ISBN 0-15-623200-6

Beyond Mindfulness in Plain English – Bhante H. Gunaratana
    Wisdom Publications – Copyright 2002
        978-0-86171-906-9

Blueprint: The Evolutionary Origins of A Good Society – Nicholas Christakis
    Little, Brown and Company – 2019
        978-0316230032

Comfortable with Uncertainty – Pema Chöndrön
    Shambala Publications - 2003
        ISBN 978-1590300787

The Wisdom of No Escape – Pema Chöndrön
    Shambhala Publications – 1991
        ISBN 978-0-87773-632-5

Psychology and Buddhism – Editors; Dockett, Dudley-Grant and Bankart
    Springer Press - Copyright 2002
        ISBN 978-1590300787

Samurai Wisdom Stories; Tales from the Golden Age of Bushido
　Shambala Publications - 2011
　　Pascal Fauliot

Urban Dharma Website – Kusala Bhikshu
　urbandharma.org
　　- Wisdom and Compassion in the Present Moment
　　- Buddhist Wisdom
　　- Wisdom of Meditation

Preparing for Death and Helping the Dying - *Sangye Khadro (Kathleen McDonald) 1999*
　Kong Meng San Phor Kark See Monastery Publication
　　http://www.urbandharma.org/pdf/death_dying.pdf
　　ISBN 981-04-8920-X

Mahatma Gandhi On Ethics – Anil Dutta Mishra
　Concept Publishing Co - Copyright 2010
　　ISBN 978-8180696817

Lectures on Greek Philosophy, and Other Philosophical Remains Vol. I – James Frederick Ferrier.
　W. Blackwood and Sons - 1866
　　Dowloaded from archive.org

The Assault on Reason – Al Gore
　Penguin Press - Copyright 2007
　　ISBN 978-0143113621

Wisdom: From Philosophy to Neuroscience – Stephen S. Hall
　Vintage Books - Copyright 2010
　　ISBN 978-0307389688

How to Sit – Thich Nhat Hanh
  Parallax Press - Copyright 2009
    ISBN 978-1937006587

Buddha's Brain – Rick Hanson Pd.D.
  New Harbinger Publication - Copyright 2009
    ISBN 978-1-57224-695-9

The Relationship between the Psychology of Religion and Buddhist Psychology –
Hiroki Kato
Kato, H. (2016), The Relationship between the Psychology of Religion and Buddhist Psychology. Jpn Psychol Res, 58: 70–84. doi:10.1111/jpr.12121

The Yoganjalisaram – T. Krishnamacharya
  Krishnamacharya Yoga Mandiram (2001)
    ASIN B003DRHHL2

The Dalai Lamas Book of Wisdom – Dalai Lama (Thupten Jinpa Translator)
  Harper Thorsons - Copyright 2015
    ISBN 978-0722539552

Ethics For The New Millennium – Dalai Lama
  Riverhead Books; Berkley Publishing Group 1999
    ISBN 1-57322-025-6

Healing Anger: The Power of Patience from a Buddhist Perspective – Dalai Lama
  Snow Lion Publications - Copyright 1997
    SBN 978-1559390736

How to Practice - Dalai Lama – (Jeffrey Hopkins, Ph.D. Translator)
  Atria Books - Copyright 2002
    ISBN 978-0-7434-2708-1

The Upanishads; A New Translation – Vernon Katz and Thomas Egenes
    Tarcher/Penguin - Copyright 2015
        ISBN 978-0-399-17423-0

The Engaged Buddhist Reader – Edited by Arnold Kotler.
    Parallax Press - Copyright 2001
        ISBN 978-0938077985

Beyond the Self: Conversations Between Buddhism and Neuroscience – Mathieu Ricard and Wolf Singer
    The MIT Press - Copyright 2017
        ISBN 978-0262036948

The Lost Art of Good Conversation – Sakyong Mipham
    Harmony Books
        ISBN 978-0-451-49943-1

Love, Freedom, Aloneness: The Koan of Relationships – Osho
    St. Martin's Edition - Copyright 2002
        ISBN 0-312-29162-0

Rebel Buddha; A Guide to a Revolution of Mind – Dzogchen Ponlop
    Shambala Publications - Copyright 2010
        ISBN 978-59030-929-2

Life-Span Development – John W Santrock
    McGraw-Hill Education; 14 edition (2012)
        ISBN 978-0078035326

Wisdom – Soka Gakkai Institute
    January *2003*, SGI Quarterly
        http://www.sgi.org/about-us/buddhism-in-daily-life/wisdom.html

The Problem With Mindfulness – Sahanika Ratnayake
- Mindfulness promotes itself as value-neutral but it is loaded with (troubling) assumptions about the self and the cosmos.
- Shank Ratnayake is a graduate student in philosophy at the University of Cambridge. Her PhD project concerns the history and philosophy of contemporary psychotherapy.

Wisdom: Its Nature, Origins and Development – Robert J. Stern
    Cambridge University Press - 1990
        ISBN 978-0521367189

Psychology of Ageing – Ian Stuart-Hamilton
    Jessica Kingsley Publishing - 2012
        ISBN 978-1849052450

Why the Dalai Lama Matters – Robert Thurman
    Atria Books (Simon & Schuster)- Copyright 2011
        ISBN 978-1582702216

The Relationship between Mental and Somatic Practices and Wisdom
    Williams PB, Mangelsdorf HH, Kontra C, Nusbaum HC, Hoeckner B (2016) The Relationship between Mental and Somatic Practices and Wisdom. PLoS ONE 11(2): e0149369. _https://doi.org/10.1371/journal.pone.0149369_.

Handbook of Intellectual Styles; Preferences in Cognition, Learning, and Thinking
    Springer Publishing
        LF Zhang, RJ Sternberg and S Rayner
            ISBN 978-0826106674

Old Path, White Clouds — Thich Nhat Hanh
    Paralax Press — 1991
        Translated by Mobi Ho
            ISBN 0-938077-26-0

About the Author

Horner has been a practicing Buddhist, in the Theravada tradition, since 2003 and enjoys talking and writing about his experiences and ideas. He has been hiking, skiing and paddling throughout Ontario and Alberta for over 50 years. He's an avid photographer, cyclist and keen outdoor enthusiast. He founded Friends of Dieppe Park and is a past member of the Harbourfront Parks and Open Space Project, in Toronto.

―――――――――

"Behold, O monks, this is my advice to you. All things which are compound are changeable. They are not lasting. Work hard to gain your own salvation."

~These were the final words, attributed to The Buddha.

―――――――――

Other Books From Mind of Peace Publications

Pain and Suffering in Buddhism

Each and everyone of us shares the combined experiences of pain and suffering. It is unavoidable. The pain comes from the simple fact that we are human and that our physiology and psychic makeup allow it to arise. Suffering is a different matter. It will arise when our ego isn't being stoked. It will arise when we experience loss. It will be experienced when our expectation is not met. Whenever anything happens to us that our ego isn't ready for, or desirous of, we will suffer.

In Pain and Suffering, we explore the relationship between these two afflictions as we look deeply into how our ego drives us ever towards disappointment and regret. However, we don't leave the reader with just an understanding of how we suffer and why we have pain. We take a serious look at how, with diligence and patience, we can apply a specific program to escape or at the very least, lessen our suffering.

ISBN 978-0-9953161-9-5

Paperback, 108pp

Death and Dying
In Buddhism

Edward Horner

Death and Dying in Buddhism

No human being, animal, plant nor smallest microbe manages to escape death. It's the ultimate end of everyone now living or that ever will live. There is no "cure" and no avoiding it, but from a Buddhist perspective, suffering over this inevitability is something we can reduce and maybe even sidestep.

In Death and Dying, Horner gives us hope that we can shake off the fear of death and bring a clear mind to the process.

ISBN 978-1-7771539-0-8

Paperback 108pp

Index

A

Adaptiv Resilience Factor Inventory 215
Against the Stream 61
Ageing xvi, 46, 71, 122, 137, 138, 140, 146, 228, 241, 288, 326
Alison White 89
Anatta 102. Ego
Anchoring Bias 183, 184, 188, 191, 194
Anticipatory Anxiety 29
Apple Inc xix, 132, 134, 135, 189, 190, 291
Arcana Imperii 41, 67, 68
Aristotle xxii, 272
Arthur Henning 183
Assortive Mating 285
Attribution Theory 197, 199
Awakening 28, 115, 239, 244, 266, 300. Enlightenment
Azi Paybarah 63

B

Betty Birner 131
Bhante Henepola Gunaratana 261
Bill Clinton 60
Blind Spot Bias 192, 195
Bodh Gaya 228
Bodhicitta 156, 158, 164, 248, 300
Brefczynski-Lewis 139
Buddha 304
Buddhahood 73, 301, 308

C

Calm Abiding 270, 301, 309

Caspar van Hilten xx

Catholic Church 62

Challenger ix

Christy Price, Dr. 289

Clustering Bias 186, 187

Co-Dependency 222, 223

Cognitive Style 214, 217

Colonial Advocate xx

Columbia-Southern Chemical Corp 134

Commitment Bias 185, 186, 194

Common Good
xii, xiii, xxiii, 16, 23, 39, 44, 51, 106, 110, 113, 115, 116, 142, 171–174, 192, 213, 214, 216, 217, 296

Communication xiii, 1, 2, 16, 211, 249, 250, 288

Compassion xiv, xxii, 7, 9, 13, 47, 80, 105, 108, 120, 142, 155–160, 162–
164, 174, 225, 247, 248, 251, 256, 257, 259, 264, 271, 296, 300–302, 323

Compound Mind xxii

Concentration
xiv, xv, xxii, 57, 75, 104, 105, 112, 125, 126, 139, 157, 212, 225, 227, 260–263, 267, 270, 271, 290, 296, 297, 301, 303, 309, 310

Confirmation Bias 129, 179–182, 194

Conservatism Bias 188

Critical Therapy Center 107

D

D4 Disorder xxii

Daily Tribune 183

Dalton State College 289

Decision Making
xiii, xiv, 13, 129, 133, 167, 170, 171, 175, 181, 192, 193, 203, 211, 224, 290

Delusion 94–96, 235, 241, 242, 263, 264, 302, 311, 312. *Ignorance*

Denialism xxii, 96–99, 232

Dependent Arising 26, 236, 238, 240, 302

Dependent Origination 26, 122, 302

Dhammacakkappavattana Sutta 115

Dhammapada 111, 131

Dr. John Cacioppo 177

Dukkha 110, 172, 230, 240, 300, 303, 309

E

Ego 8, 66, 95, 102, 103, 105, 110, 122, 164, 169, 199, 250, 251. *Anatta*

Elon Musk 214

Emmanuel Macron xxii

Emotional intelligence 138, 209, 217

Emotional Stability xiv, xxii, 174, 209, 217, 297

Energy Vampire 57–59

Enlightenment
xii, 40, 52, 86, 111, 228, 242, 243, 258, 293, 295, 300, 301, 305, 306, 311. *Awakening*

Erin McCormick 192

Ethics
xiii, 5, 35, 36, 41, 42, 44, 45, 47, 50, 53, 61, 62, 65, 94, 172, 245, 249, 272, 303, 323, 324

F

Fake news 97, 127, 128

False Attribution 129

Family Compact (The) xx

Five Precepts xiii, 50, 53, 54, 94, 106, 113, 172, 239, 253, 304

Francesca Fortenbaugh (Dr.) 139

Frank, Anne 65

Freda Blanchard-Fields (Dr.) 137, 138

G

Garry Kasparov 126

Generosity 74, 75, 80, 82, 111, 162, 246, 254, 256–258

George W. Bush 123
Georgia Institute of Technology 137
Gies, Miep 65
Gold, Michael 63
Good Samaritan Laws 168
Greed 3, 30, 94, 105, 106, 111, 113, 171, 250, 254. *The Three Mental Defilements*

H

Hannah Arendt 65
Harvard University 139
Harvey Weinstein 60
Hatred 3, 89, 90, 94, 107, 109–111, 113, 243, 247, 250, 264. *The Three Mental Defilements*
Heraclitus of Ephesus 126, 145, 148
Humility xiii, 79, 86, 87, 93, 297
Humour xiii, xxii, 79, 87, 89, 93, 105, 174, 296, 297

I

Ignorance xv, 33, 46, 94, 95, 97, 102, 103, 107, 111, 113, 120, 173, 179, 181, 184, 232, 242, 245, 254, 269, 279, 308. *The Three Mental Defilements, Delusion*
Impermanence xiv, 74, 95, 122, 123, 147–149, 223, 263, 296, 300, 305, 311
Independence 47, 171, 178, 189, 235, 236, 305
Innovation Bias 189, 190, 194
Intelligence 124, 138, 172, 173, 210, 284, 292, 322
Interdependence 47, 236, 305
Intoxicant 53, 71–73, 77, 94, 106, 172, 253, 305
iPhone 134

J

Jeffrey Epstein 62, 63
Jimmy Carter 212
Joan Halifax, Roshi 66
Jodi Kantor 60

Joe DeGutis (Dr.) 139
John Cacioppo, Dr. 177
Juan Pascual-Leone 122

K

Karma 2, 54, 56, 57, 77, 236–238, 240, 251, 258, 306, 308, 309
Ken Greenberg. Teach
Khajjaniya Sutta 304
Krishnamacharya, T. 100

L

Learning xv, 87, 112, 113, 123, 136, 279, 281, 284, 285, 288, 289

M

Mahatma Gandhi xxii, 212, 323
Mahayana 74, 301, 306, 308
marijuana 71–73, 77, 181
meditation ix, xv, 61, 74, 84–86, 103, 104, 111, 122, 123, 139, 156, 157, 178, 227, 239, 243, 259–271, 274, 290, 301, 303, 307, 309, 311, 312
Merit 2, 41, 283, 307
Metropolitan Correctional Centre 63
Michael Esterman (Dr.) 139
Mindfulness 258–260, 307, 322, 326
Mirror Neuron 201
Mirror Neurons 199, 200
Morality xiii, 5, 35, 36, 39–41, 43, 44, 47, 48, 53, 56, 75, 86, 94, 105, 254, 295, 308
Moscone Centre 134
Myers-Briggs 215

N

Nancy Merz Nordstrom 288
Nathaniel, Naka 62
Negativity Bias 175, 194
New Millennial Learners 288

Nirvana xii, 28, 52, 64, 238, 240–242, 244, 252, 258, 295, 300, 301, 308
NMLs 289
Noah Levine 61
Noblesse Oblige 287
Norm Larsen 134
Northern Illinois University 131

O

Odysseus 272
Ohio State University 177
Osho 90
Outcome Bias 191

P

Palden Gyatso 120
Patience 4, 75, 104, 125, 126, 190, 227, 261, 271, 272, 274, 281, 297, 324
Pirkei Avot xviii
Political Proficiency 213
Portapique ix. *Wortman*
Post-Traumatic Stress 121
Predictive Index 215
Price, Christy Dr. 289
Psychology Today 209
Psychotherapy 14, 222

R

Rebirth 238–240, 242, 306–308
Recency Bias 184, 185, 191
Renunciation 247
Richard Nixon 64
Right Actions 252
Right Concentration 260, 303
Right Effort 254, 303
Right Intention 246, 247

Right Livelihood 253, 254, 303
Right Speech 249, 250, 303
Right View 245, 246, 303
Rocket Chemical Co 134

S

Samatha 139, 263, 290, 301, 309, 311. *Vipassana*
Samsara 240–242, 245, 300, 301, 308, 309
Samuel Johnson 67
Samurai 6, 248, 323
Selectivism xx, xxv
Sexual Misconduct 50, 60–62, 94, 174, 252
Siddhartha Gautama 111, 228, 293, 301, 310. *The Buddha*
Silva Dutchevici 107
Skandhas 102, 103, 232–234, 241, 304, 305
SpaceX 214
Stereotyping Bias 189
Steve Jobs 134
Suffering
xiv, 11, 25, 28, 31, 35, 46, 50, 52, 55, 56, 71, 74, 77, 80, 86, 87, 96, 110, 111, 115, 120, 121, 123, 137, 142, 148, 155–157, 160–164, 171, 172, 200, 201, 205, 211, 227–232, 235, 238, 240–246, 248, 253, 257, 258, 263, 274, 293, 295, 296, 300–303, 306, 308, 310, 311, 333
Susan Krauss Whitbourne 210
Suzanne M. Skevington 89

T

Teach 24, 82, 83, 85, 86, 108, 114–116, 155, 158, 228, 243, 280, 287, 289, 292, 293, 301, 302, 305, 306, 311
Tesla Motors 214
The Buddha
xxiii, 8, 66, 87, 108, 109, 111, 115, 116, 122, 148, 228, 239, 240, 242–244, 253–255, 262, 266, 267, 270, 293, 295, 298, 300–303, 305, 310, 328. *Siddhartha Gautama*
The Eight Vicissitudes 64, 176, 211

The Eight Worldly Concerns 133, 176, 239, 292, 304

The Eightfold Path 4, 111, 122, 239, 243, 245, 246, 295, 300, 305, 308. *The Four Noble Truths*

The Five Remembrances 90

The Five Stages of Wisdom 111

The Four Noble Truths 74, 96, 111, 122, 227, 239, 244, 246. *The Eightfold Path*

The Idler 67. *Samuel Johnson*

The New York Times 60, 63

The Odyssey 272

The Paramitas 73

The Three Mental Defilements 94, 232

Theory of Mind xiv, 130, 197

Theravada 94, 249, 263, 306, 308, 311

Thich Nhat Hanh 183, 266, 324

Thomas Merton xxii, 35, 125

Three Fires of The Mind 64, 252

Three Poisons of The Mind 242, 308

Tonglen 156, 157, 159, 164

Tourettes Syndrome 200, 201

Traitify 216

Trojan War 272

Trump, Donald 126–129, 174, 212

U

Ultimate Limit Events xiii, 119, 121

Universal Responsibility 45, 49, 114

V

Vajrayana 306

Values xii, xiii, xxiii, 35–38, 94, 172, 295

Vanijja Sutta 253

Vipassana 263, 311, 312. *Samatha*

W
Weiser, Benjamin 63
William Lyon Mackenzie xx
Winston Churchill 284
Wortman. Portapique

Z
Zero Risk Bias 191, 192, 195

www.ingramcontent.com/pod-product-compliance
Lightning Source LLC
Chambersburg PA
CBHW071802080526
44589CB00012B/656